CHINA AND EAST ASIA

After the Wall Street Crisis

Series on Contemporary China   (ISSN: 1793-0847)

Series Editors: Joseph Fewsmith *(Boston University)*
Zheng Yongnian *(East Asian Institute, National University of Singapore)*

Published*

*To view the complete list of the published volumes in the series, please visit:
http://www.worldscientific.com/series/scc

Series on Contemporary China – Vol. 33

CHINA AND EAST ASIA

After the Wall Street Crisis

editors

LAM Peng Er

East Asian Institute, National University of Singapore, Singapore

QIN Yaqing

China Foreign Affairs University, China

YANG Mu

East Asian Institute, National University of Singapore, Singapore

World Scientific

NEW JERSEY · LONDON · SINGAPORE · BEIJING · SHANGHAI · HONG KONG · TAIPEI · CHENNAI

Published by

World Scientific Publishing Co. Pte. Ltd.

5 Toh Tuck Link, Singapore 596224

USA office: 27 Warren Street, Suite 401-402, Hackensack, NJ 07601

UK office: 57 Shelton Street, Covent Garden, London WC2H 9HE

British Library Cataloguing-in-Publication Data
A catalogue record for this book is available from the British Library.

Series on Contemporary China — Vol. 33
CHINA AND EAST ASIA
After the Wall Street Crisis

Copyright © 2013 by World Scientific Publishing Co. Pte. Ltd.

ISBN 978-981-4407-26-7

In-house Editor: Agnes Ng

Typeset by Stallion Press
Email: enquiries@stallionpress.com

Printed in Singapore by World Scientific Printers.

CONTENTS

Introduction

CHINA AND EAST ASIA: AFTER THE WALL STREET CRISIS

LAM Peng Er, YANG Mu and QIN Yaqing

2008 might well be a pivotal year in which the pecking order of the global political economy was reshuffled. The collapse of Lehman Brothers and the AIG (American Insurance Group) that year threatened to trigger the collapse of the US financial system. While the US eventually avoided a financial meltdown, it sunk into a great recession with sub-prime mortgage defaults, housing foreclosures and high unemployment. This American Financial Crisis was a harbinger of the economic turbulence — including sovereign debt crisis and financial contagion — which engulfed the PIIGS (Portugal, Ireland, Italy, Greece and Spain) economies and threatened to suck the banking lenders of France and Germany into this vortex of financial gloom. Indeed, the Eurozone was in deep financial trouble by 2011. That East Asia emerged relatively unscathed and stronger economically may mean that the power shift from the West to the East (with China at its core) will take place sooner than later in the 21st century. Indeed, China is poised to overtake the US and become the largest economy in the world by 2019.[1]

---

[1] "The world's biggest economy: When will China take over from America?" *The Economist*, 16 December 2010.

One sanguine view is that East Asia has emerged the "only bright spot amid the economic turbulence".[2] Moreover, Asian firms are well placed to exploit growth opportunities in at least three areas: the wave of urbanization sweeping across Asia and the resultant demand for substantial infrastructure development; the increased regional connectivity which has created unprecedented flows of goods, capital and people across borders; and that East Asian economies are now more integrated, resulting in bigger, more efficient markets and increased liquidity.[3]

Notwithstanding the American Financial Crisis and the Eurozone debt problem, Asia's rapidly growing middle class is projected to comprise half of the world's middle class by 2020.[4] According to an analyst, the Asia Pacific region's share of the world's middle class was

---

[2] Speech by Singapore Trade and Industry Minister Lim Hng Kiang at the GES Business Leaders Summit. "Emerging Asia a bright spot amid turmoil", *Straits Times*, 19 October 2011. While East Asia has outperformed other regions, it is an overstatement to say that East Asia is the "only bright spot" amidst economic turmoil.

It is a misnomer for the Western media to label the 2008–2009 American Financial Crisis a Global Financial Crisis simply because the world did not sink into a global depression. Besides, the steady economic growth of East Asia and India, even Sub-Sahara Africa was chalking up 5% economic growth in 2011 and projected to rise to 6% in 2012. See International Monetary Fund, "IMF outlook for Sub-Sahara Africa perceives good recent progress on growth and inclusiveness, but cautions on downside risks to global economy", Press release, No. 11/366, 19 October 2011.

The economic performance of Latin America and Caribbean countries in 2011 was also fairly good. The IMF projected: "Driven by commodity producers, Latin America and Caribbean economies should expand 4.5% this year (2011) ... Argentina and Chile will lead the region, growing 8% and 6.5% respectively, while the region's biggest and second-biggest economies — Brazil and Mexico — will both climb 3.8 percent". See "IMF cuts Latin America 2011 GDP forecast on slowing demand", *Bloomberg*, 20 September 2011.

[3] Lim, HK (2011). "Emerging Asia a bright spot amid turmoil", *Straits Times*, 19 October.

[4] See "The rise of Asia's middle class" from DBS Bank, "Imagining Asia 2020" in *Straits Times* (Singapore), 23 October 2011. There is no standard definition or measurement of the middle class in Asia by income or consumption. In DBS Bank's report, *Imagining Asia* 2020, it defines the middle class as those individuals who spend more than US$10 a day.

Table 1.   Share of the world's middle class.

	Population (million)	2009 Share (%)	Population (million)	2020 Share (%)
Asia Pacific	525	28	1,740	54
Europe	664	36	703	22
N. America*	338	18	333	10
C./S. America**	181	10	251	8
M.E./N. Africa***	105	6	165	5
Sub-Sahara Africa	32	2	57	2
Total	**1,845**	**100**	**3,249**	**100**

Note: *North America; **Central/ South America; ***Middle East/North Africa.
Source: DBS Bank, *Imagining Asia 2020*.

28% in 2009 and is likely to capture a 54% share of the world's middle class by 2020 (Table 1). Presumably, the rise of the Asian middle class is a juggernaut that will have implications for the global economy.

Though impressive and prominent, the phenomenal rise of the Chinese economy is only one part of the East Asian developmental story. Besides South Korea, the post-colonial ASEAN countries are doing quite well and aiming to achieve an economic community by 2015. ASEAN, as a sub-region along with China, South Korea and Japan, may well become the lynchpin of a broader East Asian Community (EAC) with a single market within a few decades.

Singapore's Minister of Trade and Industry Lim Hng Kiang notes: "As individual economies, ASEAN may not feature highly in the minds of potential investors, but collectively, the region represents a market of over 550 million people with a GDP of US$1.1 trillion and total trade of about US$1.6 trillion".[5] If we were to consider the ASEAN Plus Three (China, Japan and South Korea) as one potential market with rising consumer demand, its combined population in

---

[5] Lim, HK (2011). *Op. cit.*

2011 is around 2.065 billion people.[6] Their combined GDP by end 2010 is an estimated US$13.5 trillion.[7]

While the ASEAN Plus Three (APT) countries cannot decouple themselves totally from the financial crises of the US and the Eurozone in a globalized and interdependent world, the economic engines of China, South Korea and some ASEAN countries (especially Indonesia) are firing at full cylinders. Arguably, there is a "partial decoupling" from the economic woes of the West because many East Asian countries — though affected by the financial crisis — continue to register impressive economic growth.

That the American Financial Crisis did not worsen into a Global Financial Crisis (engulfing East Asia) is significant. Not only was there no doom and gloom among many APT countries, they demonstrated a national and regional resilience and a sobriety in their financial system. Moreover, the experience of the APT countries in 2008 was a contrast to the 1997–1998 Asian Financial Crisis (AFC) triggered by the rapid inflow and outflow of "hot" and speculative funds from the West. That AFC resulted in the massive devaluation of certain Asian currencies (Thai baht and Indonesian rupiah), economic crisis, and political unrest and change in Indonesia, South Korea and Thailand. Ironically, some Western analysts then castigated the East Asian countries of nepotism, cronyism and corruption and claimed that these practices were the root causes of the AFC.[8] In actuality, the Western toxic products like derivatives ("financial weapons of mass destruction") or CDO (collateralized debt obligation), property bubbles, unsecured "cheap" credit, the hubris of market deregulation and "market rationality" of financial products, the lack of proper state regulation of the financial system, and malfunctioning rating agencies poignantly reveal that malfeasance, greed, incompetence and hubris are common to the West too.

---

[6]The estimated population of the Plus Three countries in 2011 is: China (1.34 billion), Japan (127 million) and South Korea (48 million).
[7]The nominal GDP of the Plus Three countries in 2010 is: China (US$5.93 trillion), Japan (US$5.46 trillion) and South Korea (US$1.0 trillion).
[8]See Lam, PE (2000). The Asian financial crisis and its impact on regional order: Opening Pandora's box. *Journal of Pacific Asia* (Japan), 6, 57–80.

However, to the APT countries (which apparently learnt the lessons of the 1997–1998 Asian Financial Crisis to strengthen their banking systems), there is a "silver lining" to the dark economic clouds from the US and the Eurozone. That there is the political temptation within the US to look for Asian scapegoats (especially China for its alleged currency "manipulation") to explain its economic difficulties means that there is an additional incentive for the APT countries to enhance their cooperation, including the building of an insipient EAC. Nevertheless, the APT countries should avoid *schadenfreude* (maliciously delighting or gloating over the suffering of another) or triumphalism towards the West.

While East Asia is doing well economically, its international relations are more problematic.[9] Indeed, the inter-state relations in East Asia are not comparable to the European Union (EU) where there are no expectations of war among member states. Regional tension in 2010 included the sinking of the *Cheonan* (South Korean naval ship) allegedly by North Korea, and competing territorial claims in the South and East China Seas between China and its neighbors. The US has also taken advantage of these problems to become more assertive in the region notwithstanding China's self-declared "peaceful rise". The big picture in East Asia, therefore, appears mixed — strong economic development and progress in regional free trade agreements and multilateral processes coupled with intensifying geo-strategic competition.

There are at least two compelling reasons why the APT should enhance regional cooperation despite their political differences. First, the East Asian countries are emerging as one another's best trading partners and creating a synergy of economic growth which is good for national resilience, a better life for their masses, and social and political stability. Indeed, the shares of global trade and GDP among APT countries continue to rise inexorably (Fig. 1). Moreover, intra-APT trade is also rising (Fig. 2).

---

[9] The exception is Japan which suffered from two decades of economic stagnation since 1991 and a triple disaster of earthquake, tsunami and nuclear radioactivity in the coast of Northeast Japan in 2011.

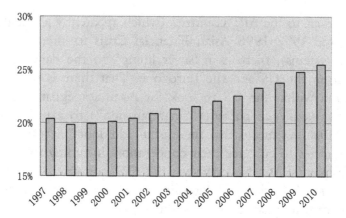

Fig. 1. ASEAN's plus China's, Japan's and Korea's share in global GDP, 1997–2010.

Source: World Economic Outlook Database, IMF, April 2011.

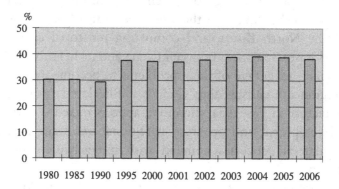

Fig. 2. Intra-regional trade share in ASEAN Plus Three.

Source: Bui Truong Giang (2008). Intra-regional Trade of ASEAN Plus Three: Trends and Implications for East Asian Economic Integration, CNAEC Research Series 08-04, Korea Institute for International Economic Policy.

The second reason is that a habit of regional cooperation and the construction of a common Asian identity will mitigate against the threat of inter-state wars. However, rising economic interdependence and nascent efforts at East Asian regionalism are necessary but not sufficient for regional peace and stability. Diplomacy, wisdom and political goodwill among top Asian leaders, national resilience among the APT countries, an epistemological community of East Asian opinion shapers advocating shared interests and a common identity, and a balance of power are other conducive conditions for a peaceable and prosperous region.[10]

This edited book examines the need for greater East Asian cooperation and the challenges to this grand endeavor. It also examines the political and economic relations between Beijing and its neighbors against the backdrop of two trends: the power shift from the West to the East in the aftermath of the American Financial Crisis and the rise of China. With differing national outlooks, how can East Asia preserve peace, prosperity and stability amidst geo-political competition?

The approach to this edited book is eclectic. Given the diverse scholarly background of scholars from the APT countries, the editors have not sought to impose any orthodoxy of theory and methodology to intellectual enquiry. Rather, each scholar is given a carte blanche to analyze his or her topic to address the broad dialectical theme of cooperation and competition among the East Asian countries in the aftermath of the American Financial Crisis. Such an approach is a better reflection of the different individual and national viewpoints of scholars in a very diverse and pluralistic East Asia. The hope is that a unity (of common themes and concerns) in diversity (of ideas) will emerge in this edited volume.

Indeed, common themes can be drawn from the diverse chapters. Most analysts in this volume are optimistic about the future of East Asia, the economic benefits of China's rise (a powerful economic engine of growth for the region), and the potential of an insipient EAC. However, some analysts are less sanguine about international relations in East Asia. Some of the problems identified are: competition among the vehicles of an East Asian regionalism — between the APT and the broader East Asian Summit (EAS) in which the US, Australia, India and Russia are also members; geo-strategic competition between a rising China and a US superpower in relative decline

---

[10] To some ASEAN countries, a balance of power means a distribution or equilibrium of power *among* great and middle powers in East Asia and not "bandwagoning" with the US *against a rising* China.

(but with a hub and spokes alliance system in East Asia and still the biggest global spender on armaments); the ambivalence among some ASEAN countries and the fear within Japan of China's rise.

The future of East Asia is, therefore, promising yet open ended. While a nascent EAC is conceivably beneficial to East Asians, there is no certainty that notions of state sovereignty, virulent nationalism, territorial feuds, the fear of China's rise among some countries within and outside East Asia, and the resultant political miscalculations will not threaten to derail East Asian regionalism despite market integration.

Chapter Summaries

This edited book is organized in two parts. The first section deals with China's rise and East Asia's political and economic architecture. In the first chapter, Qin Yaqing anchors a rising China within the horizontal networks of East Asian regionalism and not a vertical hierarchy of Asian powers with China at its apex. He argues that East Asian integration has developed multi-layered and pluralistic ways to regional governance. He notes that this regional cooperation has followed a process-oriented model with ASEAN centrality and three conspicuous features: pragmatic functionalism, cooperative multilateralism and open regionalism. Qin highlights at least two necessary features of East Asian regionalism. First, "East Asian regionalism cannot and should not blindly copy European regionalism or other models". Second, "with a group of smaller states (ASEAN) playing the pivotal role, inventing and spreading norms to bigger powers and socializing them [...] it is most desirable for major players to cooperate rather than compete for leadership in the community building process of the region". Simply put, China will cooperate with and not dominate its smaller neighbors in an East Asian regionalism.

In the second chapter, John Wong observes that within six weeks after Lehman Brothers collapsed on 15 September 2008, the Chinese government announced a stimulus package of a whooping 4 trillion RMB to stimulate and stabilize the Chinese economy. This package, he opines, was beneficial not only to China but also to East Asia's economic recovery. Wong perceives that, buoyed by their strong economic development, a relatively more ascendant China and East Asia emerged by 2009. However, he wryly warns that the historical pattern is that all established hegemonic powers (read: the US superpower) will block the rise of another new power. Moreover, the lack of trust and a common identity between a rising China and a US in relative decline will complicate America's acceptance of a China-centric East Asian economy. Implicit in this argument is that growing "trust" between China and its APT neighbors is not sufficient because the attitude and behavior of the US towards China will have consequences for the peace and stability in East Asia.

He Liping in Chapter three examines China's emergence as the world's second largest economy. He explains that, in actuality, the Chinese economy had already surpassed the Japanese economy as early as 2001 by the purchasing power parity method of calculation. He Liping also notes that the rise of the Chinese economy means that its catching-up with the world's advanced economies is now at an end. This implies that China must seek its own model of development in the years ahead. Less pessimistic than John Wong, He believes that the rise of the Chinese economy is not necessarily threatening or destabilizing to others (especially status quo great powers) because China is committed to pursuing greater international cooperation at the global level and East Asian economic integration at the regional level.

Which is the likely tendency or outcome? Will economics trump geo-politics (He Liping) or will geo-politics trump economics (John Wong) in East Asia? Obviously, it is too early to tell. Social science theories of economic integration, institutional building, construction of a common identity, and "realist" geo-strategic competition are only suggestive. Despite the uncertainties of East Asian regionalism and geo-political competition, the editors believe it probable that East Asia today is in the best position to shape its common destiny after the past two hundred years of Western imperialism and colonialism and subsequent decolonization. The American Financial Crisis and the Eurozone Debt Crisis are additional milestones of this structural power shift from West to East.

In Chapter four, Fan Ying and Li Wentao argue that the 2008 Financial Crisis suffered by the West and the sterling performances by the emerging economies of East Asia have transformed the world's economic and political landscape. The fact that some East Asian countries are now G-20 members at global economic governance (in contrast to only Japan in the G7/G8) shows the ascendance of East Asia in the global economic order. Fan and Li argue for even greater cooperation among East Asian countries such as TIF (trade and investment facilitation) in international trade and FDI. Implicit in the argument is that if East Asia can further strengthen its cooperation, it will be in a better stead to weather future global financial storms.

Bill K. P. Chou in Chapter five notes that Hong Kong has weathered the 2008–2009 Financial Crisis well due, in part, to its strategic location next to a booming Mainland China. However, Hong Kong's unique association with China under the "one country, two systems" formula may be a "double-edged sword" because its democratization has also been circumscribed by Beijing and its allies within Hong Kong. To Chou, the biggest problem of Hong Kong's electoral design is the lack of fair representation of the whole society — the interests of businesspeople and pro-Beijing forces are over-represented while the working class and democrats are marginalized. He concludes that this system is "detrimental to the building up of the necessary social solidarity for effective governance". Implicit in Bill Chou's argument is that "man cannot live by bread alone". Even though Hong Kong has benefited materially from its close association with the Mainland, many Hong Kongers aspire for greater democratic reforms.

The next section of the book (Chapters six and seven) addresses the challenges of East Asian regionalism. Wei Ling observes that in the post-financial crisis world, East Asian regionalization has witnessed new complexities, growing political and security concerns and intensified architectural competition. Nevertheless, she opines, "the fundamental themes of the region remain unchanged — peace, development and prosperity. The chances for another Cold War breaking out are small". Wei Ling notes that East Asian regionalization is still at the primary stage of integration. She then proposes that the practical and desirable way forward for East Asian regionalism is "soft institutionalism, 'asymmetrical' interaction and process-oriented construction. Consistent priorities should be given to practical cooperation based on the principles of ASEAN centrality, strategic coordination between major powers and '10+1' as the primary framework". Despite China's economic rise, it should continue to support ASEAN as the hub of East Asian regionalism in the years ahead.

In Chapter seven, Lam Peng Er observes that while East Asia is enjoying remarkable economic growth despite the 2008–2009 American Financial Crisis, political tensions persist in this region. How should order and harmony in East Asia be maintained amidst nation-states jealously guarding their sovereignty and national interests? Conceivably, an East Asian Community can be built around common interests, institutions and an Asian identity for peace and order, and to mitigate parochial nationalism. Lam's central argument is that the EAC should not mimic the European Union but must be based on "Asian" characteristics and the "consent" of both big and small nations in the region. Lam writes: "This includes a 'New Thinking' that moves beyond an obsolete and fatalistic Cold War mentality that conflict (including war) is often inevitable between rising and status quo powers". He then suggests an alternative "Hoi An" model based on regional history, mutual economic gain, multiculturalism, tolerance and cooperation as a "once and future" model for East Asia. Lam explains: "In the 17th and 18th century, Hoi An was a bustling cosmopolitan port-city in central Vietnam which serviced merchants from Asia and beyond. I will explain Hoi An as a model and metaphor for East Asian cooperation".

Cheong Young-Rok and Song Mee Joo present a South Korean perspective of Sino–South Korean relations in Chapter eight. They note that bilateral relations have been less rosy since 2008 when the American Financial Crisis erupted. Some Korean analysts wondered whether Chinese attitudes towards South Korea have changed because it has become the G2 alongside the US in the global hierarchy of power. The co-authors opine that Beijing seeks to maintain stability on the Korean peninsula. They also argue that China has a grand strategy of linking the North Korean issue with Taiwan: "Having two theaters, both serving as likely sources of war, divides

US' attention. ... By locking US attention on the North Korean issue, North Korea serves a means of diverting US attention from the Taiwan issue. As such, North Korea still is a key chip with which China negotiates a workable relationship with the US. [...] When the time is ripe, with its increased economic potentials that exceed that of US, China can fulfill its reunification with Taiwan".

The remaining chapters of the book examine the interaction of China and Southeast Asia against the backdrop of a structural shift from West to East, and the American–European financial crises. In Chapter nine, Yang Mu and Catherine Chong argue that the 1997–1998 Asian Financial Crisis and the 2008–2009 American Financial Crisis were golden opportunities for China and Southeast Asia to broaden and deepen their economic ties for mutual benefits. Indeed, the latest financial crisis will allow China to diversity and increase its economic influence in this region. This closer economic partnership is evidenced by the China–ASEAN Free Trade Area (CAFTA) which took off in January 2010. By that year, China–ASEAN bilateral trade reached US$292.8 billion with a year-on-year increase of 37.5%. In 2009, China established an ASEAN Cooperation Fund valued at US$10 billion and intends to set up a US$15 billion loan to invest in ASEAN's infrastructure, energy, resources, information technology and telecommunication industries.

In Chapter ten, Indonesian scholar Syamsul Hadi examines the aftermath and implications of the American Financial Crisis, China's rise and the prospects of East Asian regionalism. He explains that Indonesia affirms the centrality of ASEAN in the architecture of East Asia. There is also some ambivalence in Jakarta towards an East Asian Community because it would mean that the significance of ASEAN would be diluted in a bigger and more prestigious EAC with richer "+3" countries. Syamsul Hadi observes that amidst the debates on the new configuration in East Asia, Chinese Premier Wen Jiabao visited Indonesia and other ASEAN countries in April 2011 and signaled Beijing's intentions to substantially help in the construction of transportation and other infrastructure projects in Indonesia and ASEAN. He notes that notwithstanding intractable territorial disputes between China and some ASEAN countries, the former is offering the latter tangible material benefits to cement their relations.

In the following chapter, Lye Liang Fook examines two decades of China–Singapore relations since the establishment of diplomatic relations in 1990. In his assessment, China–Singapore relations are broad, strong and substantive. Besides the good personal rapport between their leaders, there is a high-level institutional mechanism in place to drive bilateral cooperation. Moreover, flagships projects like the Suzhou Industrial Park and the Sino–Singapore Tianjin Eco-city have reinforced bilateral ties. In the midst of the global economic uncertainty, it is even more important for the two countries to maintain a stable and mutually beneficial relationship. In this regard, Singapore's good relations with the US superpower and even Taiwan have not hindered the development of closer ties with China.

Contemporary Sino–Vietnamese economic relations are the theme of Chapter twelve. Do Tien Sam and Ha Thi Hong Van note that although Vietnam's foreign trade suffered heavily at the outset of the 2008 Financial Crisis, Vietnam–China trade relations gained momentum. Indeed, China has already surpassed Japan to become Vietnam's largest trading partner by 2003. They opine that the ASEAN–China Free Trade Agreement may not benefit every member due to their different levels of development. Thus, Vietnam will face a big challenge when participating fully in this free trade area in 2015 and its trade deficit with China might well increase. Notwithstanding territorial disputes in the South China Sea, Vietnam–China economic relations in recent years have indeed been enhanced.

In Chapter thirteen, Lee Kam Hing examines Sino–Malaysian economic ties between 2000 and 2010. He observes that further growth in bilateral trading and investment ties is underpinned by China's economic rise as the world's second largest economy and its strong and sustained demand for Malaysian commodities. Although the 2008–2009 American Financial Crisis and its aftermath have impacted China and Malaysia in a globalized world, both countries have fared better economically than the US, EU and Japan. Economic relations between Malaysia and China are anticipated to deepen and broaden notwithstanding the above mentioned financial crisis. Lee also points out that Malaysia is China's largest trading partner in the ASEAN region with almost a quarter of China's trade with the region in 2009. Lee also notes the irony: "Wariness of a rising China, noted among the dominant Malay political elites, is blunted by a growing involvement in China's trade by the mainly Malay-led state-linked companies".

In the final chapter, Andrea Chloe A. Wong examines Philippines–China economic relations. The Philippines values its economic ties with China but is ambivalent about its rise as a great power. Their territorial dispute in the South China Sea remains intractable. Wong notes: "While prudently promoting long-term cooperation and engagement with a rising China, the Philippines remains an ally of the US superpower. Moreover, the Philippines seeks to gain economic benefits from China, given that the US and EU are mired in economic crisis since 2008". She argues that the Philippines seeks to strike a balance between its economic and geo-strategic interests by pursuing its national interests while developing a mutually beneficial partnership with China.

What are some insights drawn from these chapters? First, the American Financial Crisis and Eurozone Crisis did have an impact on the East Asian economies but their growth and development have not been derailed. That reveals the resilience of the Asian economies. Second, China has now become an important engine of growth for East Asia and this is welcomed by its neighbors despite their concerns and ambivalence about geo-politics and economic competition. Third, China and East Asia support the grand enterprise of an insipient East Asian Community but have no consensus on how to attain this lofty goal. Although there is no present agreement on the modalities of East Asian regionalism — such as its geographical boundaries, primary institutions (APT or EAS?), membership, timetable and functions — the East Asian countries have pragmatically adopted an ASEAN-centered regionalism based on the norms of "consensus" and proceeding at a comfort level acceptable to most East Asian countries.

It is difficult to predict the future trajectory of East Asia: will the region be locked in a geo-political struggle (against the backdrop of China's rise and the US' insistence on maintaining its hegemony as the sole superpower) or able to manage existing political differences peacefully while cooperating on trade and regionalism? Notwithstanding these uncertainties, China and East Asia can exude quiet confidence and hope for a better future after weathering the American Financial Crisis and the Eurozone Crisis. China and its neighbors have indeed emerged from these financial storms relatively unscathed, even stronger and perhaps paving the way for an East Asian Renaissance by the mid-21st century.

Acknowledgments

The editors are grateful to Professor Zheng Yongnian, Director of the East Asian Institute for his kind intellectual support in bringing this project into fruition. We extend our appreciation to the World Scientific editorial team of Sandhya Venkatesh, Agnes Ng and Samantha Wong for bringing this edited volume out in a timely manner.

Bibliography

DBS Bank (2011). The rise of Asia's middle class. From DBS Bank, "Imagining Asia 2020", *Straits Times*, 23 October.

International Monetary Fund (2011). "IMF outlook for Sub-Sahara Africa perceives good recent progress on growth and inclusiveness, but cautions on downside risks to global economy", Press release, No. 11/366, 19 October.

Lam, PE (2000). The Asian financial crisis and its impact on regional order: Opening Pandora's box. *Journal of Pacific Asia* (Japan), 6, 57–80.

Lim, HK (2011). "Emerging Asia a bright spot amid turmoil", *Straits Times*, 19 October.

EAST ASIA'S POLITICAL AND ECONOMIC ARCHITECTURE

Chapter 1

EAST ASIAN REGIONALISM: ARCHITECTURE, APPROACH AND ATTRIBUTES

QIN Yaqing

East Asian regionalism has progressed remarkably in many areas but is now at the crossroads. While the region continues to be dynamic and progressive, it is confronted by many challenges: ASEAN seems to lack a strong leadership, the "ASEAN Way" faces new problems, institutional progress lags behind expectations, the major countries need to strengthen their bilateral relations and engage in regional cooperation, and "power rivalry" has intensified after the so-called United States (US) "return" to East Asia during the Obama Administration. Moreover, East Asia has the challenge and opportunity to cooperate and prosper together against the backdrop of the 2008–2009 American Financial Crisis, and the 2011 Eurozone Crisis triggered by the potential financial defaults of the PIIGS (Portugal, Ireland, Italy, Greece and Spain). This chapter raises the following questions: What are the possibilities for an East Asian architecture? What forms will and should East Asian regionalism take? And what are the distinctive features that have developed in the regional processes that we should be mindful of?

Regionalism gained momentum in East Asia after eruption of the Asian Financial Crisis in 1997. The crisis was a catalyst to the ASEAN Ten establishing the ASEAN Plus China, Japan and

Republic of Korea (ROK) cooperation framework to bring Northeast and Southeast Asia together to deal with common problems. Within a decade, East Asian regionalism, led by ASEAN and characterized by openness, informality and consensus, saw unprecedented dynamism and development. In 2005, countries like Australia, New Zealand and India joined the East Asian Summit held in Malaysia and provided momentum for regional cooperation. In 2010, Russia and the US decided to do likewise. Simply put, great, middle and small powers alike have seen the need to participate in East Asian regionalism.

During the Cold War, East Asia was sucked into the vortex of great power confrontation. Wars in Vietnam, Laos and Cambodia also broke out in the region. However, in the post-Cold War era, East Asia has avoided inter-state wars. Nevertheless, East Asia today neither possesses a clear hierarchy of power for regional order (as in the case of the North American continent) nor approximates the European Union (EU) with a high level of institutionalization. Indeed, East Asia's regionalism is different from the North American Free Trade Agreement (NAFTA) dominated by the US superpower and the pooling of national sovereignty with a supranational parliament in Brussels and a common currency. Indeed, it is unreasonable to use NAFTA or the EU as benchmarks for East Asia because its history, culture, geographical footprint and the distribution of power is different from North America and Europe. This chapter will discuss the architecture, forms and features of the East Asian regionalism within the menu of possibilities.

The chapter argues that East Asian integration has developed multi-layered and pluralistic ways to regional governance. This regional cooperation has followed a process-oriented model with ASEAN centrality and has demonstrated three conspicuous features: Pragmatic functionalism, cooperative multilateralism and open regionalism. Moreover, the openness of East Asian regionalism is shaped in the practices of Asian nations, bears the marks of history and is driven by market-oriented integration and parallel developments between internal and external linkages.

I. Architecture: Multi-layered and Pluralistic Governance

The multi-layered and pluralistic architecture is a distinctive mode of governance in East Asia. Although European scholars think European integration is characterized by multi-layered governance and diversity,[1] the diversity, multiplicity and pluralism in East Asia is far more conspicuous. Regional cooperative mechanisms are based on two somewhat overlapping geographic regions — East Asia and the Asia Pacific. East Asia in geographic terms hosts ASEAN, ASEAN Plus Three (APT), ASEAN Plus One — for instance, China, Japan and ROK, Trilateral Cooperation (China, Japan and ROK), and the Greater Mekong Sub-region mechanisms.

Cooperation mechanisms expanded to the Asia Pacific mainly include the East Asia Summit, ASEAN Regional Forum and the Trans-Pacific Strategic Economic Partnership (TPP). There is neither a clear hierarchical order nor specific division of labor among these mechanisms, some of which overlap not only in geographical coverage but also in functional areas. Even under one framework, the cooperation process can be quite complicated, with dialogues, meetings, workshops and consultations and different foci, in different forms and at different levels. For example, the ASEAN Plus Three alone has over 60 cooperative mechanisms in more than 20 areas. All these regional institutions and arrangements co-exist and develop in a parallel pattern, unfolding in a complicated, tangling networking process of East Asian integration.

Such complexity in the regional architecture is sometimes called a "noodle bowl" — too messy, interlocked and complicated to be a feasible form of regional governance. Some analysts believe that so many institutions, mechanisms and platforms can frustrate state leaders who have neither time nor energy to participate in such frequent meetings and consultations. However, despite the complexity, this architecture not only reflects the basic reality of the region, but also promotes regional cooperation and development in different respects. Moreover, these overlapping and entangling mechanisms

---

[1]Jachtenfuchs, M and B Kohler-Koch (2004). Governance and institutional development. In *European Integration Theory*, A Wiener and T Diez (eds.), pp. 97–115. Oxford: Oxford University Press.

and platforms have helped nurture and develop, to some extent, a culture of cooperation among the nations in East Asia in the post-Cold War era.

In turn, such a culture, together with its principal norms, has further promoted cooperation in the region. On the one hand, they exemplify a respect for the regional reality of diversity and pluralism; on the other hand, they have made positive contributions to promoting pragmatic cooperation. In the East Asian cooperation process, diversified mechanisms at various levels have, in a pragmatic manner, improved state-to-state relations, nurtured friendship among state leaders, promoted substantive transnational cooperation and produced tangible and significant results. Therefore, the multi-layered, plural and pluralistic architecture has indeed been an effective way of governance in East Asia.

II. Approach: ASEAN-led "Processualism"

The major form of East Asian cooperation is ASEAN-led "processualism".[2] Regional integration models in the Western IR context are often based on law, treaties and formal institutions, with the EU as a typical example. A high level of institutionalization with the capability and effectiveness of establishing binding treaties is considered necessary to guarantee institutional cooperation. Because a relatively high level of institutionalization makes it reasonably easy to predict the conduct of relevant parties and to obtain expected results, it is believed to be the most effective way of regional governance.[3] Almost

---

[2] A definition of processualism is: "the study of social structures and cultures by analyzing and comparing their processes and methodologies". See Qin, Y and Wei, L (2008). Structures, processes and the socialization of power: East Asian community building and the rise of China. In *China's Ascent: Power, Security and the Future of International Politics*, RS Ross and Zhu, F (eds.), pp. 115–138. Ithaca, New York: Cornell University Press.

[3] Keohane, R (1984). *After Hegemony: Cooperation and Discord in the World Political Economy*. Princeton, NJ: Princeton University Press; Martin, LL and BA Simons (1999). Theories and empirical studies of international institutions. In *Exploration and Contestation in the Study of World Politics*, PJ Katzenstein, RO Keohane and SD Krasner (eds.), pp. 89–117. Cambridge, MA: The MIT Press.

every milestone in European integration is marked by legal documents, which are tangible results in themselves. To some extent, European integration has been result-oriented, aiming at tangible results with existing institutions and through enhancing institutionalization.[4]

However, East Asia tells a different story. East Asian regionalization is process-oriented because the ASEAN Way emphasizes informality and minimum organization while paying great attention to safeguarding, maintaining and balancing all the processes that favor cooperation.[5] To institutionalists, such cooperative mechanisms are loose frameworks rather than formal institutional arrangements on legal bases, for they cannot constrain the behavior of member nation-states by issuing effective sanctions or authoritative orders. However, the process-oriented model in East Asia has propelled the continuous development and advancement of various under-institutionalized cooperative processes. The long-term goal of East Asian regionalism, set at the 2004 10+3 summit, is to build an East Asian community.[6] Tenacious efforts have resulted in an important achievement — creating a process of East Asian regional cooperation. It is true that the initial dynamic for this process is economic in nature, and it is true that the most tangible achievements in the region are functional. But at the same time, the process itself produces certain dynamics. Norms of cooperation have been established and spread, gradually incorporating the major powers in the region.

An important feature of processualism is gradualness, that is, the seeking of incremental changes rather than revolutionary transformation. East Asian cooperation is characterized by minimal institutionalization, which often lags behind practical cooperation. The aim is not to negate institutionalization, which is still a most

---

[4] European integration is marked by treaties, while East Asian regionalization is marked by declarations. The difference between treaties and declarations demonstrate that the two regional processes depend on different paths.

[5] Acharya, A (2001). *Constructing a Security Community in Southeast Asia*, p. 5. London and New York: Routledge.

[6] ASEAN Secretariat (2004). Strengthening ASEAN + 3 cooperation — Chairman's statement of the 8th ASEAN + 3 summit. Vientiane, 29 November 2004. http://www.aseansec.org/16847.htm [accessed 20 November 2010].

important way of governance. But it reflects the reality of the region and the practice of the nations. When ASEAN was established in 1967, it was largely a political forum to guarantee the collective strategic position of member states and to resolve internal conflicts. It was not until the 1990s that substantive functional cooperation began to develop. The first ASEAN Summit was held eight years after its establishment and its non-binding and informal nature was maintained till the 1990s. While the first APT meeting among heads of states was held in 1997, the APT structure was only institutionalized in 1999. The ASEAN Secretariat remained small from the 1970s to the 1990s. Even in 2011, the coordinating office for APT was still a unit in the ASEAN Secretariat, with functions limited to managing economic and technical cooperation. For a long time, the APT was regarded as a forum for information sharing, a platform for policy coordination, a market for bargaining, and sometimes just a talking shop. However, habits and norms have been nurtured and produced in dialogues, consultations and interactive socialization processes. Mechanisms like the East Asia Summit are even looser than ASEAN and the APT due to its diverse membership including non-Asian countries.

What is closely tied to processualism in regionalization is the phenomenon that major powers do not necessarily lead. In result-oriented interactions, leadership by material power seems to be a main factor, and regional integration or cooperation is to be led or even dominated by major powers. For example, European cooperation after World War II was launched to avoid war among the major powers in Europe, especially France and Germany. In the post-war integration process, France and Germany have indeed made significant contributions. For instance, at the initial stage of European cooperation, almost all important ideas and concepts were developed and proposed by the French. Those ideas and concepts have provided a direction and blueprint for European integration.

However, the East Asian process is entirely different. From the very beginning, ASEAN has played a major or leading role. In process-oriented regionalism, cooperation is led by a group of smaller states — ASEAN — and radiates from this core to other countries in the region. Such East Asian cooperation was first practiced by small and medium-sized countries in Southeast Asia and was later led by ASEAN. Despite challenges and doubts, ASEAN insists on and adheres to its leadership, centrality and driving role in regional processes, for which major countries have also expressed their support time and again.[7]

Some may believe that major regional powers are the natural leaders based on either the North American or the EU models. In addition, they even talk about regional power transition and Sino–Japanese rivalry for the leading role in the regional process. This so-called rivalry is not feasible or desirable because neither China nor Japan can lead the process of the East Asian regionalism, let us leave alone community building at present. China used to have problems with many ASEAN nations and only began to improve relations with them after the adoption of the reform and opening-up policy in the late 1970s. As a latecomer, China joined the regional process first as ASEAN's guest, then as a dialogue partner, and then finally as a member of the enlarged structure of 10+1, 10+3, and the EAS. Therefore, China is not positioned to lead the process.

Moreover, self-restraint by the big powers is a necessary condition for community building and for the formation of a collective identity.[8] As the rapid rise of a country with 1.3 billion people is unprecedented, there is still suspicion and uncertainty about China both inside and outside the region. What China needs to do now is to strengthen trust and relations with other actors in the region, to demonstrate its intention and determination for peaceful development, and to join the regional integration process for a better regional order, which is even more urgent, especially when one thinks about the domestic developmental strategy of China.

---

[7] At a press conference on 7 March 2010, Chinese Foreign Minister Yang Jiechi said, "I want to point out that China always holds that ASEAN should play a pivotal role in regional cooperation in East Asia. We support ASEAN leadership." http://www.fmprc.gov.cn/chn/pds/sp/t662298.htm [accessed 21 March 2010].

[8] Wendt, A (1999). *Social Theory of International Politics*, pp. 357–363. Cambridge: Cambridge University Press.

Japan is not in a position to lead either. There are three main reasons. First, like China, Japan is also a latecomer being positioned in the enlarged structure of APT and EAS. Although it once led regional economic growth through the "Flying Geese" pattern, it is very much a follower that joined the ongoing regional process initiated by ASEAN. Second, Japan has an identity issue. The debate over joining the West or the East has continued and even today people in Japan continually argue over whether Japan should promote East Asian community building. Third, there is a lack of trust in Japan by the region. Especially in recent years, Japan's relations with neighboring countries have been problematic.

Realistically speaking, ASEAN is the only qualified driver in the regional process if the goal is to make East Asian regional integration possible and workable. As a hub of the regional institutional and normative structure, ASEAN has been playing a pivotal role in coordinating cooperation. It has developed extensive connections with not only China, Japan and ROK, but also major players outside the region. The ASEAN way, characterized by informality, consensus and respect for each other has been expanded to the Plus Three and to some extent the bigger countries such as China and Japan have been socialized into this ASEAN way. In addition, the most important role played by ASEAN has been as a norm entrepreneur and norm propagator.[9] This is a role that no other country is able to replicate.

It is important, however, that we should realize the weakness of ASEAN. In the 1980s and 1990s, ASEAN played an extremely important role in regional affairs, especially among the original Five, namely, Indonesia, Malaysia, Thailand, the Philippines, and Singapore. In recent years, ASEAN leadership has been challenged by many factors. First, domestic problems, such as economic recession and political instability, have haunted some of these countries and impaired their capabilities to lead. Second, non-traditional security challenges are on the rise. Terrorism and natural disasters

---

[9] Finnemore, M and K Sikkink (1999). International norm dynamics and political change. In *Exploration and Contestation in the Study of World Politics*, PJ Katzenstein, RO Keohane and SD Krasner (eds.), pp. 247–277. Cambridge, MA: The MIT Press.

have added to the difficulties faced by some ASEAN nations. Third, ASEAN cohesiveness has been somewhat weakened in the past few years. Border disputes and occasional conflicts have caused tensions. There were debates among ASEAN members over the ASEAN Charter regarding its binding force. There were proposals to reform the ASEAN Way and make it more efficient. There were debates within Indonesia on whether it should go beyond ASEAN to play a significant role in the G20.[10] There have been doubts and pessimism about the realization of an ASEAN Community in 2015.

Thus it is important to realize that a prosperous and stable ASEAN is an asset to the regional process. Major countries in particular should express strong political will to support ASEAN for its continued leading role in regional cooperation, for whether ASEAN is able to play the leading role at present will very much decide whether or not the regional cooperative process will continue.

III. Attributes: Pragmatic Functionalism, Cooperative Multilateralism and Open Regionalism

In the past decade, East Asia's regional processes have developed and displayed three distinctive attributes: Pragmatic functionalism, cooperative multilateralism and open regionalism. It is not like the EU, which started from the desire to eliminate the possibility of war and whose functionalism, therefore, had a clear security orientation and a political connotation.

Pragmatic functionalism means that regional cooperation in East Asia and the Asia Pacific is most active and fruitful in functional areas. East Asia is the most economically dynamic region in the world, which would not have been possible without substantive regional cooperation in functional areas. Both ASEAN and APT have developed specific work plans for many years. The EAS, though designed to be a

---

[10] Hadi, S (2010). Defending the centrality of ASEAN: Indonesia and the politics of regional architecture in East Asia in the post global crisis. Paper presented at the "International Conference on China and East Asia in the Post Financial Crisis World. Beijing, 2–3 December.

strategic leaders-led forum, is increasingly pragmatic, especially in functional areas like finance, trade, energy and non-traditional security. The ASEAN Connectivity Master Plan and China–ASEAN Free Trade Area are both examples of successful functional cooperation.

Cooperative multilateralism is also conspicuous in East Asia. ASEAN plans to realize an ASEAN Community by 2015, with three pillars of ASEAN economic community, ASEAN security community, and ASEAN socio-cultural community. The Chiang Mai Initiative is a typical example of cooperative multilateralism in the very important functional area of finance. Nonetheless, cooperative multilateralism in East Asia is based on sovereign states, which is a major difference from the pooling of sovereignty practiced in the EU with supranational institutions (including a European parliament) in Brussels.

East Asian regionalism is by nature and necessity open; open in geographical boundaries, institutional establishments and cooperative processes. Not only has functional cooperation been expanded to countries outside geographical East Asia, but also institutions have been open and flexible to integrate newcomers, and processes open to positive contributions from both within and outside East Asia. There are three important factors that have shaped this openness of East Asia.

First, openness is shaped by history. After World War II, the US established alliances with several East Asian countries and set up a hub-and-spoke security system. Such a system has made the region porous.[11] Thus, in politics and security East Asia is closely connected with actors in other regions, especially the United States. When more countries join, the degree of openness will further increase.

Second, the openness is determined by its market-oriented nature. Both the development of the Asian four tigers in the 1980s and China's recent rise have followed an export-oriented strategy. Although the intra-regional trade of East Asia is over 50% of the total,[12] the growth of East Asia relies heavily on the consumption of

---

[11] Katzenstein, PJ (2005). *A World of Regions: Asia and Europe in the American Imperium*. Ithaca, New York: Cornell University Press.

[12] Wen, J (2003). Jointly compose a new chapter of East Asian cooperation. Speech delivered at the 7th ASEAN Plus Three Summit, 7 October 2003, Bali, Indonesia. http://ie.china-embassy.org/chn/xwgg/t27172.htm [accessed 20 November 2010].

foreign markets in other regions. The market-oriented nature of East Asian regionalism makes the region inseparable from the world economic system.

Third, the internal process of East Asian integration with ASEAN as the core parallels the development of the region's linkages with the outside world. ASEAN was designed to be an open process and continues to work towards further openness. It first enlarged the core from five countries to 10, and then further opened the process to other nations. The 10+3, 10+1, and other 10+*x* are all examples of this openness. It is open to countries in both Southeast Asia (Vietnam, Laos, Myanmar, etc.) and Northeast Asia (China, Japan, and ROK). In addition, the EAS has been opened further to countries outside the region, including Australia, India, New Zealand, and very recently Russia and the US. The APT has been recognized as the main vehicle of East Asian community building, and the EAS as an important forum for strategic architecture of the region.[13] The enlargement of the EAS has increased the economic openness of East Asia to the outside world.

IV. Powers and the Region: China, Japan and the US

ASEAN leadership or centrality in regional processes by no means reduces the significance of the roles of major powers in the region. In fact, an important strategy taken by ASEAN has been to keep a balance among the major powers. In the East Asian context, we need to discuss China, Japan and the US, as it is of paramount importance for the regional process that major powers cooperate rather than rival, coordinate rather than show discord, and complement one another rather than conflict with each other.

China is an important actor in the region. China has been an active participant in multilateral cooperation and important promoter of stability and economic development in East Asia. China supports regional economic cooperation, from which all participants can benefit. After the Asian Financial Crisis broke out in 1997, China played a responsible role and did not depreciate the Chinese currency, the *Renminbi*.

---

[13] ASEAN Secretariat. Strengthening ASEAN + 3 Cooperation — Chairman's Statement of the 8th ASEAN + 3 Summit.

China supported the Chiang Mai Initiative and became the biggest sponsor along with Japan for this regional reserve pool of funds.

China has actively participated in and supported the development of Asian bond markets. The China–ASEAN Free Trade Area boasts US$6 trillion GDP and benefits 1.9 billion people. China is the biggest trading partner of ASEAN, Japan and ROK. In 2010, China's trade with ASEAN reached US$292.78 billion and recorded an increase of 37.5% in comparison with that in 2009. China's trade with Japan and ROK reached around US$300 billion and US$207 billion, respectively. China has also become the largest export market of Japan, ROK, Malaysia, Thailand, and Indonesia.[14]

Beijing advocates common and cooperative security. To maintain regional stability and peace, as a responsible and important state in the region, China proposed the "new concept of security" with common and cooperative security at its core. To maintain regional stability and economic development, China supports ASEAN centrality in the regional process. For regional flashpoints, for example, the DPRK nuclear issue, China has been an active coordinator and promoter of peaceful resolution through talks and consultations. On disputed territorial issues, China adheres to the principle of "shelving disputes for joint development". China was the first among ASEAN's dialogue partners to sign the Treaty of Amity and Cooperation of Southeast Asia. Beijing also signed other important political and security documents, such as the Declaration on the Conduct of Parties in the South China Sea. Moreover, the improvement of cross-strait relations between Mainland China and Taiwan has also contributed to regional peace and stability.

China has been a supporter of open regionalism at critical junctures in East Asian cooperation. For instance, China welcomes the accession of the US to the EAS because China hopes to promote multilateral cooperation in the Asia Pacific together with the US for peace, stability and development of the region where the interests of the two countries

---

[14] Interview with Assistant Foreign Minister Hu Zhengyue (2011). Xinhua News Agency, 16 January. http://news.xinhuanet.com/world/2011–01/16/c_12985983. htm [accessed 20 January 2011].

interact most. In recent years, China's participation in the East Asian cooperation process has become even more active than before. In the meantime, the rapidly growing Chinese economy is a catalyst for regional economic development. The history and reality of East Asia has shown that a stable, prosperous and progressive China is of great significance to peace, development and cooperation in East Asia.

China–Japan cooperation is necessary for furthering East Asian regionalization. Beijing and Tokyo have had troublesome political relations in the past because of disputes over history, territory, and resources. However, the two countries and the two people have enjoyed friendship for more than three decades since the establishment of diplomatic relations. Sino–Japanese relations are also well-developed economically. The two countries are highly interdependent in terms of trade and investment. By November 2005, FDI from Japan into China amounted to US$52.8 billion. Japan was China's biggest trading partner from 1993 to 2003. Japan's economic aid has supported China's reforms and the rapid development of China has helped the economic recovery of Japan.[15] Thus there is plenty of room for cooperation between China and Japan.

For example, China is confronted with environmental problems and the issue of large energy consumption. Japan has first-rate environmental protection and energy conservation technologies. Also, regional integration and community building call for cooperation and joint efforts by Beijing and Tokyo. As the two biggest economies in the region, China and Japan account for an overwhelming proportion of the regional economy. It is thus evident that successful East Asian regionalism needs cooperation between the two nations. Under such circumstances, should rivalry exist between China and Japan for leadership in regionalism, the process itself will be doomed. At the same time, a deterioration of Sino–Japanese relations would also be harmful to this regional process aimed at peace and prosperity.

---

[15] The Trilateral Committee. Challenges to trilateral cooperation. Report of the Trilateral Commission Tokyo Plenary Meeting 2006. http://anomalies.net/archive/trilateral/trialogue_series/T57%20-%20The%20Tokyo%20Plenary%20Meeting%20(2006).pdf [accessed 30 November 2010].

The US also has important interests in East Asia and China–US cooperation in regional processes is highly desirable. Traditionally, the US was not very keen about East Asian multilateralism and sought to materialize its interests mainly through bilateralism, especially by maintaining relations with its allies and friends in the region. In fact, it did not adopt a policy of supporting East Asian multilateralism in the early years of the Cold War. Even in the early 1990s, the US did not welcome the idea of the former Japanese Foreign Minister Nakayama to establish a forum to discuss regional security issues and the idea of the former Malaysian Prime Minister Mahathir for an East Asian caucus. During the Clinton administration, the US somewhat shifted its attitude and began to join some of the region's multilateral activities, notably the APEC and ARF.

When the rise of China coincides with the development of East Asian regionalism, some people in the US are concerned, thinking that China may replace the US in terms of influence in the region. Thus, for the US, its policy seemed for a time somewhat unclear: While it was not opposed to East Asian multilateralism, it was not actively supportive of it. Some major concerns of the US were repeatedly reflected in many discussions of Washington's Asian strategy. For example, whether East Asian regionalism should replace or threaten US bilateral alliance system, i.e., the hub-and-spoke structure; and whether this regional multilateral process would be dominated by China, i.e., the emergence of a regional hegemon. Washington is deeply concerned that this would diminish the US role and damage its interests in the region.

It is out of these worries that the US made up its mind to take a more active part in the EAS. These worries exist and will continue to do so, given the fact that East Asia is still very much a region dominated by the state-centric Westphalian system. Moreover, events that occurred in 2010 concerning the South China Sea and other parts of the region have caused even more concerns. On further evaluation, however, these concerns are not as serious as originally thought.

First, the US interests in the region are longstanding and China recognizes this. The fundamental and foremost task for Beijing at present and for a long time in the future is the improvement of the well-being of its own people and the development of its own nation. Second, China does not have the capacity to reduce American influence in the region underpinned by its military presence and economic strength. To be sure, China is rising but its capability is exaggerated.[16] The US still plays a key role in regional security, both traditional and non-traditional, as well as in economic affairs.

Third, the East Asian regionalism is not a zero-sum game between Beijing and Washington. China's rise does not come at the expense of US interests or result in the automatic decline of American influence in the region. Asian countries do not, will not, and should not have to choose between China and the US. Fourth, nations in the region in general and ASEAN nations in particular do not want to take sides between China and the US. The worst scenario seems to be that they would have to choose. It is not likely that such a situation would emerge, but it is an indicator that China and the United States have complementary rather that conflicting roles to play. Better coordination and cooperation between them will benefit not only these two countries, but also nations and peoples in the region.

Experience has proven that East Asian regional integration can bring about stability and prosperity in the region, which is also in the interests of the US. It is time that the US joined, in one way or another, the regional process and made constructive contributions to dynamic regional cooperation. It is highly desirable that China and the US cooperate to make the region more peaceful, prosperous and progressive. For such a purpose, a win–win mentality is a necessity.

V. East Asian Regionalism: Prospects and Limits

East Asia's multi-layered, plural and pluralistic architecture will remain relatively unchanged for a long time. The highly institutionalized, formal and binding, rule-based nature of the EU is unlikely to occur in East Asia. The existing mechanisms will expand and deepen for future development, each playing a role in the complex processes.

---

[16]Nye, JS Jr (2010). American and Chinese power after the financial crisis. *The Washington Quarterly*, 33(4), 143–153.

Any attempt to overhaul and integrate the regional mechanisms into one neat whole is unlikely to succeed.

The ASEAN-led processualism will also continue to work in the region. Despite the goal of an ASEAN Community by 2015, it is not going to be as institutionalized as the EU. The East Asian community remains as a long-term goal, a direction for regional cooperative efforts and an ideal for sustained regional endeavor. Nonetheless, the processes to achieve the goal can shape common interests, build a basic consensus, establish a peaceful code of conduct, and construct a shared identity among participants. Moreover, ASEAN is likely to continue playing the pivotal role in the regional processes in the foreseeable future. It is unrealistic to hasten to obtain substantive results or to establish a regional community. Open regionalism will become an increasingly prominent feature in the years ahead because outside powers have been paying increasing attention to East Asia since the 2008–2009 American Financial Crisis and ASEAN is unlikely to change its basic strategy of power-balancing (by drawing the great powers into the region), at least in the near future. Open regionalism is by no means an empty slogan, but a reflection of the basic reality of East Asia.

Since the architecture and basic form of East Asia will remain unchanged, the three distinctive features of East Asian regionalism — pragmatic functionalism, cooperative multilateralism, and open regionalism — will be reinforced rather than replaced. Some are pessimistic about East Asian integration, worrying that such regionalism will not lead East Asia to the goal of a community. They are not entirely unreasonable. But they have neglected both the reality of East Asia and the sensibility and feasibility of such architecture, form and features. The multi-layered structure is mainly caused by the interlocking interests of different actors in the region. Various factors and forces have various impacts and roles to play in the regional processes. And thus the regional architecture naturally evolves into a multi-level and multi-process complex, resting on a relatively stable "balance of relations".[17]

---

[17] Qin, Y (2009). Relationality and processual construction. *Social Sciences in China*, 30(4), 5–20.

It is such a balance that has enabled peace, stability and development in East Asia.

Nonetheless, a negative effect of multi-layered and pluralistic architecture is the overlap and even redundancy of mechanisms. Most cooperative mechanisms in East Asia develop in a parallel pattern without a hierarchical order or clear division of labor. For example, the APT and the EAS have almost become parallel mechanisms in the region, with their respective functions in constant consultations and debates. In financial cooperation and FTA building, multilateral arrangements often encounter much more difficulties than the bilateral ones and hence lag far behind.

The negative part of processualism is the slow pace of integration and under-development of institutions. ASEAN has exposed its inefficiency and ineffectiveness to some degree in solving problems among its member states. It has become a critical question in East Asian cooperation as to how to strike an appropriate balance between processes and results, between informality and formality, between gradualness and efficiency, and between ASEAN leadership and ASEAN capability. Open regionalism enlists constructive contributions to the region on the one hand, but increases the risk of losing geographic boundaries on the other. Although regions are heavily influenced by political, strategic and social specifications rather than determined by geographic units, the distinctiveness of a region calls for a necessary geographic boundary with an Asian cultural core. Otherwise, it would be extremely difficult to realize a comprehensive community with economic, security and socio-cultural pillars.[18]

Solving these problems is a long-term goal of the region, which requires ongoing cooperation. At present, it is important to coordinate thoroughly various mechanisms, adopt an open and inclusive attitude toward the multi-layered, plural, and pluralistic architecture, promote mutual complementariness and reinforcement of various mechanisms, and maintain and enhance the momentum and dynamism of East Asian cooperation.

---

[18] Buzan, B (2010). China in international society: Is "peaceful rise" possible? *The Chinese Journal of International Politics*, 3(1), 5–36.

VI. Conclusion

East Asian regionalism, after rapid development for over a decade, has taken the shape of a multi-layered, plural and pluralistic architecture, in the form of ASEAN-led processualism and distinctive features of pragmatic functionalism, cooperative multilateralism and open regionalism. The reality both within and outside of the region has made it what it is. East Asian regionalism cannot and should not blindly copy European regionalism or other models, although the valuable experiences should be learnt and the eventual goal may be the same, that is, a peaceful, prosperous and progressive region which is at the same time a political, economic, and socio-cultural community.

East Asian regionalism today faces new problems. Worries about competition for regional leadership, the maneuvering of major powers, a lack of cohesiveness within ASEAN, and China's continued rapid growth have brought the region to a crossroads. Moreover, a globalized East Asia in 2011 is faced with the US and European economies mired in a deep recession. At this crucial moment, it is important that the regional process itself is preserved and promoted even as an end in itself. If the process is maintained, cooperation will continue and new platforms for developing common interests and norms will be created. Otherwise, regional cooperation will be derailed. Thus it is imperative that all sides have adequate political will and broad vision to keep the process of East Asian regionalism going. To make this possible, we should not treat the multiple mechanisms and channels as a negative factor. Rather they are part and parcel of this process, naturally being there at this evolutionary stage of East Asian regionalism. If we look at the development of East Asian regionalism with the menu of possibilities in mind, 10+1, 10+3, the EAS, etc. are all products of this process and may well complement each other. Simply out, they are part of East Asia's institutional "eco-system". It is important to streamline and institutionalize the existing mechanisms for better cooperation, but we must also remember "more haste, less speed".[19]

---

[19] This idiom means: "The faster you try to do something, the more likely you are to make mistakes that make you take longer than it would had you planned it". See "Using English". http://www.usingenglish.com/reference/idioms/more+haste, +less+ speed.html.

Keeping all channels open and moving the process forward — this is perhaps the most important thing at present.

Although the regional order, institutional arrangement and regional identity of East Asia are still at the incipient stage of development, and although the road to an East Asian community is long and tortuous, East Asian regionalism has already displayed its distinctiveness. With a group of smaller states playing the pivotal role, inventing and spreading norms to bigger powers and socializing them, with the successful experiences East Asian nations have accumulated, it is most desirable for major players to cooperate rather than compete for leadership in the community building process of the region. At least, we need to pool sufficient political will to keep the regional process going because it has already proved conducive to regional peace, stability, and prosperity.

Bibliography

Acharya, A (2001). *Constructing a Security Community in Southeast Asia.* London and New York: Routledge.

Buzan, B (2010). China in international society: Is "peaceful rise" possible? *The Chinese Journal of International Politics*, 3(1), 5–36.

Finnemore, M and K Sikkink (1999). International norm dynamics and political change. In *Exploration and Contestation in the Study of World Politics*, PJ Katzenstein, RO Keohane and SD Krasner (eds.), pp. 247–277. Cambridge, MA: The MIT Press.

Jachtenfuchs, M and B Kohler-Koch (2004). Governance and institutional development. In *European Integration Theory*, A Wiener and T Diez (eds.), pp. 97–115. Oxford: Oxford University Press.

Katzenstein, PJ (2005). *A World of Regions: Asia and Europe in the American Imperium.* Ithaca, New York: Cornell University Press.

Keohane, R (1984). *After Hegemony: Cooperation and Discord in the World Political Economy.* Princeton, NJ: Princeton University Press.

Martin, LL and BA Simons (1999). Theories and empirical studies of international institutions. In *Exploration and Contestation in the Study of World Politics*, PJ Katzenstein, RO Keohane and SD Krasner (eds.), pp. 89–117. Cambridge, MA: The MIT Press.

Nye, JS Jr (2010). American and Chinese power after the financial crisis. *The Washington Quarterly*, 33(4), 143–153.

Qin, Y (2009). Relationality and processual construction. *Social Sciences in China*, 30(4), 5–20.

Qin, Y and Wei, L (2008). Structures, processes and the socialization of power: East Asian community building and the rise of China. In *China's Ascent: Power, Security and the Future of International Politics*, RS Ross and Zhu, F (eds.), pp. 115–138. Ithaca, New York: Cornell University Press.

Wendt, A (1999). *Social Theory of International Politics*. Cambridge: Cambridge University Press.

Chapter 2

CHINA IN THE POST-FINANCIAL CRISIS EAST ASIA: TOWARDS A NEW REGIONAL ECONOMIC ORDER

John WONG

The US financial sector was the world's most dynamic financial sector from 1990 to 2007 by absorbing surplus capital from all over the world and by promoting financial innovations. However, this has resulted in what now appears to be "over-growth" and "over-expansion". As financial activities such as sub-prime mortgages, collateralized debt obligations (CDOs), credit default swaps (CDSs) exceeded their institutional limits and market capacity, the US financial sector started its self-correcting process between 2007 and 2008.

When financial institutions were losing their mutual trust and spiking off a confidence crisis, the US Government stepped in to bail out the larger ailing institutions. However, this also created what economists call a "moral hazard" i.e., while the CEOs in Wall Street could earn good salaries and huge bonuses, they did not need to take responsibility for their bad decisions. It made ordinary American people (who were coping with a higher unemployment rate and lower incomes) angry and the crisis persisted. At the same time, there was a different story in China and East Asia. Within six weeks of Lehman

Brothers' collapse in 15 September 2008, the Chinese Government announced a stimulus package worth RMB4 trillion to stabilize China's economy. It was China and then East Asia which brought the recovery to the world in 2009. Therefore, we can say that a different China and East Asia emerged in 2009.

I. China's Economic Rise

China's economy has chalked up a spectacular performance since reforms started in 1978, growing at an average of 9.8% a year for over three decades. It did not suffer from the 1997 Asian financial crisis. It was also relatively unaffected by the recent global financial crisis which brought most economies to grief, with many experiencing negative growth. China's economic growth for 2009 remained at 9% and is widely forecast to register another 9.5% growth for 2010. In fact, China's economy has quickly bounced back to high growth from the crisis; it has also been leading the global economy to recovery.

With its total (nominal) GDP at about US$5 trillion, China has just replaced Japan as the world's second largest economy. In purchasing power parity (PPP) terms, China has long been the world's number two economy after the USA. For a few years now, China has already been the world's largest exporting country. In the post-crisis world, China has further distinguished itself as a country with the largest foreign reserves of US$2.7 trillion, and as the only large country not burdened by domestic and external debt. Figure 1 shows China's economic growth process.

China's economy is set to continue with its rapid growth in the medium term at least while it undergoes rebalancing and restructuring at the same time. As China's economy today already has a large base, further rapid growth will produce its own dynamics of "speed being compounded by scale". The next phase of China's economic rise will produce profound regional and global impact, altering the geo-economic and geo-political landscapes in both East Asia and the world at large.

Regionally, China's economy has become an important engine of growth for its neighboring economies, which are making use of China's huge domestic markets as a source of their own growth by

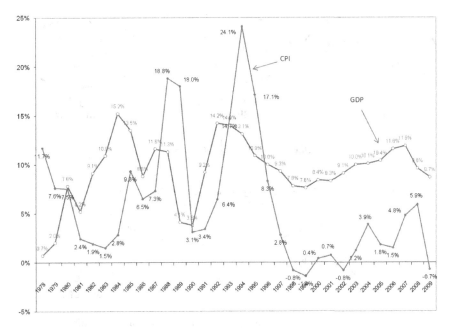

Fig. 1. China's economic growth and inflation, 1978–2009.

Source: *China Statistical Yearbook* (Various Years).

exporting both manufactured products (parts and components) and primary commodities to China. This is because China is home to many regional supply chains (or regional production networks). China's rise has also radically altered the region's trade patterns and financial flows, catalyzing the process of regional economic integration. As a capital surplus economy, China's outward foreign direct investment (FDI) to the region is becoming increasingly important. Beijing has reinforced these trends by initiating several regional economic cooperation schemes, including the China–ASEAN FTA. (see Fig. 2 showing the China-led pattern of regional economic integration).

The economic rise of China has, therefore, led to the rise of East Asia. This is not the first but the second time that people are talking about East Asia's rise. Japan's economic rise some two to three decades ago had also given rise to the notion of East Asia's rise. That was the "First Rise of East Asia" (or EA-I), which was associated with Japan's economic growth. This time round, it is about the "Second

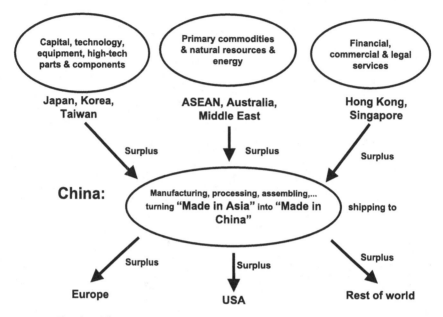

Fig. 2. The pattern of China-led regional growth and integration.

Rise of East Asia" (or EA-II), which is clearly dominated by China's economic growth. The main difference is that the China-led EA-II this time promises to be much more formidable in geo-economic and geo-political terms than the Japan-led EA-I of the past. China's rise has indeed brought about a much stronger impact on the region, not just as its powerful engine of economic growth, but also as a significant catalyst for regional economic integration as shown in Fig. 2.

II. East Asia as a Dynamic Economic Region

East Asia is historically defined to comprise Japan, China, the four NIEs (newly industrialized economies) of South Korea, Taiwan, Hong Kong and Singapore; and the four ASEAN economies of Indonesia, Malaysia, the Philippines and Thailand. All these were known to be high-performance economies, having chalked up rapid growth at various periods of time. Because of this, East Asia became the world's most dynamic economic region in the second half of the 20th century.

Overall, East Asia's growth process is marked by three distinctive waves. Japan led the first wave by sustaining near double-digit rates of high economic growth from 1950 to the 1970s. The four NIEs (dubbed East Asia's four "little dragons") led the second wave, with high economic growth spanning the period of the early 1960s to the early 1980s. The ASEAN-4 and China took up the third wave, starting their high economic growth from the late 1970s to the early 1980s onwards. Japanese economists called this the "Flying Geese" pattern, with Japan taking the lead in the formation while others progressing in succession in an orderly manner[1] (see Table 1 as the statistical expression of the "Flying Geese" pattern).

The underlying economic theory for such a growth pattern is associated with shifting comparative advantage. In other words, high costs and high wages caused Japan to lose its comparative advantage for labor-intensive manufactured exports to the NIEs, with the NIEs similarly passing their comparative advantage to other latecomers in East Asia later on. To achieve high growth, all these East Asian economies had high levels of domestic investment matched with equally high levels of domestic savings. Furthermore, all of them pursued export-oriented development strategies, reinforced by frequent pro-growth and pro-market government intervention — the so-called "Developmental State" model. The World Bank referred to this whole phenomenon as the "East Asian Miracle"[2] (see Fig. 3 as the graphic expression of the "Flying Geese" pattern).

East Asia clearly owed its first two waves of growth to the economic rise of Japan. By the mid-1980s when Japan's economic growth was at its peak, there was frequent talk of the rise of East Asia as the world's most dynamic economic region. Soon after this, however, particularly following the Plaza Accord in 1985 when the Japanese yen was forced to undergo significant revaluation, Japan the "leading goose" not only lost its economic growth momentum, but also plunged into a

---

[1] The "Flying Geese" concept of development was first coined by the Japanese economist, Kaname Akamatzu, see A historical pattern of economic growth in developing countries. *The Developing Economies,* 1(S1), 3–25.

[2] World Bank (1994). *The East Asian Miracle.* New York: Oxford University.

Table 1. East Asian economic performance indicators.

	Population (Mn)	GDP Per Capita (US$)	Total GDP (US$ bn)	Growth of GDP (%)						
	2008	2008	2008	1960–1970	1970–1980	1980–1990	1990–2000	2000–2008	2008	2009
China	**1,338**	**3,248**	**4,222**	**5.2**	**5.5**	**10.3**	**9.7**	**10.4**	**9.6**	**8.7**
Japan	127	38,100	4,844	10.9	4.3	4.1	1.3	1.6	-0.6	-5.3
NIEs										
South Korea	48	17,445	857	8.5	10.1	8.9	5.7	4.5	4.6	0.2
Taiwan	23	17,340	401	9.2	9.7	7.9	5.7	4.1	1.9	-4.0
Hong Kong	7	31,867	224	10	9.3	6.9	3.8	5.2	2.8	-3.0
Singapore	4.6	33,475	154	8.8	8.3	6.7	7.4	5.8	1.9	-2.1
ASEAN-5										
Indonesia	240	2,175	510	3.9	7.2	6.1	3.8	5.2	6.1	4.5
Malaysia	25.7	8,497	215	6.5	7.9	5.3	6.5	5.5	5.1	-2.2
Philippines	98	1,735	169	5.1	6	1	3.3	5.1	4.6	0.9
Thailand	66	4,179	272	8.4	7.1	7.6	3.8	5.2	3.6	-2.8
India	1,166	1,060	1,237	3.4	3.5	5.8	5.5	7.9	6.6	7.4

Source: World Bank.

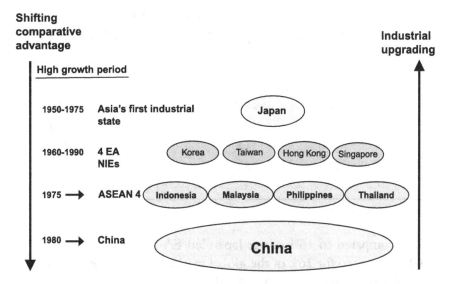

Fig. 3. Japan-led "Flying Geese" pattern for EA-I's growth and integration.

prolonged recession. In the meanwhile, economic growth of the NIEs had also come down a lot, partly because their economies became mature. East Asia had lost its glitter as a dynamic economic region.

By the turn of this century, however, the notion of East Asia as the world's most dynamic economic region was revived, this time because of the economic rise of China. In fact, East Asia's third wave of high growth, heavily gravitating towards China, has proved to be economically far more enormous than the previous two.

China's prolonged high growth has been far more "dynamic" than Japan's past process of growth because of China's huge size and diversity, which by themselves can generate a lot of growth potential. With greater internal dynamics, China promises to sustain its growth much longer than Japan's. China's role as an engine for East Asia's growth is by far more powerful than that of Japan in the past. China has also played a much larger role in integrating the East Asian economies, thanks to operation of its numerous regional production networks.

Not surprisingly, China has eclipsed Japan's economic leadership role in East Asia. The China-led EA-II is quantitatively and qualitatively different from the Japan-led EA-I. The China-led EA-II accounted for 22% of global GDP in 2009 (same as the EU's but slightly less than the

Table 2.   Comparing East Asian economies 1985 and 2009.

	Japan-Led EA-I, 1985		China-Led EA-II, 2009	
	World GDP Share (%)	World Export Share (%)	World GDP Share (%)	World Export Share (%)
East Asia	15.2	24.2	21.6	25.8
Japan	(11.1)	(11.6)	(8.7)	(4.3)
China	(2.2)	(1.8)	(8.6)	(9.6)
USA	33.0	23.7	24.5	8.4
EU	—	—	21.4	12.5

Source: World Bank.

USA), compared to 15% of the Japan-led EA-I in 1985. For exports, EA-II accounted for 26% of the global market share, compared to 24% of EA-I (see Table 2 comparing EA-I and EA-II).

While Japan's past growth potential had quickly dissipated, China is able to sustain its high growth far longer. Following the global financial crisis, most developed economies including Japan were saddled with serious structural problems such as high unemployment, troubled property markets, and government debts. They are also facing a looming public finance crisis in the longer run. In contrast, China's economy is still steaming in high growth, backed by strong fundamentals and good internal and external balances. China is widely expected to continue its high growth for the next 10 to 15 years.

In fact, with the relative decline of the developed economies after the financial crisis, the China-led EA-II will become the world's largest economic entity in a few years. This explains the clear shift of global economic gravity towards East Asia (see Fig. 4 highlighting China's economic size in EA).

III.   Towards a China-centric Regional Economic Order

China's development strategies will remain pro-growth while undergoing rebalancing gradually and addressing its many domestic economic and social issues at the same time. Overall, China has started to exert strong geo-economic influence on the East Asia region as a

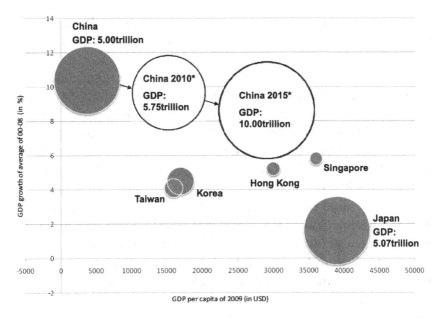

Fig. 4. Comparing East Asian economies, 2009.

Note: *indicate forecasts from 2009.

whole, with its economic activities increasingly drawn to China. China's growth will affect the growth of other East Asian economies, and China's pace of economic restructuring will also set the tone for other East Asian economies to rebalance themselves i.e., if China's economy were to cut down its exports to the world, other East Asian economies will feel the pinch first as their exports to China fall in tandem. As Singapore's former prime minister Lee Kuan Yew recently stated, "None of the economies on (China's) periphery can resist the attraction of its market. Slowly, but inexorably, we are being drawn into China's economic orbit".[3] It is sufficiently evident that a China-centric East Asian Economic Community is slowly taking shape.

While East Asia's emerging geo-economic pattern is sufficiently clear, its geo-political landscape is much more complicated. By virtue of its size, the rise of China can be considered disruptive to many of its smaller neighbors in geo-political terms, who have not unequivocally accepted China's message of a "peaceful rise". China also lacks

---

[3] *The Straits Times*, December 9, 2010. p. A31.

effective "soft power" to sell such a message. In particular, Japan still has problems of coming to terms with its relative decline and the rise of China.

It is easier for the region to embrace China's economic leadership because economic relations are essentially market-driven, with clear mutual benefits. It is far more difficult for the region to accept China's political leadership over the region; certainly not before the region settles its many outstanding geo-political issues. This means that EA-II will not be an effective and cohesive political grouping. For a long time to come, it will remain "hot in economics" but "cold in politics".

An even more complicated issue is how EA-II will integrate itself with the existing global order dominated by the USA in the future. The problem is already seen by the shift of US strategic focus to East Asia, promptly in response to the shift of global economic gravity towards the region. The presence of such extra-regional political forces is likely to further "muddy" the region's geo-political water. (See Fig. 5 showing the relative economic strength of the three big players).

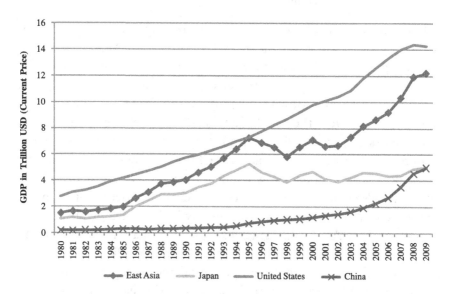

Fig. 5. GDP of East Asia, Japan, China and the United States since 1980.

Note: East Asia includes China, Japan, HK, Taiwan (ROC), Korea, Singapore and ASEAN4.
Source: World Bank Database.

Historically, all established hegemonic powers had strived to prevent the rise of another new power. The rise of the Japan-led EA-I posed no threat to the existing US geo-political interests because Japan's economic rise was under the US security umbrella. The rise of the China-centric EA-II this time will clearly be considered a challenge to the established global order, partly because China is perceived to carry far greater economic potential and partly because China's political and social systems are so much at odds with those of the West.

Great Britain once did try to prevent the rise of Germany. But it did not do much to prevent the rise of the USA, largely because of their political and social similarities, which in turn gave rise to mutual trust. In the case of China's rise, the factor of trust is missing; but it is an important factor that will complicate the acceptance of the China-centric EA-II by the existing global order.

Bibliography

Akamatzu, K (1962). A historical pattern of economic growth in developing countries. *The Developing Economies*, 1(S1), 3–25.

China's Statistics Yearbook (2011). Beijing: China's Statistics Publishing House.

Direction of Trade Statistics Year Book 2010 (2011). New York: International Monetary Fund.

World Bank (1994). *The East Asian Miracle*. New York: Oxford University.

Chapter 3

CHINA AS THE WORLD'S SECOND LARGEST ECONOMY: QUALIFICATIONS AND IMPLICATIONS

HE Liping

China's economy surpassed Japan's and became the world's second largest by 2010. This was not a surprise because the country has the largest population in the world and its economy has been growing rapidly for more than two decades. In terms of purchasing power parity (PPP) method, China's economy has already surpassed Japan's since 2001. The method of comparison using nominal gross domestic product (GDP) is, however, greatly affected by price and exchange rate factors, which are frequently subjected to cyclical changes. Moreover, the rise of China's economy may suggest that its catching-up with the world's advanced economies has approached an end. In addition, China has relied on foreign trade and capital inflows for its economic development during the past few decades, and would remain so in the foreseeable future. An important implication of the rise of China's economy is that it might pursue more international cooperation at the global level and East Asian economic integration at the regional level.

China's economy has been growing at an average rate of 8% to 9% annually since about three decades ago, and this has made China one of the largest economies in the world today. When the global financial crisis hit many of the world's largest economies from late 2008, namely, the United States, Japan and the European Union among others, the Chinese economy managed to maintain a fairly high growth rate of 8.7% in 2009 and some 9% in 2010. Thus China has become the world's second largest economy from 2010, surpassing Japan by the conventional measurement of gross domestic product in current exchange rates and prices.[1]

A more profound view is that as China has become the world's second largest economy, it is now perhaps the only contender for the position as the world's No.1 economy. Should that occur, the world's landscape of political economy would inevitably change significantly, given the fact that China's present political and economic systems are very much different from many others in certain aspects, and the uncertainty about how China would reshape its foreign policy toward international affairs.

In what follows, the chapter will mainly focus on the economics side of the issue. The first section addresses the effect of exchange rates and prices on the ranking of nations' economic size. The second section compares the Chinese economy today with the Japanese economy in the early 1980s with regard to their economic size rankings. The third section elaborates on certain characteristics of the Chinese economy that is similar to or different from the "older second largest" economy like Japan. The fourth section concludes the chapter and draws some implications from the earlier discussion.

I. Ranking of Nations' Economic Size: The Factor of Exchange Rate and Price

Some observers, both within and outside of China, predicted some years ago that China's GDP would surpass Japan's in 2009 or 2010, based on the statistical observation that the two nations' figures became close to each other in 2008. Data from the International

---

[1] Tabuchi, H (2009). "Chinese economic juggernaut is gaining on Japan", *New York Times*, 1 October.

Monetary Fund (IMF) showed that China's GDP in 2008 was $4,519.95 billion, whilst Japan's was $4,886.95 billion. The difference was remarkably small at $367 billion, which was equivalent to 8.1% of China's GDP then. Extrapolating this data, one would foresee that if Japan grew at 1% in 2009, and China grew at a little more than 9.1% in the same year, China's GDP would be larger than Japan's by the end of the year.

It turned out that in 2009, IMF estimated China's GDP at $4,984.73 billion and Japan's at $5,068.89 billion, based on current exchange rates and prices. Japan was still larger than China in the figures by a mere $84.16 billion, equivalent to 1.7% of China's GDP that year.

When data for the first half of 2010 became available, many Chinese media outlets reported that China's GDP has surpassed Japan's for the first time. A typical report went like this: "As Japanese government reveals, Japan's GDP was $1,277 billion in the second quarter of 2010. It is already known that China's GDP was $1,339 billion in the same period. China's economic size has surpassed Japan's".[2]

It thus surprised some, when Japan's figure for the third quarter turned out to be larger than China's figure. A Chinese newspaper reported in December that the Japanese government had revised its GDP figure for the first three quarters in 2010, which was given as $3,959.4 billion. And that figure was higher than China's $3,946.8 billion.[3]

Obviously, the lay reader would be misled when reading such news comparing the economic size between, say, China and Japan. Not only would a government not publish its nation's GDP figures in the US dollar for its national audience, but also international comparison of nations' aggregate output is by no means a straightforward matter, especially when the work involves change over time.

---

[2] See "China's economic total surpasses Japan and becomes the world's No. 2" (2010). *China Economic Times* (Chinese), 12 August.

[3] See "Japan revises economic data and its GDP returns to the world's number two" (2010). *Global Times* (Chinese), 10 December.

Let us elaborate on the issue by using a simple example.

Suppose there are two countries in the world and each has its total output in a given year reported in its own currency. Because the output of the various sectors and branches in an economy must be summed up by using a certain price factor, GDP in a country in a given period may be expressed in the form $Y = QP$, where Q stands for total output, P for the price factor, and Y is the nominal GDP in a given period.

At this point when comparing the two countries' GDP, the exchange rate factor also comes into play. This means that both countries' nominal GDP in a given period should be converted into a common currency. In the case of China and Japan, this would be the Chinese yuan's exchange rate with the dollar and the Japanese yen's exchange rate with the dollar respectively.

In short, for China, nominal GDP in a given period in dollar terms may be seen as $\text{GDP}^{\text{China}} = Q^c_t P^c_t e^c_t$; and similarly, for Japan, $\text{GDP}^{\text{Japan}} = Q^j_t P^j_t e^j_t$.

It is clear that when one is comparing $\text{GDP}^{\text{China}}$ and $\text{GDP}^{\text{Japan}}$, three factors are involved: Q, P, and e. A change in any one of these three factors would affect the result of comparison. Yet the purpose of comparison is really to see the relative size of the two countries' individual Q.

Over time, each of the three factors may change. A change in Q over time is called economic growth, be it fast or slow. A change in P over time is either inflation or deflation. A change in e (i.e., exchange rate) is either appreciation (revaluation) or depreciation (devaluation).

Do price or exchange rate factors matter? Yes, it does. As shown in Fig. 1, the Japanese economy has been suffering from deflation for a long time since the mid-1990s, while the Chinese economy has been on a relatively moderate inflationary path, both of which are suggested by the implicit GDP deflator depicted in the graph.

As shown in Fig. 1, Japan's nominal GDP in 1995 was $5,264.38 billion, while China's was $727.95 billion, with Japan's being 7.2 times of China's. During the period between 1995 and 2010, Japan's real GDP (Q) grew at an annually average rate of approximately 1.5%, and China's at 9.5%. If either the price factor or exchange rate factor

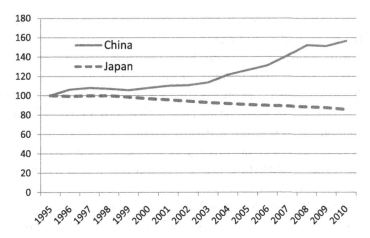

Fig. 1.   GDP price deflator index, China and Japan 1995 = 100.

Source: Compiled by the author with raw data from the International Monetary Fund (2010). *World Economic Outlook Database*, October.

remained unchanged for either of the two economies during the period, Japan's GDP would have been $6,581.69 billion in 2010, and China's $2,839.96 billion in 2010, with China's still less than half of the Japan's.

It is clear from Fig. 1 that during the period of 1995–2010, the Japanese economy suffered from deflation (about 15% negative) and China has seen significant inflation (about 55% positive), which also rendered the two economies' nominal GDP moving differently. Because of this difference, we may suppose that China's nominal GDP in 2010 had been inflated by 55% (relative to its level in 1995) to $4,401.94 billion, while Japan's nominal GDP had been contracted by 15% (relative to its level in 1995) to $5,594.44 billion. Now the two figures become closer.

Furthermore, note that between 1995 and 2010, the Chinese yuan had appreciated considerably against the dollar at some 23%, whilst the Japanese yen also appreciated to a smaller extent at some 5%. This change in currency value would also make China's nominal GDP in dollar terms augmented by some 18% to $5,194.29 billion, a figure even closer to Japan's $5,594.44 billion.

To sum up the analysis, we see that China's catch-up with Japan in nominal GDP between 1995 and 2010 is approximately contributed in half by Chinese economic growth, one-third by price changes, and one-fifth by exchange rate changes.

In other words, China's catch-up with the Japanese economy is not entirely a result of its rapid economic growth (increase in output), though this remains by all means the most important factor. Price and exchange rate are also significant factors that have helped China's rise in the ranking of economic size with Japan.

The emphasis on the price and exchange rate factors here is intended to show that these are rather cyclical ones in the sense that they may fluctuate over time. The trend we have seen for China in the past 15 years may not continue indefinitely in the future.

Needless to say, in passing, China's rise in the ranking is also in part a result of the slow Japanese economic growth since the mid-1990s.[4]

II. Is China Today as Large as Japan in 1980?

The discussion in Section I has shown certain complications in making international comparison of nations' economic size when using the nominal GDP method. Another widely used method in international comparison is based on the PPP method, which by definition excludes or is intended to exclude impacts of price and exchange rate changes or their undesirable effects (there is possible misuse of the PPP method in practice relating to Chinese economic data).[5]

Figure 2 shows the shares of world total GDP held by several nations based on the PPP method between 1990 and 2015. The data are from the IMF, and the institution' research staff have made projections for 2010–2015.

As can be seen from the graph, China's share in the world total of GDP based on the PPP method surpassed Germany's as early as in 1995, and by the same measure surpassed Japan's in 2001. By the

---

[4] Fackler, M (2010). "Japan economic decline", *New York Times*, 16 October.
[5] Gilboy, GJ and Zhong, N (2010). Measuring China's economy: The proper use of PPP methods. *Economic Research Journal* (Chinese), No. 1 (January).

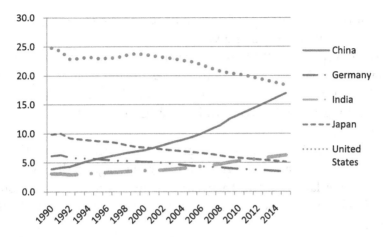

Fig. 2. Gross domestic product, based on PPP, % share of world total, 1990–2015.
Source: International Monetary Fund (2010). *World Economic Outlook Database*, October.

IMF research staff's projection, China's share would possibly rise to a level close to that of the US, with China taking some 16.5% and the US taking some 18.5% of the world total.

Figure 2 seems to suggest that China is now a definite contender for the United States' world No. 1 position in the world economy. It is no denial that the possibility is on the horizon if the Chinese economy continued to grow at its current high speed (8–9% annually) and the American economy continued to grow at its extremely moderate one (2% annually).

One may neglect certain other relevant facts while inspecting Fig. 2. First, the relative decline of the American economy or other industrial economies is also in part a result of the rise in emerging market economies including China during the recent decades. It may be more accurate to say that emerging market economies as a whole are a challenge to the global status quo.

Second, even if taking a look at individual nations, one may have to consider certain other emerging market economies other than China, e.g., the Indian economy. Like China, the Indian economy has been growing rapidly in the recent years since the early 21st century. By the PPP method, India had surpassed Germany in 2007 in terms of its share of global GDP, and would possibly surpass Japan in 2012.

In the foreseeable future, India would become the world's third largest economy after the US and China.

Moreover, as the PPP method excludes the impact of price and exchange rate factors and therefore gives greater weight to population factors than otherwise, one may consider the difference in population growth between India and China for their economic growth outlooks.

At present, India's economic growth has been close to that of China, but its population growth has been higher than China's. Should these factors retain their current momentum, the economic size of India would be increasing faster than that of China in the future.

As such, the Indian economy may become as large as China's one day in the future. In this situation, the world economy would see co-contenders for the No. 1 position, or even co-No. 1.

As mentioned earlier, international comparison of nations' economic size using the PPP method involves the factor of population, we need to consider GDP per capita, which is also relevant in thinking of any possible implications of a nation's rising economic size.

Figure 3 compares Japan's and China's per capita GDP based on the PPP method for selected years between 1980 and 2010, both of which are seen as a percentage of the US level. When Japan was the world's second largest economy, its per capita GDP was only moderately lower than the US level at between 70% to 80%. But the Chinese level was and still is remarkably lower than either the US or Japanese level. As recently as 2010, China's level was still only some one-sixth of the US level.

To answer a question about the implications of China becoming the world's second largest economy, at least we now see it does not follow that it has become the world's second richest one, or even among the rich economies in the world today. The gap between China and the industrial economies with regard to per capita GDP remains considerable.

Is the Chinese economy as large as Japan's in the early 1980s? Let us return to the measure of nominal GDP in current prices and exchange rates. Figure 4 shows the US, Japan, and China's share of

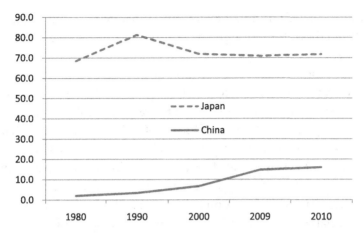

Fig. 3. Japanese and Chinese per capita GDP as a % of the US level, by PPP method, selected years 1980–2010.

Source: International Monetary Fund (2010). *World Economic Outlook Database*, October.

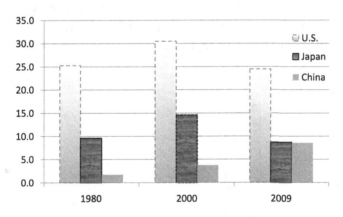

Fig. 4. The US, Japan, and China's shares in the world's total GDP, by current exchange rates and prices, selected years 1980–2009.

Source: The World Bank (2010). *World Development Indicators* online, November.

the world's total GDP in current prices and exchange rates for selected years between 1980 and 2009. We can see that China's share of the world total by this measure (8.6%) is smaller than Japan's in 1980 (9.6%).

The point here is that China's large economic size today may be not *that* large as it appears to be. Above all, China's rise in its share of the world's total GDP, either in current exchange rates and prices or by the PPP method, has been greatly contributed by its huge population endowment.

In addition, perhaps we can look at how large Chinese firms are ranked with their overseas peers. It seems to be a usual pattern that the larger an economy is, the more its corporations feature in the world's top rankings, e.g., the Fortune Global 500. China has pursued hard in recent years to promote the growth of large (and also state-owned) corporations. A result is that the number of Chinese companies in the list has increased rapidly. However, as a matter of fact, the number is still smaller than what Japan once had and still has (see Fig. 5).

The relative under-development of large corporations might be seen as a sign of weakness in Chinese economic growth. But more profoundly, it is rooted in the course of recent Chinese economic development that has been remarkably different from earlier examples in many aspects. We will explore this in detail in the next section. Here, it is sufficient to note that despite China's outstanding record of economic growth and its rapid advance in the world's total output

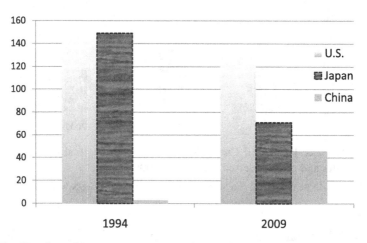

Fig. 5. Number of American, Japanese, Chinese firms in the Fortune Global 500, 1994 and 2009.

Note: 1994's Chinese figure does not include a Hong Kong-based firm; and 2010's figure includes four Hong Kong-based firms.
Source: *Fortune*, 7 August 1995 and 26 July 2010.

ranking, its economic development is still very much behind many of the industrial economies, not only from today's point of view, but also to a certain extent from yesterday's.

III. How will the Chinese Economy Rely on the Outside World?

In world history, the rise of a great power would often mean a new, emerging challenge to the existing international political order. When a great power gains economic might and hence military capacity, it might be tempted to use force in dealing with its international affairs from time to time.

Would an economically rising China be like this in the future? My answer is that it would probably not. The fundamental reason is that post-1978, economic growth of China has occurred with extensive use of external resources in and within the existing international political and economic order, and that has in turn made China a great beneficiary of globalization. As such, the nation sees no incentive to depart from the existing international systems.

Below are highlights on some characteristics of post-1978 Chinese economic growth relevant to its external relations. Much of the information displayed in the following charts is already well known to observers of the Chinese economy. We bring them together here for a quick review.

Figure 6 shows indicators of China's trade dependence from 1978 to 2009, i.e., exports or imports in commodities as a percentage of China's nominal GDP. The trend of a steady rise in the indicators is clear, except for 2008 and 2009 when the ratios were falling. The exception was apparently caused by the global financial crisis that crippled world trade. The relatively stable time trend over a long period since 1978 suggests that Chinese economic growth has greatly relied on foreign trade.

Figure 7 compares China with three references, namely Japan, the US, and the world average, in the measure of exports of goods and services as a percentage of GDP. As can been seen, in 1980 the Chinese level was similar to the US and smaller than both Japan's and

Fig. 6.   Trade dependence in China, 1978–2009.

Source: China Statistical Yearbook.

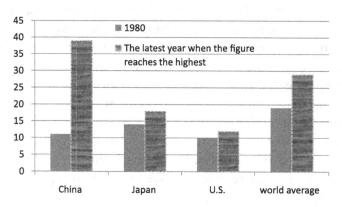

Fig. 7.   Exports of goods and services as a % of GDP, 1980 and the latest year.

Note: The second figure for China is of 2006, and that for the other three is of 2007.
Source: The World Bank (2010). *World Development Indicators* online, November.

the world average, but in recent times it has been the highest among all. The Chinese economy's reliance on foreign trade is most outstanding in contemporary world economy.

Two developments in post-1978 China's external economic development are most notable. One is known as "processing trade", a term used to categorise a type of trading and producing activity that has been solely for the purpose of exports in the country. Figure 8 shows that the share of processing trade accounts for more than half

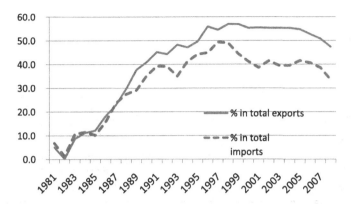

Fig. 8. Role of processing trade in China's trade growth, 1981–2008.
Source: China Statistical Yearbook.

of China's total exports in goods in recent years. It is obvious that without development in processing trade, China's foreign trade could not have seen a rapid growth.

Another is the role of foreign firms in Chinese trade development. As can been seen from Fig. 9, foreign firms' trading and producing activities contribute to more than half of China's total exports and imports in goods, similar to that for processing trade. Foreign firms have been attracted both by China's favorable policy and low-wage labor force, thus helping the country's exports to grow at a rapid pace.

Scarcely in modern economic history has a nation of China's size seen such huge foreign capital and trade flows. Neither Japan nor South Korea did so in their post-war economic development. China has obviously made good use of international resources to overcome certain internal obstacles in the course of post-1978 economic development.

The "international resources" China has used are mainly foreign markets for its products ("Made in China") and foreign primary goods supplies for its domestic needs. Figures 10 and 11 show that manufacturing goods have dominated China's total exports, and the share of primary goods has been increasing faster than other imports to China in recent years. It is foreign markets that provide opportunities for "Made in China" products and foreign primary goods supplies that support the country's domestic economic growth.

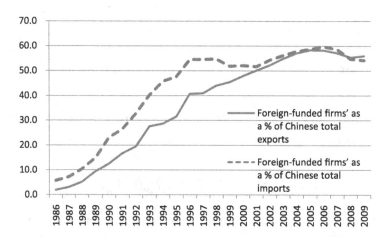

Fig. 9. Role of foreign firms in Chinese trade growth, 1986–2009.
Source: China Statistical Yearbook.

A new question is whether China's economic growth can be sustained in the future with its reliance on exports and foreign capital inflow reduced. The question can be looked at from two different perspectives. First, as the size of the economy increases, the degree of reliance on foreign trade and capital inflow would tend to decline. Second, the decline would not necessarily mean that the role of foreign trade and capital inflow becomes less significant over time.

In a broader sense, the important role of foreign trade and capital inflows towards Chinese economic growth in the future may be conceived in several different ways. First, as China is still short in capacity for technological innovation due largely to domestic institutional obstacles, trade and capital inflow as a channel of transmission are essential for further economic growth. Second, also due to certain institutional obstacles, China's domestic market has been growing slower than the overall economy, and this pattern would possibly remain in the foreseeable future. For this reason, China still needs foreign markets to absorb its production capacity in manufactured goods. Third, as a "world factory", China's needs for primary imports, energy and industrial raw materials, will grow steadily over time.

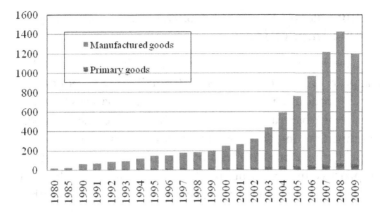

Fig. 10. Major composition of Chinese exports, $ billions, selected years 1980–2008.

Source: China Statistical Yearbook.

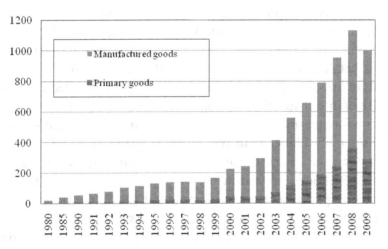

Fig. 11. Major composition of Chinese imports, $ billions, selected years 1980–2008.

Source: China Statistical Yearbook.

In short, international trade and capital flows are necessary for China's sustainable economic growth in the future. It is in the nation's best economic interests to support the existing world economic and political systems.

IV. China as the World's Second Largest Economy: Some Implications

There have been quite some voices, both within China and abroad, that appear to call for changes in China's foreign policy amid the country's economic rise.[6] Our discussion in previous sections has led us to several observations on China's economic rise with regard to some immediate implications of its rising economic rankings.

First, China is now perhaps on the frontline to lead the development process in emerging market economies, yet this does not mean that China is itself approaching the end of its "catching-up" process.

Second, by certain significant measures, the Chinese economy today is not as large as the Japanese economy in the early 1980s. This suggests that China's catching-up task remains tremendous.

Third, because population is one of the main determinants of nations' economic size, China has advantages and potential to become a contender for top positions in the world economy. But other emerging market economies would soon join the race as well.

More importantly, as post-1978 China has emphasized the extensive use of international resources, the Chinese economy today greatly relies on foreign trade and capital flows, to an extent that this reliance is considerably higher than that of many other economies and the world average. International trade and capital flows have helped Chinese economic growth in the past three decades, and they will continue to play a necessary and important role in the future as well.

This suggests that to sustain economic growth, China needs to continue its economic development strategy as well as its foreign policy that is derived to support the development goals, which ultimately provides a basis for domestic social and political stability. Any attempt to deviate from the principles in China's overall economic development strategy and foreign policy would possibly do more harm than good in net terms. To put it simply, the economic foundations of China's foreign policy have not changed in general.

---

[6]Wang, Y (2010). To become a great but moderate nation: China desperately needs a new East Asia strategy. *Southern Weekend* (Chinese), 23 December, p. F35.

In particular, China's external economic development over the past decades, based on trade and foreign direct investment, has been closely intertwined with the East Asian region. A "production network" has evolved in the region, where numerous firms from different countries or territories have taken part in forming supply chain networks that run from raw material procurement through intermediate good processing to final good assembling to marketing. Though much of the raw material supply source and ultimate markets are outside of the East Asian region, the bulk of manufacturing and distributing are located within the region, especially in mainland China's coastal industrial belts.

The relatively successful story of "made in China" should be largely attributed to such market-driven regional economic integration. It is also due to strong links existing in the region that China's trade relations with its East Asian partners have grown rapidly through the 1990s and the early 21st century. Figure 12 shows how important mainland China's East Asian trading partners have been in the country's total external trade. Notably, Japan and Hong Kong were the largest trading partners in the 1990s, and their declining shares since then

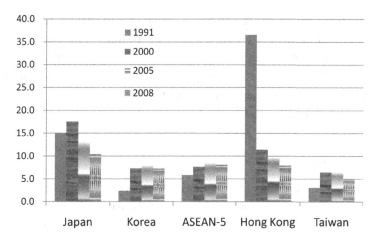

Fig. 12. China (mainland)'s main EA trading partners, % of China's total trade in goods, selected years 1991–2008.

Note: ASEAN-5 here refers to Indonesia, Malaysia, the Philippines, Singapore, and Thailand.
Source: China Statistical Yearbook.

have been compensated to a certain extent by rising shares of other East Asian trading partners such as South Korea, ASEAN-5 and Taiwan.

In recent years, the share held by East Asian trading partners in China's total external trade has become smaller than before. But this should not be interpreted as a sign that the role of the region has been reduced. Rather, as the size of the economy becomes larger, diversification in trade over regions is necessary. Also, as the demand for energy and other primary goods increases rapidly, China's trade with non-East Asian regions, especially with Africa, Latin America, and Oceania, has grown faster than the country's overall external trade. The East Asian region remains the base of the supply chain networks for goods manufacturing, which is taking place and generating great benefits to Chinese economic growth. It is, therefore, reasonable to expect that China will pursue East Asian economic integration whilst continuing to support existing multilateral trade systems at the global level.

Postscript

The author recalls a short paper he wrote in the early 1990s on the economic foundations of China's foreign policy.[7] The paper's main theme was that economics has played an increasingly important role in post-1978 China's foreign policy-making, which may continue to be so after the Tiananmen Square event in 1989. Here he would like to attest the same stance for the future while writing this chapter.

Bibliography

"China's economic total surpasses Japan and becomes the world's no. 2" (2010). *China Economic Times* (Chinese), 12 August.
Fackler, M (2010). "Japan economic decline", *New York Times*, 16 October.

---

[7] He, L (1991). Economic foundations of China's foreign policy. *Cambridge Review of International Affairs*, 5(1), 32–38.

Gilboy, GJ and Zhong, N (2010). Measuring China's economy: The proper use of PPP methods. *Economic Research Journal* (Chinese), No. 1, (January).

"Japan revises economic data and its GDP returns to the world's number two" (2010). *Global Times* (Chinese), 10 December.

He, L (1991). Economic foundations of China's foreign policy. *Cambridge Review of International Affairs*, 5(1), 32–38.

Tabuchi, H (2009). "Chinese economic juggernaut is gaining on Japan", *New York Times*, 1 October.

Wang, Y (2010). To become a great but moderate nation: China desperately needs a new East Asia strategy. *Southern Weekend* (Chinese), 23 December, p. F35.

Chapter 4

TRADE AND INVESTMENT FACILITATION IN EAST ASIA: DEVELOPMENT, CHALLENGES AND COOPERATION

FAN Ying and LI Wentao

This chapter argues that East Asia needs to expand and deepen its economic operations by promoting trade and investment facilitation (TIF) to adapt to the altered external economic environment in the post-crisis era. The 2008 American financial crisis resulted in considerable readjustments and transformation in the world economic and political landscape. In the reshaping of the global economic order, performances of the emerging economies in East Asia are indeed very eye-catching. East Asia has thus become a region on the rise, both in the world economic structure and global economic governance, especially after the G-20 has been defined as "a major platform for international economic cooperation",[1] at the Pittsburgh Summit.

This fully demonstrates that the international stature of East Asia has improved remarkably after the financial crisis, and its influence is also rising. On the other hand, with profound shifts in the world economic structure, East Asia also faces major challenges as well as opportunities in economic restructuring and shifting its economic growth paradigm. Thanks to the outbreak of this financial crisis, East

---

[1] See Leaders' Statement: The Pittsburgh Summit 2009 at http://www.pittsburg hsummit.gov/mediacenter/129639.htm [accessed 24–25 September 2009].

Asian countries now have a better understanding of the importance and urgency of mutual help and self-reliance in the region as a whole against the backdrop of deepening economic globalization. Under these new circumstances, East Asia needs to expand and deepen its economic cooperation, especially in trade and investment.

Therefore, promoting cooperation in TIF is significant for international trade, foreign direct investment (FDI), as well as the recovery and sustainable development of the world economy. Closer economic cooperation and trade within the region is also especially important in reducing trade inefficiencies and market access barriers such as FDI thresholds, expanding intra-regional demand, and solidifying the foundations for East Asian economic development. In the meantime, TIF cooperation will help East Asian countries better adapt to the altered external economic and trade environment brought about by its own swift emergence in the post-crisis global economy.

This chapter is organized as follows: Sections I and II assess TIF achievements, latest developments and obstacles, as well as challenges for further TIF cooperation in East Asia respectively. Section III offers a framework and roadmap for the region on TIF cooperation; and the final section contains our closing remarks.

I. TIF Achievements and Latest Developments in East Asia

TIF cooperation in East Asia has great potential. At present, all countries in the region have participated very positively in various kinds of TIF cooperative mechanisms.

1. *TIF cooperation under APEC*

Since the issuance of the Asia-Pacific Economic Cooperation (APEC) Economic Leaders' Declaration of Common Resolve ("Bogor Declaration"), APEC members have made remarkable achievements in TIF, especially in customs procedures, standardization and unification, movement of business people and e-commerce. They have also formulated and implemented two action plans. All these developments have helped decrease their business transaction costs by 5% between 2002 and 2006 and again between 2007 and 2010. In addition, APEC has implemented a massive TIF action plan, contributing to a relatively transparent, stable and efficient trade and investment environment with comparatively low cost in the Asia-Pacific region.

2. TIF cooperation under AFTA

To achieve its goal of building the Association of Southeast Asian Nations (ASEAN) Community by 2015, ASEAN members have conducted TIF cooperation in an orderly manner through such arrangements as the ASEAN Customs Valuation Guide and Single Window Agreement.

In trade facilitation, after seven years of extraordinary efforts, ASEAN Customs has been able to reduce time required for Customs clearance from several days to about two hours on average. The Green Lane system provides speedy customs clearance for CEPT goods. Similar initiatives have also been adopted by several ASEAN Member Countries such as the Gold Card Program in Indonesia, Super Green Lane in the Philippines and Single Window in Singapore.[2]

In investment facilitation, since the signing of the ASEAN Investment Area Framework Agreement in October 1998, ASEAN members have been constantly making efforts to integrate their regional markets and build a unified, transparent and free "single investment area". For instance, they have activated the ASEAN Investment Area Framework Agreement, which aims at removing intra-regional investment hurdles through implementing an investment liberalization plan such that ASEAN investors are able to invest freely in all fields by 2010 while non-ASEAN investors will be able to do so by 2020.

---

[2]ASEAN Secretariat (2004). Trade Facilitation in ASEAN. http://www.aseansec. org/pdf/BrosurTradeFacility.pdf.

3. *TIF cooperation under GMS*

Since the Eighth Ministerial Conference on Sub-regional Cooperation of ASEAN added trade facilitation into its scope of cooperation, Greater Mekong Sub-Region countries (GMS) have made notable progress in this regard, as exemplified by the Ten-Year Strategic Framework for the GMS Program formulated in 2001, GMS Cross-Border Transport Agreement in 2003, and the Strategic Framework for Action on Trade Facilitation and Investment in GMS which was formulated by the governments of China, Cambodia, Laos, Myanmar, Thailand and Vietnam together with the Asian Development Bank for a five-year period. The strategic framework has defined four priority fields for cooperation, including customs regime, quarantine measures, trade logistics, and flow of business people. These agreements and strategic frameworks serve as guidelines for sub-regional trade as well as investment facilitation and cooperation, and are conducive to coordinated and concerted actions among its members and capacity-building for those less developed members. In the meantime, they can also share their experience in the sub-region and a better trade and investment environment for enterprises.

4. *TIF cooperation among China, Japan and ROK*

In recent years, TIF cooperation among China, Japan and the Republic of Korea (ROK) has made remarkable progress. They approved the Action Plan to Improve Business Environment in December 2008, and their trilateral investment agreement has undergone several rounds of negotiations and is about to come into place. In early May 2010, a joint research on a China, Japan and ROK free trade area conducted by government agencies, industries and academicians was formally launched. The 2020 Outlook issued by the third meeting of leaders from China, Japan and ROK not only sets down guiding principles for trilateral cooperation in the following decade, but also stipulates that the three countries will strengthen their cooperation in standardization, which is aimed at removing technical barriers. A permanent secretariat will be established through consultation to institutionalize trilateral cooperation.

5. *TIF cooperation under bilateral free trade agreements in East Asia*

Most bilateral FTA agreements signed and implemented in East Asia include certain trade and investment facilitation content (see Table 1).

Taking the ASEAN–China FTA as an example, The Framework Agreement on Comprehensive Economic Cooperation between ASEAN and China signed in November 2002 has agreed to "take effective TIF measures, including but not limited to the simplification of customs procedures and mutual recognition arrangements". This framework agreement also includes other TIF-related clauses such as promoting and facilitating commodity trade and service trade as well as investment (which includes standard unification evaluation, technical barriers, non-tariff measures, customs cooperation, etc.), improving competitiveness of small and medium enterprises, promoting e-commerce, capacity building and technological transfer. In addition, the ASEAN–China FTA, ASEAN–ROK FTA and Japan–ASEAN FTA also include investment liberalization agreements, improving TIF cooperation levels in the region as a whole (see Table 2).

Table 1.   TIF-related provisions of the concluded FTAs in East Asia.

TIF-related Provisions	Customs Procedures	Standards & Conformance	Sanitary & Phyto-sanitary Measures	Movement of Natural Persons	Paperless Trading E-commerce	Total 5
JM EPA	√	√	√	√		4
JV EPA	√	√	√	√		4
JS EPA	√	√		√	√	4
JP EPA	√	√		√	√	4
JT EPA	√	√		√	√	4
JI EPA	√	√		√		3
KS FTA	√	√		√	√	4
AC FTA	√	√				2
AK FTA	√	√	√			3
AJ CEP	√	√	√			3

Sources: Official texts of the concerned FTAs. *Final Report on EAFTA Phase II Study* (2009).

Table 2. Areas for cooperation in ASEAN+1 FTAs.

Category	Areas for Cooperation	ACFTA	AJCEP	AKFTA
Trade and Investment	Customs procedures	√		√
	Trade		√	√
	Investment	√	√	√
	Information and communication technology	√	√	√
	Standards and conformity assessment			√
	Sanitary and phytosanitary measures			√
	Shipbuilding and maritime transport	√	√	√
Industrial Cooperation	Tourism	√	√	√
	Financial services	√		√
	Agriculture, fisheries, livestock, plantation commodities, and forestry	√	√	√
	Environmental industry	√	√	√
	Broadcasting			√
	Mining	√		√
	Energy	√	√	√
	Natural resources			√
	Film			√
	Industrial cooperation	√		
	Biotechnology	√		
	Construction technology			√
Industrial Competitiveness	Small and medium-sized enterprises	√	√	√
	Human resource management and development	√	√	√
	Science and technology			√
Regional Dev't	Sub-region development	√		√
Others	Intellectual property rights	√	√	√
	Competitive policies		√	

Sources: Official texts of the concerned FTAs. *Final Report on EAFTA Phase Study (2009).*

All the above-mentioned TIF cooperative mechanisms are mutually enhancing and complementary. While upgrading TIF cooperation levels in the region, they have also laid a solid foundation for further TIF cooperation in the post-crisis era.

II. Obstacles and Challenges for Further TIF Cooperation

In a nutshell, TIF cooperation in East Asia is faced with both "hardware" challenges as manifested in its weak infrastructure, as well as "software" challenges in its institutional design.

1. *Varying levels of infrastructure among countries in the region, resulting in hardware insufficiency for furthering TIF cooperation in East Asia*

As is known to all, infrastructure is the key to achieving TIF and economic growth. Without a certain degree of investment of infrastructure TIF is unlikely to materialize. However, some countries in East Asia have very poor infrastructure with respect to transportation, communication, quarantine and customs clearance, and their investment in these aspects is also seriously inadequate (see Table 3). This not only makes it hard for these countries to meet the needs of rapidly increasing trade and FDI in this region, it also seriously hinders the free flow of goods and capital, posing obstacles to continued TIF cooperation.

2. *Disparity in development levels leading to different perceptions about TIF and different capabilities to participate in TIF*

Although there has been a common understanding that TIF helps to promote international trade and FDI, East Asian countries are at varying stages of development, and thus have different perceptions and receptivity towards TIF. Such differences actually hinder further TIF cooperation in the region.

Table 3.   Quality of infrastructure in some East Asian economies, 2009.

	China	Japan	Korea	Brunei	Cambodia	Indonesia	Malaysia	Philippines	Singapore	Thailand	Vietnam
Quality of port infrastructure (1)	5.4	5.2	5.1	4.8	3.5	3.4	5.5	3	6.8	4.7	3.3
Quality of air transport infrastructure (1)	4.3	5.1	6	5.2	4.1	4.7	5.8	3.7	6.9	5.9	4.1
Quality of internet Infrastructure (2)	7.2	7.8	9.5	6.7	4.5	6.8	8.8	7.5	9.8	7.4	4.3

Sources: (1) *The Global Competitiveness Report 2009–2010*, Section II Infrastructure, pp. 365–373. (1 = extremely underdeveloped; 7 = extensive and efficient by international standards); (2) *The World Competitiveness Yearbook 2009*, http://www.imd.ch/research/publications/wcy/World-Competitiveness-Yearbook-Results/#/wcy-2010-rankings/ (1 = extremely underdeveloped; 10 = extensive and efficient by international standards).

Generally speaking, a country's efficacy in TIF is directly related to its level of economic development. That is to say, the more economically developed a country is and the higher its per capita GDP, the greater its ability to conduct foreign trade and overseas investment, and the higher its efficacy in TIF. Thus, such countries will have greater initiative to promote TIF. Due to large disparities in their development, East Asian countries have different TIF levels, resulting in different dynamisms for TIF among them (see Table 4).

Certain East Asian countries such as Singapore, Malaysia and Japan enjoy higher levels of TIF and thus are more proactive in promoting TIF; they also possess greater capability to implement it. However, less developed East Asian countries with lower TIF levels display less dynamism in promoting and less capability in implementing TIF. Such circumstances not only constrain their foreign trade and FDI inflows, but also impede further development of intra-regional trade and investment in East Asia, exerting negative impact on the sustainable development of the region as a whole.

Table 4. Typical cargo dwell time and customs procedures in some East Asian economies.

Economies	M/X Dwell Time (days)	M/X Customs Procedures	Economies	M/X Dwell Time (days)	M/X Customs Procedures
Singapore	3/5	4/4	Brunei	19/28	6/6
Korea	8/8	6/4	Vietnam	23/24	8/6
Japan	11/10	5/4	China	24/21	6/7
Thailand	13/14	3/4	Indonesia	27/21	6/5
Malaysia	14/18	7/7	Cambodia	30/22	11/11
Philippines	16/16	8/8	Laos	50/50	10/9

Source: http://econ.worldbank.org/WBSITE/EXTERNAL/EXTDEC/0,menuPK:476823~pagePK:64165236~piPK:64165141~theSitePK:469372,00.html.

To sum up, such huge disparities in development among East Asian countries are an obstacle to the progress of the TIF process in the region.

3. *High cost of TIF unaffordable for comparatively less developed countries in the region*

A study conducted by APEC in 2000 on its 21 members' customs procedures, standards and unification, as well as movement of goods and people revealed that complicated customs procedures and legalities were as restraining as tariffs in preventing trade facilitation. Therefore, reform of customs authorities is vital to the success of TIF measures. But for most developing countries in East Asia, especially the less developed ones, the required reforms (such as modernization of customs clearance, setup, maintenance and upgrading of electronic data interchange (EDI), as well as connection of networks of government departments, customs and enterprises) all involve high costs that are not affordable for them.

In addition, TIF cooperation is different from trade and investment liberalization in that TIF requires constant improvements to the government's administrative capability and quality of its human resources. TIF calls for a more transparent, convenient and efficient trade and investment management system. It even involves revision of domestic laws and reform of economic systems, and needs greater coordination and collaboration among countries. To East Asian countries that have very different political and social systems, especially to the comparatively less developed ones with levels of TIF at the initial stage, these are all arduous tasks which cannot be accomplished within a short time span.

4. *Complex international investment policies with different standards in the region*

The network of international investment agreements (IIAs) has expanded to encompass more than 5,700 different agreements, with almost every country in the world being part to at least one of the bilateral investment treaties, double taxation treaties and other international agreements with investment provisions, such as free trade agreements and economic cooperation agreements that make up this system. The universe of IIAs has not only grown in number, but also in complexity as agreements increasingly become multifaceted and overlap each other. Besides, East Asian countries have unaligned national laws, procedures, rules and regulations for investment. Such a complex system of agreements and domestic institutions lacks coordination and unification. Therefore, it is an urgent task for East Asia to coordinate and harmonize international investment policies in order to make them more consistent with one another.

5. *Difficulties in quantifiable assessment of TIF costs and effects*

Though TIF can apparently contribute to reducing governments' administrative cost while reducing the operational cost of enterprises and help increase revenues, it is very difficult to evaluate the costs and benefits in a quantifiable manner. In the meantime, since East Asian countries are in varying development stages, it is easy to anticipate how difficult it would be to coordinate their customs procedures, rules and policies, labor standards, and safety and technical standards. It would be all the more difficult to measure the effects of facilitation. Unlike trade liberalization, TIF statistics are very hard to obtain, so it is difficult to conduct a cost-effect analysis from an economic perspective. Without knowing the expected effect in a quantifiable manner, there would be greater uncertainty regarding the will of policy-makers in stepping up TIF cooperation.

In a nutshell, East Asia has on one hand made remarkable progress in TIF; on the other hand, difficulties and problems loom ahead, as disparities in nations' development levels, lagging infrastructure levels, poor management, and inconsistent policies and legislations all need to be addressed. In the post-crisis era, it is imperative to expand and deepen trade and investment cooperation by upgrading TIF cooperation in East Asia to a higher level.

III. A Framework and Roadmap for East Asia Trade and Investment Facilitation Cooperation

1. *Goals*

1.1 *General goals*

As an important route to realize East Asian economic integration, East Asian TIF cooperation aims at narrowing the development gap, sustaining economic development and promoting common prosperity of the people in the region.

1.2 *Specific goals*

Guided by the above-mentioned general goals, this Network of East Asian Think Tanks (NEAT) Working Group set the following specific goals for East Asian trade and investment facilitation cooperation, taking into account the varied conditions of the Member States.

- To ameliorate the trade and investment environment in East Asia. The cooperation intends to expand the width and depth of trade and investment facilitation measures, create more opportunities for trade and investment and make East Asia more competitive in the global economic system.
- To put in place a comprehensive cooperation mechanism. It is urged to present a practical action plan with specific trade and investment facilitation measures, whose implementation will serve the process of East Asian economic integration and make an institutional preparation for East Asian FTA building.
- To create a safe, stable, facilitative and predictable trade and investment environment. This requires eliminating administrative, institutional and technical barriers in trade and investment, standardizing institutions, policies and practices in relation to trade and investment, and providing maximum facilities for cross-border transport of goods flow and of people. It is an important step towards bringing down transaction costs of intra-regional trade by 5% by 2016.

2. Guiding principles for cooperation

Due to the big difference in development levels among the Member States, the performance of trade and investment facilitation varies remarkably across the region. Under such circumstances, East Asian trade and investment facilitation cooperation should be complete, flexible, transparent, comparable and inclusive.

2.1 Being complete

Being complete means that the cooperation should include all Member States, cover all aspects of trade and investment facilitation, and benefit all Member States to the fullest extent.

2.2 Being flexible

Being flexible means that each Member State decides the width and depth of the cooperation in which it would like to participate according to its own conditions; the Member States activate and give impetus to the cooperation process together, but are allowed to follow individualized timelines.

Trade and investment facilitation cooperation tends to stagnate, for it involves coordination of all Member States, revision of the Members' domestic laws and regulations and reform of their institutions. With a flexible approach, the process would not be suspended, if some Members are not ready for deep cooperation; neither would the standards of facilitation be compromised to accommodate the less developed Members. It is a way to both meet the high expectations of the Members at an advanced stage and to bring along the Members at the initial or medium stages through example-setting and experience-sharing.

Being flexible also means the facilitation performances of both individual Member States and that of the ASEAN 10+3 as a whole should be assessed. It is improper to use the same set of indicators to assess and compare Member States' facilitation performances at varying development levels. A common set of indicators would be too demanding for some developing Member States, which might lead them to retreat from the process and result in cooperation stagnating.

Too much flexibility and self-determination might lead to low efficiency and free riding, such problems should be solved by calibrating an overall timescale and institutionalizing facilitation measures.

2.3 *Being transparent*

Being transparent means that the Member States should make prompt publications of domestic laws, regulations, trade polities, technical standards and management rules, so that other Members can have full and fast access to relevant information for monitoring and gaining maximum benefits from the facilitation measures.

2.4 *Being comparable*

Being comparable means that the cooperation timelines and facilitation measures should be practical and quantifiable, so that the outcomes can be assessed quantitatively through horizontal and vertical comparisons. Quantitative assessments are important references for designing follow-up actions.

2.5 *Being inclusive*

Being inclusive means that policy-making for regional trade and investment facilitation cooperation should involve participation by the public sector, the private sector and academia together through close cooperation, dialogues and consultations.

3. *Approaches of cooperation*

East Asia should take varied and flexible approaches to improve the region's trade and investment facilitation performance, and to achieve the goal of reducing transaction costs of intra-regional trade by 5% by 2016.

3.1 *Consensus-based collective action*

Consensus-based collective action is the major approach of cooperation. As a key process to build the East Asian FTA, East Asian trade and investment facilitation cooperation is expected to make fast, consistent and tangible progress. This can only be realized through consensus-based collective actions by all Member States; all participate in, make endeavors to and share benefits from the cooperation.

3.2 *Pathfinder pattern*

APEC's pathfinder pattern is recognized as a successful approach to promote trade facilitation cooperation. It can be drawn upon in some areas of cooperation. To make a specific cooperation program/process successful, the Member States with similar conditions reach a consensus and activate the program/process first; other Member States can join in later when their domestic conditions become mature. It is an effective way to expand the scope of cooperation.

3.3 *Narrow the development gap through capacity building*

Capacity building is an important aspect of East Asian trade and investment facilitation cooperation. The less developed Members should be given technical assistance in formulating and implementing facilitation measures through seminars and trainings, in which the developed economies from both within and outside the region can share good practices.

It is necessary to seek cooperation with OECD, WCO, ISO, WTO, IBRD[3] and other international organizations in capacity building, and to draw upon their experience in increasing the administrative capacity and capability of Members States.

---

[3] OECD — Organization for Economic Co-operation and Development;
WCO — World Customs Organization;
ISO — International Organization for Standardization;
WTO — World Trade Organization;
IBRD — International Bank for Reconstruction and Development (World Bank).

3.4 *Synergy of the public sector, the private sector and academia*

The public sector, the private sector and academia should make joint efforts to push forward East Asian trade and investment facilitation. The governments should seek to understand the needs of the private sector, and designate priority areas for cooperation. Academia will conduct analytical studies on goals, strategies, costs, and potential benefits of facilitation measures, and make scientific and feasible policy recommendations. With the partnership of the public sector, the private sector and academia, East Asian trade and investment facilitation cooperation can be more effective and efficient.

3.5 *Quantitative assessment mechanism*

A quantitative assessment mechanism ensures tangible outcomes of the cooperation, which includes the following elements:

- Key Performance Indicators (KPIs). KPIs should be defined for each priority area in consultation with the World Bank (WB), APEC and GMS and be used in measuring the progress of the action plan.
- Regular reporting mechanism. Consultative Working Groups and KPI reporting formats should be set up for the priority areas. The consultative groups are responsible for updating the Ministers' Meetings with the latest progress made in the priority areas by the Member States individually and by the ASEAN 10+3 collectively.
- Independent experts' team. An independent experts' team should be formed and tasked to make a mid-term assessment of the implementation of the action plan in late 2013 and early 2014, and ensure the final goal of lowering transaction costs by 5% is to be achieved by 2016.

3.6 *Steering committee for East Asian trade and investment facilitation cooperation*

It is necessary to establish a steering committee, which is responsible for converting the agreements of the ASEAN 10+3 Summit and

Ministers' Meeting into a specific action plan, facilitating communications and resources-sharing among the Member States and the Working Groups of the priority areas, monitoring and reviewing the cooperation process, updating the Economic Ministers' Meeting and Foreign Ministers' Meeting with the latest developments, and making policy recommendations.

4. Priority cooperation areas

Since East Asian trade and investment facilitation cooperation remains at the initial stage, a consensus has not been reached by the Member States on the width and depth, modes and timetable of cooperation. Therefore, the priority should be given to those areas that are better-conditioned and where it is easier to achieve tangible results. It not only resonates with the agreement of the ASEAN 10+3 Summit to activate cooperation soon, but also sets a good example for future cooperation in other areas.

4.1 Country of origin principle

Principal actions: harmonize the country-of-origin (COO) principles of the three 10+1 FTAs; make them more transparent; bring down transaction and administration costs; avoid "spaghetti effect" as much as possible.

4.2 Procedures of customs

Principal actions: simplify and harmonize the procedures of customs; make them more transparent; encourage free flow of goods within the region; improve efficiency and quality of trade data collection; optimize trade database; provide the business sector with more accurate, compatible, convenient and timely information service.

4.3 Standards and conformance

Principal actions: harmonize the Member States' domestic standards with the international standards; spread good practice of technical regulation formulation and implementation; ensure transparency of the Member States' standards and conformance measures; set up information-sharing and consultation mechanisms to monitor and review the standards and conformance measures.

4.4 *Construction of logistic network*

Principal actions: harmonize the Member States' rules and regulations on trade logistics; simplify the formalities for cross-border transport of goods; standardize transportation technologies; optimize infrastructure facilities, and raise the speed and efficiency of regional trade logistics.

4.5 *Mobility of business people*

Principal actions: strengthen facilitation and cooperation on visa application procedure and standardization for cross-border movement of business people; simplify the formalities of travel document inspection and immigration legislature; follow the APEC Business Travel Card Scheme and simplify cross-border personnel movement with in business purposes such as signing contracts, participating in business meetings, negotiating investment; provide visa facilitation; make visa information and application documents available on the Internet.

5. *Roadmap*

March 2011

Design and present a five-year action plan for East Asian trade and investment facilitation cooperation; solicit recommendations from the public sector, the private sector and academia.

July 2011

Convene a high-ranking officials' meeting to examine and finalize the action plan; submit it to the ASEAN 10+3 Economic Ministers' Meeting in August 2011.

2012–2015

Set individualized goals by each Member State based on the action plan; take well-planned actions according to the overall timescale; designate a country reference point responsible for monitoring the implementation of the action plan; submit reports to the Ministers' Meeting.

Form Consultative Working Groups comprising officials, business persons and scholars from the Member States for the priority areas to monitor and assess the implementation of the action plan in the areas. The Groups will hold regular meetings, coordinate with the ASEAN counterparts, and submit reports to the Ministers' Meeting.

Late 2013–early 2014

Make a mid-term assessment of the implementation of the action plan.

2016

Final assessment of the action plan's implementation and submit a report to the Ministers' Meeting.

IV. Conclusion

In recent years, East Asian countries have been making remarkable achievements through varied cooperation mechanisms in improving regional performance of trade and investment facilitation. In the post-crisis era, when the world economy is at a critical moment of recovery, it is an appropriate choice for East Asia to strengthen cooperation in this field as a means to tackle the problems and challenges of the regional economy. With political will and feasible measures from all Member States, the cooperation can certainly expand the width and depth of regional economic cooperation, narrow the development gap across the region, sustain regional economic development, and give an impetus to regional economic integration.

Bibliography

ASEAN Secretariat (2004). Trade Facilitation in ASEAN. http://www.
aseansec.org/pdf/BrosurTradeFacility.pdf.

China's Statistics Yearbook (2011). Beijing: China's Statistics Publishing
House.

Direction of Trade Statistics Year Book 2010 (2011). New York: International
Monetary Fund.

Chapter 5

ELECTIONS IN HONG KONG: INTERNATIONAL PERSPECTIVES AND IMPLICATIONS FOR CHINA

Bill K.P. CHOU

Hong Kong is a prosperous and globalized city with a rising China as its natural hinterland. That Hong Kong has weathered the 2008–2009 American financial crisis well is, in part, due to its strategic location next to a booming Mainland China. However, Hong Kong's unique association with China under the "one-country-two-systems" scheme may well be a double-edged sword. Although the city has benefited enormously from China's impressive economic growth, its democratization has also been circumscribed by Beijing (with a communist party at its helm) and its allies within Hong Kong.

This chapter first examines Beijing's three major considerations in planning Hong Kong's electoral reform. Further reform depends on the ability of pro-Beijing politicians in winning elections and restraining democrats — the major opposition forces in town. Then the power distribution of pro-Beijing politicians and democrats is discussed. Pro-Beijing forces are unable to triumph the democrats in fair and contested elections. Their grip on most of the seats in the Legislative Council and Election Committee (formed to return the Chief Executive) is contingent on an electoral system biased towards business and professional classes, whose commercial interests are

subject to Beijing's interests. Following that, the chapter investi-
gates the electoral system that is in conflict with the principle of fair
representation but enables the pro-Beijing forces to rein in
democrats.

Hong Kong's democratic development is under international
scrutiny. The governments of the EU, the US and the UK are obliged
to deliver reports on Hong Kong's democratization. Taiwan watches
closely for the impact of sovereignty retrocession on Hong Kong's
autonomy and the people's right to change its government.[1] In addition, elections and the democratic development of Hong Kong are
central to the conflicts between Beijing and Hong Kong's democrats,
who form its *de facto* opposition parties.

The political landscape of Hong Kong is roughly divided into
pro-Beijing (and pro-establishment) and pro-democracy (or pan-
democracy) camps based on their attitudes toward Hong Kong elections and democratization. The pro-democracy camp which
constantly grosses around 60% of the votes in the Legislative
Council's (LegCo) geographical constituency elections, demands
universal suffrage of the Chief Executive and the full house of
LegCo. They have organized protests with hundreds of thousands
of participants who are urging for democratization. They are closely
related to the Hong Kong Alliance in Support of Democratic
Patriotic Movements in China, which is actively involved in the res-
cue of the Chinese political dissidents and is labeled as "subversive"
by the government. Since their political demands and perceived
subversion challenge Beijing's political control, Beijing refused any

---

[1] European Commission (2009). *Report from the Commission to the Council and the
European Parliament Annual Report Hong Kong 2009*, p. 2. http://www.eeas.
europa.eu/hong_kong/docs/com_242_10_en.pdf; U.S. Department of State (2010).
Diplomacy in Action. http://www.state.gov/r/pa/ei/bgn/2747.htm; Secretary of
State for Foreign and Commonwealth Affairs (2008). *Six-monthly Report on Hong
Kong*, 1 July–31 December. http://www.official-documents.gov.uk/document/
cm75/7541/7541.pdf; Huang, T-L (2005). "Chen rejects 'one country, two systems'", *Taipei Times*, 29 April. http://www.taipeitimes.com/News/taiwan/
archives/2005/04/29/2003252405.

direct negotiations with pan-democracy camps.[2] The deadlock lasted until May 2010 when the constitutional reform package prepared by the Hong Kong government and endorsed by Beijing risked being defeated. An investigation of Hong Kong elections can help to understand Beijing–Hong Kong relations, reveal the dynamics behind the central-local disputes, and conceive ways of addressing these disputes.

In Hong Kong, elections are used for returning four types of politicians. The Chief Executive is elected every five years. The LegCo election is held every four years returning 70 legislators, District Council elections held every four years, and the election of Hong Kong deputies to the National People's Congress in Beijing held every five years. The 18 District Councils are consultative organs; most of its members are directly elected. The elections of District Councilors and Hong Kong deputies to the National People's Congress are limited in their implications on the relations between China and Western countries, cross-straits relations, and further democratization in Hong Kong. Their role in Beijing–Hong Kong conflicts is minimal and is seldom discussed by Hong Kong observers in the international community. Consequently, this chapter focuses on the first two types of elections.

I. Beijing's Position

Under the notion of "no taxation without representation", the representative of any executive and legislative branches provides legitimacy for a government over the taxation — a fiscal basis for other powers. To realize its representative function, a legislature has to be formed by contested and fair elections framed by the "one-person-one-vote" principle. Each vote is of equal importance through dividing the voters into constituencies with similar number of voters.

Beijing's position is the most important factor in deciding the pace of democratization and electoral reform in Hong Kong. Political

---

[2] Sing, M (2009). Hong Kong's democrats hold their own. *Journal of Democracy*, 20(1), 98–112.

scientist Sonny Lo pointed out Beijing's three major considerations on Hong Kong's democratization:

1) Can the pro-Beijing forces perform well in elections and grasp more seats than the democrats?
2) Are the business elites confident of maintaining their political influence over the Chief Executive and the entire LegCo after universal suffrage is introduced?
3) Can the democrats be effectively checked by the pro-Beijing forces?[3]

The answers to the three questions are negative. Among the pro-Beijing forces, the Hong Kong Federation of Trade Unions (FTU) has the largest membership of around 300,000. Established in 1948, the FTU was a mass organization directed by Beijing's United Front policy to penetrate into the working class so that the Chinese Communist Party (CCP) could remain underground and avoid offending the colonial administration.[4] After the passage of the Hong Kong Basic Law in 1990, Beijing felt a pressing need to set up a pro-Beijing political party in order to participate in future elections for the formation of LegCo, municipal councils, and district boards. This consideration led to the establishment of the Democratic Alliance for the Betterment of Hong Kong (DAB) in 1992. Before the handover of sovereignty, Hong Kong people were wary of pro-Beijing forces due to the chaos associated with the various political campaigns during the Mao era and the 1989 Tiananmen incident. The first-past-the-post electoral system was also unfavorable to such small parties as DAB. Hence in 1992, DAB could only win one seat in the LegCo election. With the rise of China in global politics and economy (as well as the increasing number of new Chinese immigrants becoming voters), the Chinese regime and pro-Beijing forces have become more and more acceptable to Hong Kong

---

[3] Lo, SS-H (2010). *Competing Chinese Political Visions: Hong Kong vs. Beijing on Democracy*, p. 135. Santa Barbara, Denver, Oxford: Prager.
[4] Loh, C (2010). *Underground Front: The Chinese Communist Party in Hong Kong*, pp. 79–98. Hong Kong: Hong Kong University Press.

Table 1. Directly elected Legco members: Pro-Beijing forces and democrats.

Pro-Beijing Forces

Jasper TSANG Yok-sing, CHAN Kam-lam, TAM Yiu-chung, Christopher CHUNG Shu-kun, James TIEN Pei-chun, WONG Kwok-hing, CHAN Hak-kan, "Ann" CHIANG Lai-wan, Priscilla LEUNG Mei-fun, Regina IP-LAU Suk-yee, WONG Kwok-kin, Paul TSE Wai-chun, LEUNG Che-cheung, Alice MAK Mei-kuen, Michael TIEN Puk-sun, CHAN Han-pan, Elizabeth QUAT
(Total: 17 members)

Democrats

LEE Cheuk-yan, SIN Chung-kai, "Helena" WONG Pik-wan, CHAN Ka-lok, Claudia MO Man-ching, WU Chi-wai, KWOK Ka-ki, Ray CHAN Chi-chuen, CHEUNG Chiu-hung, Gary FAN Kwok-wai, Emily LAU Wai-hing, LEUNG Yiu-chung, Ronny TONG Ka-wah, Cy HO Sau-lan, Alan LEONG Ka-kit, LEUNG Kwok-hung, Albert CHAN Wai-yip, WONG Yuk-man
(Total: 18 members)

voters. The change into a proportional representation electoral system that favors small political parties has also increased the chances of DAB and FTU candidates to be elected.

DAB and FTU form the core of pro-Beijing forces. Besides them are the right-leaning Liberal Party representing business and middle classes, Heung Yee Kuk representing rural interests and indigenous inhabitants, and independents who are not affiliated to any political parties or major societal associations. In the current session of LegCo, the pro-Beijing forces won 17 directly elected seats compared to the democrats' 18 members. However, Beijing is not confident that they could grasp most of the votes in elections and control the LegCo if all LegCo seats were directly elected. (See Table 1.)

The second consideration concerning the confidence of business interests is significant. For the sake of social stability, the colonial government relied on Chinese business people to liaise with a Chinese society whose languages and culture were alien to most British officials. These groups are the most firmly rooted in Hong Kong because of their investments and ownership of local assets. They had vested interests in maintaining stability and supporting the regime, and therefore were the natural allies of the colonial government. Chinese business leaders, especially those who undertook extensive charitable work and led such charitable organizations such as Tung Wah Group of Hospitals (its predecessor Kwong Fook I-tse established in 1851) and Po Leung Kuk (established in 1878) were appointed to various consultative committees and decision-making organs to reflect the opinions in Chinese communities.

In the 1980s, many foreign investors withdrew from Hong Kong in face of an uncertain political future. Local Chinese business tycoons expanded their investment to take up the market share left behind by emigrating capitalists. Their contribution to Hong Kong's economic prosperity, their conservative political outlook and the shift of their loyalty from London to Beijing induced Beijing to protect their privileges. Many of them and their children were appointed to national and local legislatures and advisory organs. The values that the pan-democracy camp advocate, including individual liberty, labor and social rights, and participation do not sit comfortably with business people's commercial interests and political privileges, and could potentially destabilize the business-friendly environment.[5]

The defeat of all pro-business candidates fielded by the Liberal Party in the 2008 LegCo direct elections further alarmed the business class and reminded them that they could not protect their power through direct elections. They had to defend the current electoral system that magnifies their influence through functional constituencies in LegCo elections and the four sectors of the Election Committee returning the Chief Executive. In its submission to the government on the 2012 election of the Chief Executive and LegCo, the Hong Kong General Chamber of Commerce supported the principle of "balanced participation", literally meaning to keep the current political system. It stated:

> Functional constituencies have been providing the LegCo with members of different professional, business and community back-

[5]Yep, R (2009). Accommodating business interests in China and Hong Kong: Two systems — one way out. In *Changing Governance and Public Policy in East Asia*, Mok, KH and R Forrest (eds.), pp. 187–188. Oxon and New York: Routledge; Goodstadt, LF (2005). *Uneasy Partners: The Conflict between Public Interest and Private Profit in Hong Kong*, pp. 97–116. Hong Kong: Hong Kong University Press.

grounds, enhancing the quality of debate and providing the necessary expertise in scrutinizing bills and policies. Functional constituencies should be maintained, but in time we should consider how their present form may evolve to meet the requirements of universality and equality, while at the same time keeping in line with the spirit of balanced participation.[6]

The analysis of the first two questions leads to the answer to the third question: Pro-Beijing forces cannot effectively curb democrats' power through direct elections. Since the Basic Law explicitly stated that the LegCo would ultimately be formed by universal suffrage, Beijing could not ignore the idea of universal suffrage but instead delayed its implementation. In 2004, it ruled out the possibility of universal suffrage for LegCo in 2008 and the Chief Executive in 2007. In December 2007, Beijing announced that the entire LegCo may be elected by universal suffrage by a date no earlier than 2020, while universal suffrage for the chief executive election may be introduced in 2017.[7] In the meantime, Beijing has to assure the pro-Beijing forces and guarantee the privileges of the business class through a quasi-democratic electoral system composed of direct and indirect elections.

II. Chief Executive Election

An important means for Beijing to maintain political control over Hong Kong is to control the electoral design of the Chief Executive, in order to guarantee the victory of its designated candidates. The Election Committee indirectly elects the Chief Executive every five years. Like the political elites in Beijing, the Chief Executive can serve two terms (10 years) at most. The Election Committee consists of 800

---

[6] Hong Kong General Chamber of Commerce (2010). *Submissions and Reports: Methods for Selecting Chief Executive and for Forming Legislative Council in 2012*, 9 February. http://www.chamber.org.hk/en/information/policy_comments.aspx?ID 221.

[7] Sing, M (2009). Op. cit., pp. 99–100.

members (1,200 from 2012 onwards) returned from the following four sectors:

1) Industrial, commercial and financial sectors;
2) The professions;
3) Labor, social services, religious and other sectors, and;
4) Members of the LegCo, representatives of district-based organizations, Hong Kong deputies to the National People's Congress, and representatives of Hong Kong members of the National Committee of the Chinese People's Political Consultative Conference

Each sector returns 200 members (300 from 2012). Each sector is divided into subsectors that either elect or nominate their representatives (see Table 2 for the subsectors and the number of voters in various subsectors). Most of the subsectors are composed of body voters and individual voters. Body voters may be the persons-in-charge of member companies and member associations. Some subsectors such as commercial (first), finance, and financial services do not have individual voters at all. Owners of big conglomerates may create dozens of companies and thus cast dozens of votes. However, the unemployed, retired, students, and housewives do not have their representatives. The total number of body and individual voters of the four sectors is around 231,000, or 7% of all 3.3 million registered voters in the territory.

Business interests are over-represented in the Election Committee. The first sector of the Election Committee comprises industrial, commercial and financial interests. Although it is composed of 27,000 members, or less than 12% of the total voters, this sector can return one-fourth (200) of the Election Committee members. The subsector of hotel is the most over-represented. It has only 101 members, or less than 0.05% of the total voters, but return 1.4% (or 11) of the Election Committee seats. On the contrary, voters of the education subsector account for more than one-third of total voters, but the 20 members that this subsector returns account for only 2.5% of the total number of voters. The

Table 2. Subsectors and the number of voters in 2009.

Sectors	Voter No. (Bodies)	Voter No. (Individuals)	Total	No. of Members Returned
Sector 1				
Catering	577	7,407	7,984	11
Commercial (First)	993	0	993	12
Commercial (Second)	733	1,043	1,776	12
Employers' Federation of Hong Kong	105	0	105	11
Finance	129	0	129	12
Financial Services	578	0	578	12
Hong Kong Chinese Enterprises Association	306	8	314	11
Hotel	101	0	101	11
Import and Export	861	608	1,469	12
Industrial (First)	706	0	706	12
Industrial (Second)	798	0	798	12
Insurance	139	0	139	12
Real Estate and Construction	440	276	716	12
Textiles and Garment	3,578	130	3,708	12
Tourism	1,127	0	1,127	12
Transport	178	0	178	12
Wholesale and Retail	1,819	4,154	5,973	12
Sector 2				
Accountancy	0	22,086	22,086	20
Architectural, Surveying and Planning	0	6,115	6,115	20
Chinese Medicine	0	4,056	4,056	20
Education	0	81,025	81,025	20
Engineering	0	8,261	8,261	20
Health Services	0	36,468	36,468	20
Higher Education	0	7,887	7,887	20

(*Continued*)

Table 2. (*Continued*).

Sectors	Voter No. (Bodies)	Voter No. (Individuals)	Total	No. of Members Returned
Information Technology	360	5,381	5,741	20
Legal	0	6,020	6,020	20
Medical	0	10,491	10,491	20
Sector 3				
Agriculture and Fisheries	160	0	160	40
Labour	597	0	597	40
Religious*	N/A	N/A	N/A	40
Social Welfare	249	12,291	12,540	40
Sports, Performing Arts, Culture and Publication	2,052	155	2,207	40
Sector 4				
National People's Congress	0	36	36	36
Legislative Council	0	60	60	60
Chinese People's Political Consultative Conference	0	117	117	41
Heung Yee Kuk	0	151	151	21
Hong Kong and Kowloon District Councils	0	204	204	21
New Territories District Councils	0	220	220	21

Note: *The following are the six designated religious associations entitled to nominate members and the number of the nominated members: Catholic Diocese of Hong Kong (7), Chinese Muslim Cultural and Fraternal Association (6), Fraternal Association Hong Kong Christian Council (7), The Hong Kong Taoist Association (6), The Confucian Academy (7), and The Hong Kong Buddhist Association (7).

Source: The Government of Hong Kong Special Administrative Region. *Package of Proposals for the Methods for Selecting the Chief Executive and for Forming the Legislative Council in 2012*, pp. 45–49. http://www.cmab-cd2012.gov.hk/doc/consultation_document_en.pdf.

lack of fair representation makes it difficult for the elected Chief Executive to be the true representative of Hong Kong people. Favored under this electoral system, the business class voiced its support for the system. As the Hong Kong General Chamber of Commerce stated:

> The existing Election Committee is broadly representative and the demarcation and composition of its four sectors are in line with the principle of balanced participation.[8]

The small number of voters in certain sectors provides much leverage for behind-the-scene negotiation. Candidates who want to run in the election have to be nominated by 100 voters. With Hong Kong's economy increasingly integrated with the Chinese market and Hong Kong businesses becoming more dependent on China, the career development and business opportunities of many voters in the business and professional sectors depend on Chinese connections. This offers Beijing an opportunity to implement its United Front policies and ensure that pro-Beijing candidates are elected. The candidates without Beijing's support can hardly receive enough nominations, let alone win the election. The Chief Executive elections thus become window-dressing. Since the handover of the sovereignty, four elections have been held. The most competitive one was the inaugural election in 1997, with three candidates contesting the post. Tung Chee-hwa who received Beijing's auspice won a landslide victory. In the second and third elections, the candidates were returned uncontested. Democrats challenged the Beijing-controlled election by fielding their candidate Alan Leong in the fourth election. In order to get enough nominations, the democrats mobilized its supporters to run in the election for the Election Committee. Although Leong was finally nominated to stand in the election, his votes were far fewer than the eventual winner, Donald Tsang. (See Table 3.)

Another weakness of the current Chief Executive electoral system is such that according to the Chapter 569 Section 31, the winning

---

[8] Hong Kong General Chamber of Commerce, *Submissions and Reports.*

Table 3. Candidates in Chief Executive Elections and the votes they grossed.

Name of the Candidates	Number of Votes Received	Total Number of Voters
First Election (1997)		
Tung Chee-hwa	320	400
Tang Ti-liang	42	
Peter Woo	26	
Second Election (2002)		
Tung Chee-hwa	N/A*	800
Third Election (2005)		
Donald Tsang	N/A*	800
Fourth election (2007)		
Donald Tsang	646	800
Alan Leong	123	

Note: *The candidates were declared elected if the elections were uncontested.

Source: Electoral Affairs Commission. The Government of Hong Kong Special Administrative Regions, *Chief Executive Election*. http://www.eac.gov.hk/en/chief/cee.htm.

candidate in the election has to declare that he/she is not a member of any political party.[9] The ban aims to insulate the Chief Executive from domestic party politics. However, an unintended consequence is that political parties do not necessarily support the Chief Executive. Out of electoral considerations, Legislative Councilors (including those from pro-Beijing parties) have to oppose unpopular government bills and policies in order to appeal to voters.

To solicit political support, the Chief Executive has to offer favors to the members of pro-Beijing parties. DAB Vice Chairman Lau Kong-wah was appointed by the Chief Executive Donald Tsang to the current session of the Executive Council, the highest decision-making

---

[9] Cap 569 Chief Executive Election Ordinance. http://www.legislation.gov.hk/blis_pdf.nsf/6799165D2FEE3FA94825755E0033E532/0B621C1E1F7C5B7A48 2575EF001BF072?OpenDocument&bt=0.

body of the Hong Kong government. The Executive Council also includes Lau Wong-fat, Chairman of Heung Yee Kuk (an organization representing indigenous inhabitants in the New Territories) and Cheng Yiu-tong (FTU Chairman). Gregory So Kam-leung, appointed as Undersecretary for the Commerce and Economic Development in 2008, was a former DAB's former Vice Chairman. The Liberal Party, representing business interests, has 10 members appointed to various District Councils. The partisan politics may work well in liberal democracies in which ruling parties are elected to offices by most voters and granted with popular mandates. In Hong Kong, however, the democrats who constantly gross around 60% of the votes cast in LegCo elections are denied of these political positions. Without a popular mandate, the government has to use a unique electoral design to receive adequate support from LegCo.

III. Legislative Council Election

Similar to the Chief Executive election, LegCo's electoral method contradicts the "one-person-one-vote" principle. According to the Annex II of the Basic Law, LegCo is composed of 60 members (and 70 members starting from 2012). Thirty of them (and 35 starting from 2012) are elected from five geographical functional constituencies with over 3.37 million voters. This part of the LegCo election is generally contested, fair, and unrigged. No candidates are returned uncontested. Bribery and violence are unusual. Criticisms are occasionally leveled against Beijing and its Central Liaison Office in Hong Kong for meddling in LegCo elections. Former Liberal Party Chairman and legislator James Tien claimed that his defeat and that of fellow member Selina Chow in the 2008 LegCo election were due to lack of support from the Central Liaison Office. On the contrary, the pro-Beijing FTU mobilized its members to vote for independent candidate Priscilla Leung who eventually won the election. Some voters who ran businesses in the Mainland said that local Chinese officials persuaded them to vote for pro-Beijing candidates.[10]

---

[10] Lo, S S-H (2010). *Op. cit.*

It is the functional constituency election that contradicts with the fairness and "one-person-one-vote" principles. Functional constituencies were first introduced in the formation of LegCo in 1985, when the British government prepared to retreat from Hong Kong. Initially, they were meant to be a transitional arrangement between a fully appointed and a fully elected LegCo. Similar to the four sectors of the Election Committee electing the Chief Executive, the functional constituencies are formed on occupational and professional categories. The functional constituencies enfranchise only 226,591 voters (see Table 4).[11] A total of 15 out of the 28 functional constituencies are related to business interests. Business people can also run in the election in the non-business functional constituencies such as Heung Yee Kuk, District Council, and Sports, Performing Arts, Culture and Publication. Starting from 2012, five more members will be introduced in the functional constituency of District Council. The candidates from this functional constituency will stand in the election by all qualified voters who have no right to vote in other functional constituencies.

Functional constituency elections have the same representative problem as the Chief Executive election i.e., business interests are over-represented. The number of voters varies widely among constituencies. The Education functional constituency has 88,000 electors, but the Finance constituency has only 132 electors. Yet both constituencies return one legislator respectively. Furthermore, the electors are divided into individual electors and corporate electors. Corporate electors may either be companies or societal organizations with shared common interests. Some constituencies such as Education, District Council and Legal are composed entirely of individual electors. The electors in functional constituencies such as finance, transport, and labor are all corporate. This means that bank tellers in Finance constituency, taxi drivers in Transport constituency, and factory workers

---

[11] Voter Registration, The Government of Hong Kong Special Administrative Region, *Voter Registration Statistics: Geographical Constituency.* http://www.voterregistration. gov.hk/eng/statistic20091.html#1; Voter Registration, The Government of Hong Kong Special Administrative Region, *Voter Registration Statistics: Functional Constituency,* http://www.voterregistration.gov.hk/eng/statistic20092.html.

Table 4. Functional constituencies and registered electors.

Functional Constituencies	Number of Registered Electors	Functional Constituencies	Number of Registered Electors
Heung Yee Kuk	155	Tourism	1,236
Agriculture and Fisheries	160	Commercial (First)	1,040
Insurance	141	Commercial (Second)	1,814
Transport	178	Industrial (First)	715
Education	88,964	Industrial (Second)	805
Legal	6,022	Finance	132
Accountancy	22,089	Financial Services	578
Medical	10,493	Sports, Performing Arts, Culture and Publication	2,215
Health Services	36,491	Imports and Exports	1,494
Engineering	8,261	Textiles and Garment	3,709
Architectural, Surveying and Planning	6,117	Wholesale and Retail	5,997
Labour	597	Information Technology	5,747
Social Welfare	12,293	Catering	7,996
Real Estate and Construction	727	District Council	425

Source: Voter Registration, The Government of Hong Kong Special Administrative Region, *Functional Constituencies*. http://www.voterregistration.gov.hk/eng/statistic20093.html.

in labor constituency have no right to vote in functional constituencies. On the contrary, powerful businesspeople holding many companies (such as Li Ka-Shing) and powerful societal groups with many subordinate organizations (such as FTU with over 300,000 members) may exercise huge influence in their respective constituencies. The system even allows foreign investors and governments to vote! Singapore Airport Terminal Services Ltd and Dubai Ports World have government capital. They have share in Hong Kong-based Asia Airfreight Terminal Co Ltd and CSX World Terminals Hong Kong

Ltd respectively; their interests are represented in transport functional constituency election.[12]

Although functional constituencies were planned to be phased out eventually, they created vested interests and gained their own lives, with many LegCo members returned from functional constituencies wanting to keep them. For example, Vincent Fang of the Wholesales and Retail constituency suggested keeping the functional constituency for the future in February 2010.[13] Beijing is keen on keeping functional constituencies, arguing that functional constituencies may provide an opportunity for balanced participation in politics.[14] After several rounds of redistributing LegCo seats since 1985, the "50–50" distribution between geographical and functional constituencies was set in 2004, with 30 seats assigned to each type of constituencies respectively. The "50–50" rule affects LegCo's representativeness. The pan-democracy camp consistently seized around 60% of total votes and the same percentage of seats returned from geographical constituencies. Functional constituencies were the stronghold of businesspeople and pro-Beijing politicians. Democrats could only seize only around 40% of all LegCo seats (see Table 5). The candidates of the pan-democracy camp are only able to win in functional constituencies with a large number of well-educated individual electors, such as education, social welfare, legal and medical services who are identify more with democratic values, whose numerous numbers makes it difficult for any political power to manipulate behind the scenes, and whose professional development has little to do with access to Chinese markets. As a result of the electoral system, business and professional interests are over-represented whilst the interests of working-class people are inadequately represented.

---

[12] Corporate voting in HK Elections (2005). *Webb-Site*.Com, 28 November. http://www.webb-site.com/articles/corpvote.asp.

[13] Constitutional and Mainland Affairs Bureau (2010). *Package of Proposals for the Method for Selecting Chief Executive and for Forming the Legislative Council in 2010.* http://www.cmab-cd2012.gov.hk/doc/package/package_e.pdf.

[14] Lo, SS-H (2010). Op. cit., pp. 202–227.

Table 5. LegCo members — by political affiliation and constituency.

Pan-democracy camp

From Geographical Constituency: LEE Cheuk-yan, SIN Chung-kai, "Helena" Wong Pik-wan, CHAN Ka-lok, Claudia MO Man-ching, WU Chi-wai, KWOK Ka-ki, Ray CHAN Chi-chuen, CHEUNG Chiu-hung, Gary FAN Kwok-wai, Emily LAU Wai-hing, LEUNG Yiu-chung, Ronny TONG Ka-wah, Cy HO Sau-lan, Alan LEONG Ka-kit, LEUNG Kwok-hung, Albert CHAN Wai-yip, WONG Yuk-man (Total: 18 members)

From Functional Constituency: "Dennis" KWOK Wing-hang (Legal), IP Kin-yuen (Education), Joseph LEE Kok-long (Medical Services), CHEUNG Kwok-che (Social Welfare), Charles Peter MOK (Information Technology), Kenneth LEUNG Kai-cheong (Accountancy), James TO Kun-sun (District Council Second), Frederick FUNG Kin-kei (District Council Second), HO Chun-yan (District Council Second) (Total: 9 members)

Pro-Beijing camp

From Geographical Constituency: Jasper TSANG Yok-sing, CHAN Kam-lam, TAM Yiu-chung, Christopher CHUNG Shu-kun, James TIEN Pei-chun, WONG Kwok-hing, CHAN Hak-kan, "Ann" CHIANG Lai-wan, Priscilla LEUNG Mei-fun, Regina IP-LAU Suk-yee, WONG Kwok-kin, Paul TSE Wai-chun, LEUNG Che-cheung, Alice MAK Mei-kuen, Michael TIEN Puk-sun, CHAN Han-pan, Elizabeth QUAT (Total: 17 members)

From Functional Constituency: LO Wai-kwok (Engineering), NG Leung-sing (Finance), CHUNG Kwok-pan (Textiles and Garments), Martin LIAO Cheung-kong (Commercial–Second), Steven HO Chun-yin (Agriculture and Fisheries), Frankie YICK Chi-ming (Transport), LAU Wong-fat (Heung Yee Kuk), MA Fung-kwok (Sports, Performing Arts, Culture and Publication), Abraham SHEK Lai-him (Real Estate and Construction), Tommy CHEUNG Yu-yan (Catering), Vincent FANG Kang (Wholesale and Retail), Jeffrey LAM Kinfung (Commercial–First), Andrew LEUNG Kwan-yuen (Industrial–First), WONG Ting-kwong (Import and Export), Christopher CHEUNG Wah-fung (Financial Services), Tony TSE Wai-chuen (Architectural, Surveying and Planning), POON Siu-ping (Labor), LEUNG Ka-lau (Medical), LAM Tai-fai (Industrial–Second), Paul CHAN Kin-por (Insurance), Kwok Wai-keung (Labor), IP Kwok-him (District Council First), CHAN Yuen-han (District Council Second), Starry LEE Wai-king (District Council Second), TANG Ka-piu (Labor), YIU Si-wing (Tourism) (Total: 26 members)

IV. Implications of Recent Elections

The electoral system that favored business classes may be related to the business-friendly environment and the resulting economic prosperity. Hong Kong has not yet enacted a competition law while legislation on the minimum wage was not set until 2010. Effective tax rates are among the lowest in the world. The US-based think tank Heritage Foundation often ranks Hong Kong as number one on its Index of Economic Freedom. Commenting on Hong Kong's business environment, it stated:

> Hong Kong's competitive tax regime, respect for property rights, and flexible labor market, coupled with an educated and highly motivated workforce, have stimulated an innovative, prosperous economy. Hong Kong is one of the world's leading financial and business centers, and its legal and regulatory framework for the financial sector is transparent and efficient. Business regulation is straightforward. Labor regulations are flexible... The labor code is strictly enforced but not burdensome. The non-salary cost of employing a worker is low.[15]

In spite of that, it does not mean that the negative impact caused by the electoral system on China and its relations with the international community and Hong Kong can be downplayed. Indeed, Hong Kong elections are more than a purely domestic affair that distribute political power among various local actors and define relations between Hong Kong and Beijing. They are also the concern of the international community, which believes it has moral and legal responsibilities to monitor the political development of a territory which is formerly a colony of the Western World. The elections of Hong Kong also underline the right of people to choose their government which lies at the core of human rights, a central issue in the disputes between China and the West. Although Hong Kong elections is never a core issue in the disputes, an electoral system in Hong

---

[15] Heritage Foundation (2011). *2010 Index of Economic Freedom — Hong Kong*. http://www.heritage.org/index/country/HongKong.

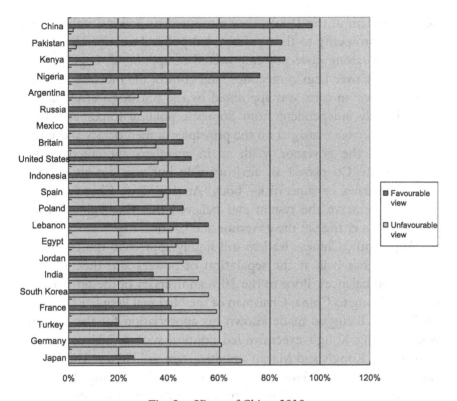

Fig. 1. Views of China, 2010.

Source: Pew Research Center, *Key Indicators Database — Opinion of China: Do You Have Favorable or Unfavorable View of China*. http://pewglobal.org/database/?indicator=24.

Kong that aligns with conventional practices in Western countries may help China to properly address the concerns of Western citizens who hold their governments responsible. As suggested by the Pew Global Attitude Survey (see Fig. 1), the citizens (and therefore voters) in Western countries and their allies largely hold mixed to unfavorable views to China in 2010. Disputes over the electoral system and voting rights do little to improve the general views to which the democratic governments in the Western countries have to be responsive to.

Furthermore, the debate on the electoral system is one of the most divisive issues both within Hong Kong and between Hong Kong and Beijing. When Chinese leaders conceived Hong Kong's post-handover political system in the 1980s, they attributed its political stability and economic prosperity to the executive-led political system. The system rested on a strong governor empowered to appoint all LegCo members, preside over LegCo meetings, and control the meeting agendas. The governor, in turn, was appointed by the British government and was relatively independent from domestic political forces. A professional civil service managed on the principles of meritocracy and integrity assisted the governor. With all its members appointed by the governor, LegCo played an advisory role but was not an effective decision-making or supervisory body. At that time, Chinese leaders hoped to preserve the system and believed that the regime change entails only a change in the governor and national flag.[16]

Apparently, Chinese leaders still highly appreciate the executive-led system but balk at the separation of powers and their roles of checks and balances. Prior to the 10th anniversary of the retrocession of Hong Kong to China, Chairman of the National People's Congress (NPC) Wu Bangguo made known his appreciation for the defining role of Hong Kong's executive-led political system.[17] In comparing both Hong Kong's and Macao's political system, Deputy Director of the State Council's Hong Kong Macao Office Zhang Xiaoming appreciated Macao's timid legislature and judiciary more, stating that Macao's political system was "more constructive". Macao's executive, legislative and judiciary branches were more cooperative and better coordinated with each other than their Hong Kong counterparts.[18]

Obviously, the democrats in Hong Kong have a different view. Unlike the halcyon days of colonial rule, more Hong Kong people are now keen on participatory politics, evidenced by the masses in various

---

[16] Scott, I (2000). The disarticulation of Hong Kong's post-handover political system. *The China Journal*, 43, 30.

[17] Yu, X (2007). Wu Bangguo you guan xianggang jianghua yinqi fanxiang (The Speech of Wu Bangguo Has Aroused Controversy), *Dajiyuan*, 9 June. http://www.epochtimes.com/b5/7/6/9/n1738423.htm.

[18] Cai, Y and Mo, J (2009). Fu zhuren Zhang Xiaoming niuqu sanquan fenli gangaoban jie aomen cai xianggang (Deputy Director Zhang Xiaoming Distorted the Concept of Separation of Three Powers. His cynicism about Hong Kong showed by his use of Macao), *Pingguo ribao* (Apple Daily), 11 November.

political gatherings and the lively debate in cyberspace. As various surveys indicate, most Hong Kong people want universal suffrage of Chief Executive and the entire LegCo rather than a political system that constrains their participation. Many civic organizations hold demonstrations, urging for universal suffrage for the LegCo and Chief Executive elections that was promised in the Basic Law, on important days such as the anniversary of Hong Kong's reunification on 1 July, the National Day of China on 1 October, and New Year's Day (i.e., 1 January).

The debates on the electoral system underline the differences between Beijing, which places high emphasis on the political control of Hong Kong on one hand, and a significant portion of Hong Kong citizens who blamed the unrepresentative electoral system for Hong Kong's governance problems on the other. The issue involves the (re) distribution of political power among the major actors in Hong Kong's political landscape, and more importantly impacts Beijing's political control on Hong Kong. The conflict can hardly be settled unless both Beijing and the democrats are willing to compromise.

Furthermore, Hong Kong and Macao are the experimental grounds of the "one-country-two-system" policy used by Beijing in its vision to ultimately unify with Taiwan. As the Foreign Affairs Ministry stated, the concept of "one-country-two-systems" proposed by Deng Xiaoping and enshrined by China's constitution is able to uphold China's sovereignty. Beijing would not interfere into Taiwan's domestic issues. Taiwan would have autonomy to choose its own social and economic systems, its way of life, and its cultural ties with other countries.[19]

Hong Kong is closely observed to see whether the autonomy — including that of forming its own government — promised by Beijing in its "one-country-two-system" policy framed by the Anglo–Chinese Joint Declaration and Hong Kong Basic Law can be maintained. Any disputes over the electoral systems may be regarded as Beijing's lack

---

[19] Ministry of Foreign Affairs. People's Republic of China (2000). *A Policy of "One Country, Two Systems" on Taiwan — 17 November 2000.* http://www.fmprc.gov.cn/eng/ziliao/3602/3604/t18027.htm.

of commitment to uphold Hong Kong's autonomy, and the failure of the "one-country-two-system" policy to insulate Hong Kong from Beijing's meddling with its domestic affairs. In view of Beijing's failure to introduce universal suffrage of the Chief Executive in 2007 and the entire LegCo in 2008, former Taiwanese President Chen Shuibian criticized that the "one-country-two-system" policy was a fraud; one country was true but the promise of two systems were false. Chen claimed that the implementation of the "one-country-two-system" policy underscored the biggest contradiction between both sides of the Straits, that is, the choice of a democratic system and lifestyle.[20]

To Taiwan, Hong Kong's experience is a negative one; any promise of broad autonomy can hardly be considered credible. A 2009 survey in Taiwan reported that only 15.7% of the respondents supported unification with China while 47.2% favored Taiwan independence.[21] Hung and Kuo even argued that the "one-country-two-system" policy had become a taboo among Taiwanese politicians across the political spectrum.[22] In order to earn trust from Taiwanese on the idea of unification, Beijing has to show its commitment to promote democratic development in Hong Kong and introduce an electoral system that lives up with the Western ethos of fair and contested elections.

V. Conclusion

Beijing's policy to Hong Kong is akin to its integrationist policy to Xinjiang and Tibet in the early 1950s: The existing social systems and ways of life were untouched. Local elites were promised with high levels of autonomy. Beijing then extended its influence through

---

[20] Huang (2005). Op. cit.

[21] Global View Survey Research Center (2009). Survey on President Ma Ying-jeou's Performance after Assuming KMT Chairpersonship, Ma-Hu Meeting, and Taiwanese People's Views on Unification with China and Independence (Ma zongtong jianren dang zhuxi ji zhizheng biaoxian, Ma-Hu hui, minzhong tongdu lichang), 20 October. http://www.gvm.com.tw/gvsrc/200910_GVSRC_others.pdf.

[22] Hung, H-F and Kuo, H-Y (2010). "One Country, Two Systems" and Its Antagonists in Tibet and Taiwan. *China Information*, 24(3), 318.

cultivating its supporters and bringing them to leadership positions.[23] What makes Hong Kong different from Xinjiang and Tibet is that firstly, Beijing uses a carefully designed electoral mechanism rather than military action and oppression to control the appointment of important personnel and wipe out opposition. Secondly, Hong Kong is much more integrated with the global capitalist economy and has received tremendous amounts of foreign direct investment. Western countries have a stake in maintaining its economic prosperity. They are naturally to be attentive to Hong Kong's democratic development and electoral reform, perceived to be important to Hong Kong's stability and prosperity. International attention to Hong Kong should not be simply dismissed and criticized as an attempt by the West to contain China.

The biggest problem of Hong Kong's electoral design is the lack of fair representation of the whole society. The interests of businesspeople and pro-Beijing forces are over-represented while the working class and democrats are marginalized. The electoral design is quite successful in maintaining Beijing's control of important personnel at arm's length, but detrimental to the building up of the necessary social solidarity for effective governance i.e., the translation of public opinion into important personnel decisions and public policies. Former Chief Executive Tung Chee-hwa won his re-election after attaining a landslide victory in the LegCo for the second term of office in 2002 despite the economic stagnation seriously affected his mass popularity. Indeed, while pro-Beijing forces can command most seats in the LegCo, they failed to win a mandate from the majority of Hong Kong people, who supported the democrats instead. To resolve this political deadlock, the electoral system has to be redesigned through wide public participation and feedback in Hong Kong's governance.

---

[23] For details about Beijing's policies to Xinjiang and Tibet, see Millward, JA (2007). *Eurasian Crossroads: A History of Xinjiang*, pp. 235–284. New York: Columbia University Press; Goldstein, MC (1997). *The Snow Lion and the Dragon: China, Tibet, and the Dalai Lama*, pp. 37–60. Berkeley, California University of California Press.

Bibliography

Cai, Y and Mo, J (2009). Fu zhuren Zhang Xiaoming niuqu sanquan fenli gangaoban jie aomen cai xianggang (Deputy Director Zhang Xiaoming Distorted the Concept of Separation of Three Powers. His cynicism about Hong Kong showed by his use of Macao), _Pingguo ribao_ (Apple Daily), 11 November.

Cap 569 Chief Executive Election Ordinance. http://www.legislation.gov. hk/blis_pdf.nsf/6799165D2FEE3FA94825755E0033E532/0B621C 1E1F7C5B7A482575EF001BF072?OpenDocument&bt=0.

Constitutional and Mainland Affairs Bureau (2010). The Government of Hong Kong Special Administration Region, _Package of Proposals for the Method for Selecting Chief Executive and for Forming the Legislative Council in 2010._ http://www.cmab-cd2012.gov.hk/doc/package/package_e.pdf.

Corporate voting in HK elections (2005). _Webb-Site_.Com, 28 November. http://www.webb-site.com/articles/corpvote.asp.

European Commission (2009). _Report from the Commission to the Council and the European Parliament Annual Report Hong Kong 2009._ http:// www.eeas.europa.eu/hong_kong/docs/com_242_10_en.pdf.

Global View Survey Research Center (2009). Survey on President Ma Ying-jeou's Performance after Assuming KMT Chairpersonship, Ma-Hu Meeting, and Taiwanese People's Views on Unification with China and Independence (Ma zongtong jianren dang zhuxi ji zhizheng biaoxian, Ma-Hu hui, minzhong tongdu lichang), 20 October. http://www.gvm. com.tw/gvsrc/200910_GVSRC_others.pdf.

Goldstein, MC (1997). _The Snow Lion and the Dragon: China, Tibet, and the Dalai Lama._ Berkeley, California University of California Press.

Goodstadt, LF (2005). _Uneasy Partners: The Conflict between Public Interest and Private Profit in Hong Kong._ Hong Kong: Hong Kong University Press.

Heritage Foundation (2011). _2010 Index of Economic Freedom — Hong Kong._ http://www.heritage.org/index/country/HongKong.

Hong Kong General Chamber of Commerce (2010). _Submissions and Reports: Methods for Selecting Chief Executive and for Forming Legislative Council in 2012._ 9 February. http://www.chamber.org.hk/en/inforation/ policy_comments.aspx?ID=221.

Huang, T-L (2005). "Chen rejects 'One country, two systems'", *Taipei Times*, 29 April. http://www.taipeitimes.com/News/taiwan/archives/2005/04/29/2003252405.

Hung, H-F and Kuo, H-Y (2010). "One country, two systems" and its antagonists in Tibet and Taiwan. *China Information*, 24(3), 317–337.

Lo, SS-H (2010). *Competing Chinese Political Visions: Hong Kong vs. Beijing on Democracy*. Santa Barbara, Denver, Oxford: Prager.

Loh, C (2010). *Underground Front: The Chinese Communist Party in Hong Kong*. Hong Kong: Hong Kong University Press.

Millward, JA (2007). *Eurasian Crossroads: A History of Xinjiang*. New York: Columbia University Press.

Ministry of Foreign Affairs, People's Republic of China (2000). *A Policy of "One Country, Two Systems" on Taiwan — 17 November*. http://www.fmprc.gov.cn/eng/ziliao/3602/3604/t18027.htm.

Scott, I (2000). The disarticulation of Hong Kong's post-handover political system. *The China Journal*, 43, 29–53.

Secretary of State for Foreign and Commonwealth Affairs (2008). *Six-monthly Report on Hong Kong*, 1 July–31 December 2008. http://www.official-documents.gov.uk/document/cm75/7541/7541.pdf.

Sing, M (2009). Hong Kong's democrats hold their own. *Journal of Democracy*, 20(1), 98–112.

U.S. Department of State (2010). *Diplomacy in Action*. http://www.state.gov/r/pa/ei/bgn/2747.htm.

Voter Registration, The Government of Hong Kong Special Administrative Region, (2010). *Voter Registration Statistics: Geographical Constituency*. http://www.voterregistration.gov.hk/eng/statistic20091.html#1.

Voter Registration, The Government of Hong Kong Special Administrative Region (2010). *Voter Registration Statistics: Functional Constituency*. http://www.voterregistration.gov.hk/eng/statistic20092.html.

Yep, R (2009). Accommodating business interests in China and Hong Kong: Two systems — one way out. In *Changing Governance and Public Policy in East Asia*, Mok, KH and R Forrest (eds.), pp. 185–205. Oxon and New York: Routledge.

Yu, X (2007). Wu Bangguo you guan xianggang jianghua yinqi fanxiang (The Speech of Wu Bangguo Has Aroused Controversy), *Dajiyuan*, 9 June. http://www.epochtimes.com/b5/7/6/9/n1738423.htm.

Chapter 6

REGIONALISM IN THE POST-FINANCIAL CRISIS EAST ASIA: DEVELOPMENTS, MODELS AND PROPOSALS

WEI Ling

In the post-financial crisis East Asia, regionalism has witnessed new complexities, growing political and security concerns and intensified architectural competition. Key players are each reshaping their own strategies in the region. Nevertheless, the fundamental themes of the region remain unchanged — peace, development, and prosperity. The chances for another Cold War breaking out are small. The prospects for regional cooperation are, therefore, good. Based on the analysis of new regionalism, the European experience and the East Asian model, the chapter emphasizes the need for the region to stick to a process-oriented approach with soft institutionalism and "asymmetrical" interaction which harmonizes relations between powers great and small. It concludes with a number of policy recommendations, including ASEAN centrality, power coordination and pragmatic ASEAN Plus One cooperation.

Since the 2008–2009 American Financial Crisis, the international system has undergone major changes in power configuration, institutional order and normative base. A new growth trend for East Asia is in place. As "the superpower relatively declines and major powers switch positions",[1] emerging powers are becoming a core force of international institutional governance; the growth model under Capitalism is questioned and challenged; democracy, human rights and green and sustainable development are gradually being promoted to be universal values by the West, while the rise of China has gained global attention.

Economies in East Asia fared relatively well in this financial crisis. However, with America's so-called strategic "return" to Southeast Asia during the Obama administration, and the strengthening of its security alliances, East Asia is directly confronted by the readjustment of global power, institutional and ideational structures. This is particularly true in 2010 — greater tension in the Korean Peninsula, intensified territorial disputes, frequent military exercises by the US and its allies, the US raising the South China Sea issue at the ASEAN Regional Forum in Hanoi, the convening of ADMM+, and the admission of the US and Russia to the East Asia Summit as member states. A string of debates ensued: The likelihood for a new Cold War in East Asia, the means to keep the region stable while pushing for the transformation of a regional order, the prospect of East Asian integration, and the need for China to reconsider its strategies in East Asia and towards ASEAN. How stakeholders view East Asian regionalism, and how key players size up the situation and make their strategic choices are crucial to the prospect of East Asian integration. Indeed, East Asian cooperation is at a crossroads.

This chapter addresses the above questions by analyzing the dynamics, theories and policy responses toward East Asian regionalization. The chapter argues that peace and cooperation remains the main theme of the region. Despite a bumpy road, the integration process is still backed by growing willingness among East Asian states and opportunities to do so. In light of this, China's East Asia strategy should stick to the principle of "respecting ASEAN, giving more and obtaining less". New regionalism and the EU experience indicate that East Asian regionalization is still at the primary stage of integration.

---

[1] Qin, Y (2010a). Continuity and change of the international system. *Foreign Affairs Review*, 27(1), 1.

Anchored by strong political will and functional cooperation, it should stick to soft institutionalism, "asymmetrical" interaction and process-oriented construction. Consistent priorities should be given to practical cooperation based on the principles of ASEAN centrality, strategic coordination between major powers and 10+1 as the primary framework.

I. Developments of Regionalization: Security Tests, Architectural Competition and Strategic Adjustments

Since the American Financial Crisis and the US' geo-strategic "return" to Southeast Asia, new complexities have emerged in East Asia. These complexities include political security, regional architecture and strategic planning, which severely challenge and pose difficulties to the East Asian regionalization. Nevertheless, the culture of peace and cooperation embodied in the regional process remains intact. There is still plenty of goodwill and opportunities to deepen regional cooperation.

1. *Political and security tests*

The political and security issues in contemporary East Asia are seen on three main fronts: The system of alliances, tension in the Korean peninsula, and territorial disputes. First, the US has reinforced its bilateral security alliances, based on a hub-and-spoke system, in Asia-Pacific by staging joint military exercises frequently. Second, the North Korean nuclear issue, and North–South Korea tension cast a shadow on regional stability as evidenced by the Cheonan and Yeonpyeong Island incidents. Third, intractable territorial disputes in the South China Sea, East China Sea and Northern islands (South Kuriles) are further sources of tension.

Between March and April 2010, China and Vietnam fell out over fishing in disputed waters. At the ASEAN Regional Forum in July the same year, the US claimed that the freedom of navigation in the South China Sea is its national interest, thus further muddying the issue despite not being a claimant state. In September 2010, after the collision between a Chinese fishing boat and two Japanese coast guard vessels in the disputed waters of the Diaoyu Islands, the US stated that the Diaoyu Islands is covered by the Treaty of Mutual Cooperation and Security between the United States and Japan. Besides, the Japan–Russia dispute over the Northern Islands (Southern Kuriles) and the Japan–Korea dispute over Dokdo Island (Takeshima) have continued to simmer.

Security tensions in East Asia seem to have been influenced by three factors. First, collective security is absent as the basis for East Asian integration.[2] Second, public and social support for regional integration is weak. Because of different social systems and ideologies, countries in the region lack political mutual trust and tend to shirk away from multilateral security cooperation, either by will or accident.[3] Third, a fast rising China and the reshaping of the power configuration in Asia are unnerving some neighboring states despite China's grand strategy of a "peaceful rise".[4] After the global financial crisis, there have been different theories about a rising China with "opaque intentions". Cynics question China's commitment to peaceful development in East Asia. With the China–ASEAN free trade area in place since January 2010, there has been even more concern

---

[2] Guo, Y (2010). America and East Asian security governance — An analysis based on the theory of public goods externality. *World Economics and Politics*, 7, pp. 36–50.

[3] Searight, A (2010). Special assessment: Asian regionalism new challenges, new visions, pedestrian progress. *Comparative Connections*, 125. http://csis.org/files/publication/1001q.pdf [accessed 30 May 2010]. The boat collision incident on Diaoyu Islands triggered an irrational or even extreme spout of nationalist behavior. According to the recent survey by Fujisankei, 80% of the Japanese people degraded China's image after the incident, and 71% saw China a threat to Japan's security. Cited from Green, MJ and N Szechenyi (2010). US–Japan relations: Hitting the reset button. *Comparative Connections*, 23. http://csis.org/files/publication/1003q.pdf [accessed 1 November 2010].

[4] Cossa, RA and B Glosserman (2010). Regional overview: They're (not quite) back! *Comparative Connections*, 6–7. http://csis.org/files/publication/1001q.pdf [accessed 30 May 2010].

among critics that China will dominate regional cooperation in East Asia.[5]

On the one hand, these issues have clouded the atmosphere for regional cooperation, deepened mutual suspicions and mistrust between certain countries, and inflamed irrational nationalisms which may drag East Asia back to a competitive and unstable balance-of-power model of international relations instead of community building. However, problems exposed in the regional process such as lagging political and security cooperation, insufficient mutual trust at the political level and low public support for regional integration may also stimulate problem-solving in some issues.

An example is the first ASEAN Defense Ministers' Meeting Plus in 2010 where disaster relief and maritime security were prioritized in regional security cooperation. The meeting itself may become the primary security institution in East Asian regionalization. The example testifies to the agreed recognition of political and security cooperation as an inevitable trend. While some issues can hardly be resolved in the near future, discussions and consultations are part of the cooperation process aimed at trust-building. More importantly, behind all the complexities in the regional security situation underlies the fact that the basic theme and culture of peace and cooperation remains unchanged across East Asian countries. The ASEAN Regional Forum-Voluntary Demonstration of Response (ARF–VDR) is another example of various ARF members engaging in multilateral exercises to deal with natural disasters based on a military–civilian model of cooperation.

Arguably, conflict avoidance is part of ASEAN's culture. When China and US fell out on the South China Sea, ASEAN countries refrained from taking sides and did not introduce sensitive topics to the East Asia Summit and the first ASEAN Defense Ministers' Meeting Plus, even when they held the prerogative to set the agenda. This shows ASEAN's adherence to the fundamental principles of maintaining regional stability and sustaining regional cooperation.

---

[5] *2010 Report to Congress of the US–China Economic and Security Review Commission.* November 2010. http://www.uscc.gov/annual_report/2010/annual_report_full_10.pdf. [accessed 10 December 2010].

2. Regional architectural competition

In recent years, another major development in East Asian integration is the competition in architecture and institution building. First, newly-elected state leaders offered competing visions of Asia, such as then Australian Prime Minister Kevin Rudd's 2008 proposal of the Asia-Pacific Community; then Japanese Prime Minister Hotoyama Yukio's 2009 concepts of "Fraternal Diplomacy" and "East Asian Community"; and President Obama's endeavor in the Trans-Pacific Strategic and Economic Partnership Agreement (TPP).[6] Regardless of their outcomes, these visions and initiatives have intensified architectural competition in the region to some extent.

Second, the existing East Asian cooperation regime has undergone major changes as evidenced by the institutionalization of China–Japan–ROK trilateral cooperation, the "Plus" of ASEAN Defense Ministers' Meeting, and the new membership into the East Asia Summit. At the third trilateral summit in May 2010, the three Northeast Asian countries embraced a roadmap of cooperation for the next ten years and agreed to complete a joint research of China–Japan–ROK FTA by 2012.[7] In October 2010, the ASEAN Defense Ministers' Meeting Plus (ADMM+) was defined as the primary mechanism for discussing security and defense cooperation between ASEAN and its dialogue partners.[8] In the same month, the East Asia Summit (EAS) convened, granting membership status to America and Russia, and thus creating the "ASEAN 10+8" architecture

---

[6] TPP is a higher standard FTA within the APEC framework. As of now, the US, Australia, Brunei, Chili, New Zealand, Singapore and Vietnam are into negotiations. Analysis of relevant initiatives can be learned from Wei, L (2010a). Norms, institutions, community — architecture and direction of East Asian cooperation. *Foreign Affairs Review*, 27(2), 74–77.

[7] *Trilateral Cooperation Vision 2020* adopted at the third Trilateral Summit on 29 May 2010, Jeju Korea. http://www.fmprc.gov.cn/chn/pds/ziliao/zt/dnzt/wjbdhrmzsfmbcxdrczrhhy/t70598.htm [accessed 5 December 2010].

[8] ASEAN Secretariat (2010). Ha Noi declaration on the first ASEAN defense ministers' meeting-plus. http://www.aseansec.org/defence/JointDeclaration101012.pdf [accessed 10 December 2010].

and reiterating that the EAS was a primary political and security forum on major strategic issues in the region.[9]

Third, the main institutions in the region have somewhat stagnated in growing competition. Under the ASEAN Plus Three framework, the most advanced trade and financial cooperation have reached a bottleneck. The East Asia Free Trade Area (EAFTA) finds itself competing against the Japanese idea of an ASEAN+6 FTA. The multilateral Chiang Mai Initiative is still struggling with poor feasibility, insufficient use of institutions and excessive reliance on the International Monetary Fund (IMF), and therefore can hardly become a full-fledged regional monetary fund in the short term.[10] The EAS may be caught in an awkward position as America and Russia (both with different strategic cultures) became new members. This means that it will have to adjust its previous pragmatic style and serve as a strategic platform[11] to accommodate America and Russia. Some scholars even view the EAS as a "counter-regionalization" factor, whose mission is to prevent the emergence of an Asian East Asian Community. Therefore, there is not much traction for the EAS to become the cornerstone of a regional community.[12]

Architectural and institutional issues tend to impact directly on the dynamism, direction and outcome of regional integration. On the one hand, architectural and institutional competition has resulted in increasingly complex regional institutional networking and slowed down progress on some fronts. It might even result in more disparate

---

[9] ASEAN Secretariat (2010). Chairman's statement of the East Asia Summit. Ha Noi, Viet Nam, 30 October. http://www.mofa.go.jp/region/asia-paci/eas/pdfs/state101030.pdf [accessed 10 December 2010].

[10] Gao, H (2010). East Asian financial cooperation in response to post-crisis challenges. presentation at the NEAT Working Group Meeting on East Asian Financial Cooperation in Response to Post-Crisis Challenges. Beijing, 21 May.

[11] Clinton, HR (2010). America's engagement in the Asia-Pacific. Speech given in Honolulu, Hawaii, 28 October. http://www.state.gov/secretary/rm/2010/10/150141. htm [accessed 5 December 2010].

[12] Breslin, S (2010). Comparative theory, China, and the future of East Asian Regionalism(s). *Review of International Studies*, 36(3), 727.

power distribution and even undermining each other's preferences. Some scholars even suggested recently that a complex eco-system has emerged in East Asia; rather than collective multilateralism, regional cooperation features "soft balancing" led by national strategies, "double hedging" and institutional Darwinism.[13] On the other hand, a pluralistic, diversified and open architecture[14] enhances East Asian regionalization, injecting vigor and broadening space for cooperation. Therefore, debates, competition and inter-compatibility at the institutional and architectural level can also inject more vigor to this process and even drive a momentum of inclusive process, open outcomes and accommodative interests.

3. *Strategic challenges facing parties concerned*

In the new context, the existing strategies of the parties concerned are challenged and need reshaping. First, with the increasing presence of major powers, ASEAN, which intends to keep its centrality in regional integration, lacks cohesiveness and leadership. This is in part due to the absence of strong leadership within the organization. Indonesia is the most likely candidate. But its government officials, business leaders and scholars (in a more pluralistic and democratizing Indonesia since the fall of the Suharto regime triggered by the 1997–1998 Asian Financial Crisis) seem to have disagreed on many issues on ASEAN institutionalization, East Asian cooperation and self-positioning. Therefore, its recent engagement in ASEAN integration seemed distracted by insufficient commitment.

Besides, some ASEAN states harbor doubts about an ASEAN community by 2015 and hold different views on a broader institutional

---

[13] Pempel, TJ (2010). Soft balancing, hedging, and institutional Darwinism: The economic-security nexus and East Asian regionalism. *Journal of East Asian Studies*, 10, 209–238.

[14] Qin, Y (2010b). Regional architecture and East Asian cooperation: A plural and multi-dimensional regional governance system. In *East Asian Cooperation 2009*, Qin, Y (ed.), pp. 8–13. Beijing: Economics and Science Publishing House.

framework.[15] This has weakened ASEAN's cohesiveness and leadership. In addition, ASEAN's key strategy to remain central in regionalization and drawing in major powers to balance each other may entail dangerous risks. Once confrontation or a power game emerges, regionalization may grind to a halt, depriving ASEAN of its driving seat and even forcing it into the reluctant dilemma of taking sides. Another party that deserves consideration is Vietnam. With rapid economic growth in recent years, Vietnam has become increasingly active on the diplomatic front. Vietnam also took advantage of its ASEAN chairmanship in 2010 to place the South China Sea issue on the agenda during the ARF meeting in Hanoi and internationalized the dispute beyond the claimant states, much to China's chagrin. The role of Vietnam and its impact on ASEAN and East Asia remains to be seen.

Second, China's East Asian diplomacy has met with some difficulties at home and abroad. First, the overall national strength of China in the post-crisis age is over-valued to some extent.[16] Some analysts even claimed China and the US was forming a "G2", thus lessening East Asia's strategic weight in China's peaceful development. Second, the 1997 Asian Financial Crisis enhanced interdependence and joint development in East Asia, and pushed for regionalization featuring pragmatic cooperation. Nevertheless, after the 2008 American Financial Crisis when world politics began to gravitate towards the Pacific region, interest in East Asian integration shifted to political security and other strategic issues. As a result, architectural disputes since the 2005 EAS have become more serious. Moreover, the rising Western view of "China uncertainty" reveals a string of disputes

---

[15] At the ASEAN Summit in January 2007, the announcement was made to advance the timetable for an ASEAN Community from 2020 to 2015. The decision was made as the Philippines, the then Chair, hoped to maintain ASEAN's competitiveness and investment appeal relative to China and India. There is certain pessimism within ASEAN on whether it will come true as scheduled or achieve the desired effects. For background information, please refer to Hadi, S (2010). Defending the centrality of ASEAN: Indonesia and the politics of regional architecture in East Asia in the post global crisis. Paper presented at the International Conference on China and East Asia in the Post Financial Crisis World. Beijing, 2–3 December.

[16] Nye, JS Jr. (2010). American and Chinese power after the financial crisis. *The Washington Quarterly*, 33(4), 143–153.

involving China and hidden behind regional cooperation. These include neighbors' concerns over China's rise, China's development model, territorial disputes and other traditional security issues. With all these new complexities, debates are also going on within China over its regional policies in the past ten years, such as respecting ASEAN leadership, "giving more and obtaining less" and maintaining the cooperation process. Realism is heading up.

Third, while the US intends to "return" to Southeast Asia by leveraging on its security alliances, and through preferred multilateral organizations and values, these approaches are not structurally compatible with the existing regional order. In the post-crisis era, non-traditional security threats have become the common and probably most urgent threats for all parties concerned. The security model advocated by the US is based on the hub-and-spoke system coupled with the ASEAN Regional Forum (ARF), EAS and other multilateral institutions. Rather than providing the collective security consonant to East Asian regionalism, it undermines the existing ASEAN-centered integration model.

At the economic level, the US is still committed to a broader sphere of cooperation across Asia-Pacific and a Free Trade Area accordingly, pushing for the signing of the TPP. Its EAS participation might further complicate East Asian economic integration. At the social and cultural level, while advocating its own values, it cannot and will not identify itself with Asia.[17] This deep-seated identity issue has presented a cultural dilemma that the US found unsolvable in its engagement in East Asian integration.

II. Theories on Regionalization: New Regionalism, the European Experience and East Asian Model

It seems that the above-mentioned challenges have dragged East Asian regionalization into troubled waters with respect to directions, structures and paths not envisaged since regional cooperation was

---

[17] Hemmer, C and PJ Katzenstein (2002). Why is there no NATO in Asia? Collective identity, regionalism, and the origins of multilateralism. *International Organization*, 56(3), 575–607.

launched in 1997. Where should East Asian regionalism go from here? Examination of mainstream regionalization theories and the East Asian experience may offer some clues, dispel confusions and uncover the dynamics and motives of regional integration.

1. *New regionalism and East Asian features*

In any regionalization theory, the first concept to be clarified is the "region" in question. Some scholars see it beyond a pure geographical concept, but more of a social construct, or a social fact manifested in geographical formats.[18] As one of the core concepts of new regionalism, regionalization is a process of cooperation and integration across economic, political and cultural fronts. It is also a process of architecture-building. The extent of regionalization is known as regionalism, which is divided into five levels according to the theory of new regionalism, namely (i) regional area, (ii) regional complex, (iii) regional society, (iv) regional community and (v) regional state.[19] New regionalism has three defining features. First, it is openness across national borders and throughout the cooperation process. Second, pluralism is reflected in the make-up of players, cultures and values, and the integration process itself. The third is "sociality". A key condition and component in regionalization toward higher levels, "sociality" is shown in mutual identification between the actors concerned, diffusion of social norms and a high level of institutionalization. For instance, the European integration has reached the stage that demands the sharing of social norms and identification. This is evidenced by the European Union (EU) efforts to save weaker members such as Greece from financial bankruptcy in the wake of the 2008–2009 American Financial Crisis.

---

[18] Pempel, TJ (2005). Introduction: Emerging webs of regional connectedness. In *Remapping East Asia: The Construction of a Region*, TJ Pempel (ed.), p. 4. Ithaca and London: Cornell University Press.

[19] Hettne, B and F Soederbaum (2002). Theorising the rise of regionness. In *New Regionalisms in the Global Political Economy*, S Breslin, CW Hughes, N Phillips and B Rosamond (eds.), pp. 33–47. New York: Routledge.

In light of the new regionalism, East Asian regionalization features openness and pluralism but lacks "sociality". In reality, openness includes geographical and process openness, as seen in the constant expansion of membership to even beyond the "East Asia" concept in the geographical sense. A pluralistic value system is underscored by the diversity of social systems, ideologies, and customs. The lack of "sociality" in East Asian cooperation is caused by three imbalances.

First is the imbalance between economic and security cooperation. While deeply interdependent economically, countries in the region are not so interdependent in security. Second is the imbalance between state and society. Prior to the official launching of the East Asian cooperation in 1997, integration in the region was largely market-driven. However, the cooperation was later led by states. There has been little bottom-up integration powered by civil society, but norm-sharing and identity-building has to be nurtured by social processes. Third is the imbalance between the institutionalizing of norms and cooperative practices. Indeed, the informal "ASEAN Way" thus far is a norm in the East Asian cooperation. While social and legal norms need to be further institutionalized, they will be challenged by the presence of non-East Asian powers (such as the US, Russia, India and Australia) which may not necessarily subscribe to the cultural norms of the ASEAN Way.

2. *European integration: Theories and their limits*

The theories of European integration have been gradually built up alongside the development of the European Union after World War II. European integration can be divided into three stages: the base-setting stage defined by power competition and state interests between 1950s and 1960s; the relatively stagnated stage from 1970s to mid-1980s and the stage of high-level institutionalization and Europeanization after the signing of the *Single European Act* in 1986. The first and second stages were governed by the theories of neo-functionalism and inter-governmentalism, focused on interpreting political process of integration, and the formation and results of an institutional system as instrumental. At the third stage of European integration, theoretical studies have concentrated on supra-national institutions and the social processes of Europeanization.[20]

Among the existing European theories and experience, only neo-functionalism and inter-governmentalism relate to practices in East Asia. A higher level of institutionalization and the East Asian integration are not yet ready to take place. While political, security and strategic guarantees are indispensable to neo-functionalism, in the European case they were delivered with support from the global hegemon and the leadership of regional powers in the European integration process. At its core was the prolonged presence of major powers. Indeed, political and strategic cooperation between powers were emphasized when the European Coal and Steel Community was first established. In respect of inter-governmentalism, although national governments have been the main facilitators of East Asian regionalization since 1997, the power transferred from nation-states to regional institutions can only be very limited given the circumstances that the regional process has been led by a group of lesser states, driven by pragmatic economic cooperation and lacking political, security and strategic guarantees.

Supported by the US hegemon and led by the major powers of France and Germany, European integration has proceeded through spilled-over cooperation and norm institutionalization. However, the European Union is merely one specific case of regionalization (an exceptional one even) rather than an exclusive model. In the comparative study of regions, a growing number of scholars began to challenge its universality. First, is high-level institutionalization really necessary for regionalization? Sometimes, a formal institution may even hinder cooperation. In contrast, shared social norms may work better for cooperation. The informality, consensus, openness and flexibility of East Asian regionalism are all major contributors to the constant progress of East Asian cooperation. Second, is it certain that homogeneity of regional countries will push for political and security

---

[20] Wiener, A and T Diez (2004). Introducing the mosaic of integration theory. In *European Integration Theory*, A Wiener and T Diez (eds.), pp. 7–10. Oxford: Oxford University Press.

regionalization? Although sharing the same language, identity and culture, some countries within the same region see little progress in their political and security integration process. A good example in point is the Arabic League. Third, is it inevitable that functional spillover will give rise to a single, regional political entity or institution? As regionalization is more diverse, pluralistic and multi-dimensional in practice, functional spillover may result in the rise of multiple sub-regions rather than the assumed unitary political unit. Indeed, the EU itself is not yet totally supranational.[21]

3. *East Asian model: Soft regionalism, asymmetrical interaction and process-orientation*

While studying the model of East Asian regionalization, some clues can be gleaned from previous experience. East Asian cooperation, if viewed as an expansion from ASEAN to East Asia, may include three interrelated key facts: first, overall peace among ASEAN member states; second, a fundamental transformation of the China–ASEAN relationship from suspicion and confrontation to strategic coopera-tion, thus generating fundamental change in the regional culture; third, dialogue and cooperation have become the dominant culture in the region since the regionalization process was initiated in 1997. With these three facts come three important lessons.

First, East Asian regionalism marked by the "ASEAN Way" is a form of soft regionalism as seen in soft borders, soft institutions and soft identity. Soft borders refer to the openness, fluidity and multi-dimensions of the regional space; soft institutions indicate that East Asian regionalization does not rely on hard-coded laws and treaties, but on "friendly relations", political will and social norms; soft iden-tity goes beyond essentialism and is defined by processes, practices and participants.[22] Regionalization, in essence, depends on the dominant

[21] Mansfield, ED and E Solingen (2010). Regionalism. *Annual Review of Political Science*, 13(1), 145–163; Breslin, S (2010). Comparative theory, China, and the future of East Asian regionalism(s). *Review of International Studies*, 36(3), 709–729.
[22] Wei, L (2010b). Post-essentialism and international politics. *World Economics and Politics*, 11, 34–44.

mode of spatial production in a particular era.[23] In the contemporary international system, nation-states and industrial civilization serves as the political and economic foundation, while political, economic, and socio-cultural spheres co-exist. However, in the post-industrialized era, the modes of spatial production are diverse and pluralistic. Known as a "noodle bowl" or regional network by some scholars, East Asian regionalization is pluralistic networking with plural players, processes and structures. Each node is a center and can stretch out to form new networks in any means or levels. Therefore, there is neither a rugged external boundary nor internal unity in East Asian integration. The socio-cultural pluralism and multi-dimensions of regional space have enabled East Asia to go beyond the essentialist identity-building and obtain special vigor and resilience in the regional processes.

Second, East Asian regionalization is pushed by asymmetrical interaction. Some scholars hold the view that hegemonic states and smaller states tend to interact in four ways, i.e., bandwagon or alliance-building, sub-regional collective defense, regional institutional constraint, and hegemonic institutional supply.[24] All these, however, contravene the reality in East Asia. The process here not only features a dominant role played by a group of smaller states, but also asymmetrical interaction between major powers and smaller ones. A classic proof here is the fundamental shift of the China–ASEAN relationship, which has contributed hugely to the dominant culture in East Asia. By asymmetrical interaction, major powers fully respect and accommodate the legitimate concerns of smaller countries, who gain more from the process, including both soft gains in institutions and norms, as well as material gains. Asymmetrical interaction features asymmetry between strengths and dominance. It is the only way to nurture trust and positive identification between countries with huge power gaps.[25]

[23] Duara, P (2010). Asia redux: Conceptualizing a region for our times. *The Journal of Asian Studies*, 69(4), November, 963.

[24] Hurrell, A (1995). Explaining the resurgence of regionalism in world politics. *Review of International Studies*, 21(4), 331–358.

[25] Wei, L (2010c). Domestic processes, asymmetrical interaction and systemic change — China, ASEAN and East Asian Cooperation. *Contemporary Asia-Pacific*, 6, 54–57.

Third, as a process-oriented model of regional cooperation, ASEAN regionalization attracts major powers to participate and gradually socialize them in the regional process. The process constructs relations, nurtures norms, builds collective identity and plays the key role in socialization. And indeed, the process is the center and core of practices. An actor may enter into the process out of consideration for its interests. However, upon its entrance, it starts to integrate and be integrated. It still weighs out its interests, which however does not follow that it can detach itself from the process. To maintain the process is to continue the interaction oriented toward identity construction. The East Asian process initiated by ASEAN and expanded to major powers is a mainstream process in the region. It is both a means and an end. As a means, it is the pathway towards the long-term goal of an East Asian community; as an end, it serves to maintain regional stability, promote regional cooperation, shape regional norms and construct regional collective identity. Therefore, maintaining the ongoing momentum of East Asian cooperation, strengthening political will and commitment to regional integration, and properly managing the regionalization process matter even more than any specific outcome of regional integration.[26]

III. Policy Proposals: ASEAN-centrality, Power Coordination, Pragmatic cooperation

When examining the development of East Asian regionalization in the post-Financial Crisis world, we probably should not worry too much about a zero-sum game among major powers or even a new Cold War in East Asia, because East Asian regionalization has become pluralistic and multi-dimensional processes. No single force alone can dominate. No single process represents the whole picture of the regionalization. In addition, social processes, soft institutions and soft norms are not merely capable of defending themselves, but also in a good position to "socialize" participants. For the participants, the cost of maintaining

---

[26] Qin, Y and Wei, L (2007). Structures, processes and socialization of power — China and East Asian cooperation. *World Economics and Politics*, 3, 7–15.

and engaging in the processes tends to be much lower than that of toppling, rebuilding and detaching themselves from the processes. Therefore, it is important to properly seize the key forces and processes of East Asian regionalization, strengthen political will, allow regional cooperation to achieve its full potential and thus guide the regional processes toward peace, progress and prosperity of the region. This paper attempts to make three policy proposals, i.e., institutional centrality of ASEAN, strategic coordination between major powers, and substantial ASEAN Plus One cooperation.

1. *ASEAN as the institutional center*

A strong and cohesive ASEAN is crucial to East Asian regionalization. However, with the growing presence of regional and global powers in the region and their increasing inputs, ASEAN centrality is being challenged. On one hand, any power should be sober-minded to realize that the ASEAN centrality has been proven to be the only feasible institutional model for the region; on the other hand, ASEAN should also be fully aware that rather than balancing among major powers, it should enhance its institutional power so as to remain central to the regionalization process, including accelerating ASEAN integration and community building, and increasing its normative capacity.

First, the success of a complete or partial ASEAN community in 2015 as scheduled is crucial to ASEAN's vigor and strength. Right now, the community building process faces tricky structural barriers caused by huge gaps in development levels, national strengths, political systems and values among member states. Therefore, a more realistic option for capacity-building is to narrow development gaps and achieve better connectivity. First and foremost is to deepen economic integration. In this process, ASEAN should make full use of major countries' strengths, particularly the growth opportunities from China, India and other emerging economies. In the meantime, integration should be a staged process. Cementing the economic basis should be the first step, while achieving political security and socio-cultural communities should be objectives for the second stage and will cost planning and consistent efforts for the next decade or even longer.

Second, ASEAN's normative power is also essential to maintaining and bolstering its institutional centrality in the regionalization. This is mainly seen in the norm-advocacy and dissemination as well as agenda-setting. The "ASEAN Way" is a good example. It is developed during the course of ASEAN processes. When applied to ASEAN's partners and other ASEAN-centered institutions, it has injected constant flows of vigor to East Asian cooperation in the past ten years through "friendly quarrels" and "friendly competition". "Cooperative Security" is a good example of ASEAN's localization of international norms. ASEAN has transformed the European norm of "common security" into "cooperative security" in the Asian context, and accordingly established the ASEAN Regional Forum (ARF). Hence, it not only defended ASEAN centrality and the "ASEAN Way", but also effectively expanded the regional agenda of security cooperation.[27] In East Asian cooperation, ASEAN has also held on to the right of agenda-setting firmly. The themes and agendas of summit meetings are usually decided by ASEAN, such as energy security, food security, and so on. Recently, the theme of connectivity, proposed and defined by ASEAN, has also come on top of the agenda in regional summit meetings. Therefore, in the future, whether ASEAN centrality can be preserved and strengthened successfully depends on whether ASEAN can move ahead of Asia as a whole in norm-building and agenda-setting. This may include reforming the "ASEAN Way" to make it efficient and adaptive to the needs of deepening cooperation and integration, harmonizing local, Western and international norms to maximize cooperation and solidarity, and developing a constructive research and cooperation agenda that benefit the region as a whole.

2. Strategic coordination between major powers

The main actors in East Asian regionalization are ASEAN and major powers. Therefore, besides the capacity building of ASEAN, strategic

---

[27]Acharya, A (2004). How ideas spread: Whose norms matter? Norm localization and institutional change in Asian regionalism. *International Organization*, 58(2), 239–275.

coordination between major powers is also crucial to the direction and efficacy of the regionalization. Strategic coordination shall be conducted with two groups of states, i.e., China–US and China–Japan–ROK. Without China–US strategic coordination, peace and development in East Asia cannot be guaranteed. The two countries need to coordinate on the following issues. First, the direction of regionalization: What kind of region should East Asia grow to be? Is the dominant culture one of cooperation, openness and diversity aiming for deeper integration, or one of confrontation, enclosure and uniformity aiming to preserve inter-governmentalism? Second, what are the core and vital interests that each wants to derive from regionalization and what are the shared interests? Third, if both agree to push for peace, development and cooperation in East Asia, what sort of risks and challenges will they encounter? What is the biggest threat? Fourth, what measures need to be taken as a joint response to the above threats?

As China's core national interests are political stability, sovereign security and sustainable economic and social development, its East Asian strategy naturally serves to "create a stable and favorable neighboring environment for its own growth". Its neighborhood diplomacy features "harmony, security and prosperity". Rather than following the "Monroe Doctrine", its strategic intention is to maintain and facilitate peace, development and cooperation in the region.[28] The biggest threat to China's regional interests is broken peace, disrupted cooperation and stagnated development. Examples are seen in the economic and financial crises, major natural disasters and regional conflicts. Therefore, China has been following a fundamental policy of respecting and supporting ASEAN, upholding open regionalism and facilitating effective cooperation across functional areas. On the part of the US, its strategic goal is to boost its leadership, promote regional security and prosperity, and advocate American values. To do so, it relies on its Asia-Pacific alliances and partnerships, and is enhancing cooperation with regional multilateral institutions.[29]

---

[28] Dai, B (2010). Adhere to the road of peaceful development. http://www.fmprc.gov.cn [accessed 20 December 2010].

[29] Clinton, HR. America's engagement in the Asia-Pacific.

Therefore, a safe and prosperous East Asia meets the shared interests of both China and the US. Besides, both countries are committed to supporting ASEAN centrality and they are increasingly interdependent on global and regional affairs. All these point to the need for strategic coordination, and the possibility for concerted efforts to facilitate common interests and coordinate differences.

Strategic coordination should also be conducted among China, Japan and ROK. Seated in Northeast Asia, the three countries share vital interests in sub-regional political stability and economic prosperity. At present, the lack of sufficient mutual trust is the biggest barrier that prevents the realization and maximization of common interests. Not only is the state-to-state political mutual trust inadequate, but the people-to-people friendship is also fragile. Despite external factors, the disputes over regional architecture and the prominence of security tensions are largely due to insufficient strategic coordination among the three countries. Therefore, East Asian regionalization calls for coordination and mutual support among China, Japan and ROK. *Trilateral Cooperation Vision 2020* prescribes the cooperation objectives in the next decade, among which the following are critical. First, develop frequent high-level exchanges and discuss the possibility for a trilateral defense dialogue; second, conclude a joint study on China–Japan–Korea FTA by 2012; third, implement the Joint Action Plan on Environmental Cooperation, in particular in cooperation on prevention and control of sand storms.[30] These three goals are the key to further cooperation in political security, economic and social areas.

3. *Pragmatic ASEAN plus one cooperation*

A key dimension to the multi-dimensional architecture in East Asia is the cooperation between ASEAN and its dialogue partners, i.e., ASEAN Plus One. Although an overarching regional architecture cannot be decided at present, with the support for ASEAN centrality from all parties, the ASEAN Plus One mechanism is actually the basic institutional frame of East Asian regionalization. Therefore,

---

[30] *Trilateral Cooperation Vision 2020.*

strengthening ASEAN Plus One cooperation can enhance the resilience and dynamism of regional networking. Among all the 10+1s, ASEAN plus China, ASEAN plus Japan and ASEAN plus Korea have been developing most rapidly and substantively.[31] Moreover, as ASEAN's FTA with the three countries are either already in place or nearing implementation, these three 10+1 have the potential to be the most promising sub-regional institutions. Pragmatic cooperation under the 10+1 regime should deliver the following:

First, respect ASEAN, and "give more and obtain less". Initiated by ASEAN as early as 1970s, dialogue partnerships have only begun to achieve robust growth in the past ten years due to two reasons. First, the rapid development of the China–ASEAN relationship has given rise to benevolent competition between the various 10+1s; second, as regional cooperation across Asia is in full swing, ASEAN centrality is widely respected and supported, making the 10+1 regime even more relevant to countries' regional strategies. One thing that can be learned from ten years of 10+1 cooperation is to show full respect to ASEAN and give due considerations for ASEAN's concerns, let ASEAN obtain more dividends of cooperation, and consider ASEAN's needs in setting the priority list for cooperation.

Second, adopt connectivity as the growth engine in the post-FTA era. At the moment, ASEAN's primary objective is to build an ASEAN community. A chief means to it is ASEAN connectivity, particularly connectivity in infrastructure networks across the transport, communication and energy fronts. The Master Plan on ASEAN Connectivity[32] is being implemented. If each 10+1 scheme can set out corresponding plans to meet the ASEAN plan, then connectivity across East Asia might come true, and thus further the regional integration process. Right now, China and ASEAN have signed the Strategic Plan on Transport Cooperation, which set out to achieve connectivity on road transport pathways within the next 10 to 15

---

[31] Ji, L (2009). ASEAN+China, ASEAN+Japan, ASEAN+ROK. In *East Asian Cooperation 2009*, Qin, Y (ed.), p. 57. Beijing: Economics and Science Publishing House.
[32] ASEAN Secretariat (2010). Master plan on ASEAN connectivity. Jakarta, December. http://www.aseansec.org/documents/MPAC.pdf [accessed 20 December 2010].

years.[33] As a result, a new construction era of connectivity may take shape under the 10+1 scheme.

Third, strengthen social and cultural exchanges within the 10+1 regime. Social and cultural exchange has recently become a priority on ASEAN's cooperation agenda,[34] starting from human resource development and educational cooperation. For instance, Thailand took the lead in setting up the ASEAN university network and began extending it to East Asia. The first preparation meeting was convened in late 2010 and a special taskforce for the East Asian university network will be launched soon. The first China-ASEAN Education Ministers' Meeting was also held in 2010. Those are all good moves that can be leveraged. Firstly, a cooperation network on education should be established and institutionalized to mark the first step in shaping institutionalized social and cultural networks in the region. Socio-cultural exchanges, once institutionalized and network-based, can improve mutual trust, friendship and identification between the peoples in East Asia. Secondly, social forces should be mobilized and guided to facilitate bottom-up regionalization process. Although the overall cooperation is still inter-governmental, socio-cultural cooperation can move a bit faster to lend more roles to social forces.

IV. Conclusion: China and East Asian Cooperation

This chapter has reviewed and analyzed the dynamics of East Asian regionalization in the post-financial crisis world. It attempts to clarify and answer a number of questions behind all the complexities. For instance, whether the basic regional culture of East Asia is peace and cooperation or confrontation and balancing, whether China enjoys an overall friendly neighborhood or suffer from a worsening neighboring environment, and whether East Asian integration is deepening or

---

[33] Wen, J (2010). Remarks at the 13th ASEAN+3 Leaders Meeting. Ha Noi, Vietnam, 29 October. http://www.gov.cn [accessed 30 November 2010].
[34] ASEAN Secretariat (2009). Chairman's statement of the 15th ASEAN Summit — "Enhancing Connectivity, Empowering Peoples". Cha-am Hua Hin, Thailand, 23–25 October. http://www.aseansec.org/23560.htm [accessed 2 December 2010].

risking stagnation. The author believes that despite all the tests, competition and difficulties, the will and opportunity for peace and cooperation is none but evident in East Asian regionalization. The immediate issue is not one about whether regionalization and China's neighborhood strategy should proceed, but rather how to seize the key elements in the process, run the current institutions and favorable conditions more effectively, push for a benevolent and interactive form of competition and strategy, and inject new vigorr and vitality to the whole process. Therefore, regionalization at the next stage should stick to soft institutionalism, asymmetrical interaction and process orientation. ASEAN should remain the regional institution -center, strategic coordination between major powers should be reinforced and pragmatic cooperation under the 10+1 regime should be furthered.

China is a pivotal, indispensable and cooperative actor in the East Asian regionalization process. The lessons that Beijing has learned from its previous engagement in regional cooperation is to support ASEAN's leadership, "give more and obtain less" and promote pragmatic cooperation. In the future, with growing interaction between China's domestic politics and diplomacy, it is increasingly significant to properly handle the relation between China's domestic economic growth and regional cooperation in order to enhance economic interdependence and the shared destiny between China and other East Asian countries. Beijing has acquired certain lessons and experience, both positive and negative. On the positive side, ASEAN countries have shared the dividends of China's growth in the past twenty years. They affirm their cooperation with China and appreciate China's role in the region. Some of them have developed beneficial interactions with China. For instance, Singapore succeeded in setting up the Suzhou Industrial Park, Tianjin Eco-city and Guangzhou Knowledge City; Malaysia rode on the trend of Chinese students pursuing overseas studies and recruited many Chinese exchange students.[35]

---

[35] Lye, LF (2010). 20 Years of China–Singapore diplomatic relations: An assessment; Wong, AC (2010). Philippines–China economic relations: A brief review; Lee, KH (2010). China–Malaysia economic relations: 2000–2010. Presentations at the International Conference on China and East Asia in the Post Financial Crisis World. Beijing, 2–3 December.

However, China's energy-intensive growth has impacted the ecology of Southeast Asia negatively. On a more positive note, the China–ASEAN Free Trade Area is now in place, and China seeks to change its economic development pattern and pursue sustainable growth. In the future, while China concentrates on its domestic development, its interaction with the rest of the region is going to be increasingly important in terms of "soft" power projection, image building, benefits sharing and the nurturing of a common Asian identity.

Bibliography

Acharya, A (2004). How ideas spread: Whose norms matter? Norm localization and institutional change in Asian regionalism. *International Organization*, 58(2), 239–275.

Breslin, S (2010). Comparative theory, China, and the future of East Asian regionalism(s). *Review of International Studies*, 36(3), 709–729.

Cossa, RA and B Glosserman (2010). Regional overview: They're (not quite) back! *Comparative Connections*, 6–7. http://csis.org/files/publication/1001q.pdf [accessed 30 May 2010].

Duara, P (2010). Asia redux: Conceptualizing a region for our times. *The Journal of Asian Studies*, 69(4), 963–983.

Green, MJ and N Szechenyi (2010). US–Japan relations: Hitting the reset button. *Comparative Connections*, 23. http://csis.org/files/publication/1003q.pdf [accessed 1 November 2010].

Guo, Y (2010). America and East Asian security governance — An analysis based on the theory of public goods externality. *World Economics and Politics*, 7, 36–50.

Hemmer, C and PJ Katzenstein (2002). Why is there no NATO in Asia? Collective identity, regionalism, and the origins of multilateralism. *International Organization*, 56(3), 575–607.

Hettne, B and F Soederbaum (2002). Theorising the rise of regionness. In *New Regionalisms in the Global Political Economy*, S Breslin, CW Hughes, N Phillips and B Rosamond (eds.), pp. 33–47. New York: Routledge.

Hurrell, A (1995). Explaining the resurgence of regionalism in world politics. *Review of International Studies*, 21(4), 331–358.

Mansfield, ED and E Solingen (2010). Regionalism. *Annual Review of Political Science*, 13(1), 145–163.

Nye, JS Jr. (2010). American and Chinese power after the financial crisis. *The Washington Quarterly*, 33(4), 143–153.

Pempel, TJ (ed.) (2005). *Remapping East Asia: The Construction of a Region*. Ithaca and London: Cornell University Press.

Pempel, TJ (2010). Soft balancing, hedging, and institutional Darwinism: The economic-security nexus and East Asian regionalism. *Journal of East Asian Studies*, 10, 209–238.

Qin, Y (2010a). Continuity and change of the international system. *Foreign Affairs Review*, 27(1), 1–13.

Qin, Y (ed.) (2010b). *East Asian Cooperation 2009*. Beijing: Economics and Science Publishing House.

Qin, Y and Wei, L (2007). Structures, processes and socialization of power — China and East Asian cooperation. *World Economics and Politics*, 3, 7–15.

Searight, A (2010). Special assessment: Asian regionalism new challenges, new visions, pedestrian progress. *Comparative Connections*, 125. http://csis.org/files/publication/1001q.pdf [accessed 30 May 2010].

Wei, L (2010a). Norms, institutions, community — architecture and direction of East Asian cooperation. *Foreign Affairs Review*, 27(2), 74–77.

Wei, L (2010b). Post-essentialism and international politics. *World Economics and Politics*, 11, 34–44.

Wei, L (2010c). Domestic processes, asymmetrical interaction and systemic change — China, ASEAN and East Asian cooperation. *Contemporary Asia-Pacific*, 6, 54–57.

Wiener, A and T Diez (2004). Introducing the mosaic of integration theory. In *European Integration Theory*, A Wiener and T Diez (eds.), pp. 7–10. Oxford: Oxford University Press.

Chapter 7

EAST ASIAN COMMUNITY: DREAM OR REALITY?

LAM Peng Er

East Asia is enjoying remarkable economic growth despite the 2008–2009 American Financial Crisis triggered by the US sub-prime mortgage problem.[1] Nevertheless, political tensions persist in this region. How should order and harmony in East Asia be maintained amidst nation-states jealously guarding their sovereignty and national interests? Conceivably, an East Asian Community (EAC) can be built around common interests, institutions and an Asian identity for peace and order, and to mitigate parochial nationalism.

To be sure, constructing an EAC is likely to be a long and winding road given the differences among regional states in their levels of economic development, regime-types and national interests.[2] Some

---

[1] I define East Asia as including Northeast Asia and Southeast Asia. According to the Asian Development Bank, East Asian economies including China and South Korea will lead growth, expanding an overall 8.4% in 2011 and 8.1% in 2012. Southeast Asia including Singapore Thailand, Malaysia and the Philippines will grow 5.5% in 2011 and 5.7% in 2012 while Indonesia and Vietnam are expected to expand more than 6% in the same period. See ADB, WB Forecast steady growth for Asia in 2011–2012 (7 April 2011), *Bernama*.

[2] For a summary of Chinese, Japanese, Korean and Southeast Asian views of East Asian regionalism, see He, B (2004). East Asian ideas of regionalism: A normative critique. *Australian Journal of International Affairs*, 58(1). See also You, J (2006). East Asian community: A new platform for Sino–Japanese cooperation and contention. *Japanese Studies*, 26(1).

of these states (Japan, South Korea, the Philippines and Thailand) are allies of the US superpower while other states eschew military alliances. Presumably, an ally like Japan is likely to be torn between the alliance with the US and an EAC. In theory, memberships in an alliance with extra-regional powers and an EAC need not be mutually exclusive. But given the fact that the US superpower watches the rise of China (as a potential challenger) and the advent of an EAC (which excludes the US) with concern, it will not be surprising if some US allies in the region are marked by ambivalence towards the EAC too.

Notwithstanding the above caveats, an East Asian aphorism instructs: The journey of a thousand miles begins with a single step. At the outset of the 21st century, that regional aspiration may appear more of a dream than a reality. However, it is not impossible for realities to change and sometimes dreams do become realities.[3] At the risk of sounding like a cliché, the dreams of today may become the realities of tomorrow.

In actuality, the EAC is an evolutionary process and therefore very much a work-in-progress. Sometimes, it may be a case of "one step backward, two steps forward" or "one step forward, two steps backward". Though community-building is likely to be a protracted project, there is no need to give in to despair and despondency and believe that the East Asians are less capable and pragmatic than the West Europeans in constructing their own community.

Economically, the region is increasingly tied together by an Asian production network.[4] Politically, the East Asia has yet to become one.

---

[3] Just before taking office, Hatoyama Yukio expressed his desire for an EAC. He said: "It is not a bad thing to have a dream. Even dreams come true in the end". Unfortunately, Hatoyama did not stay long as a Prime Minister to pursue his dream of anchoring Sino–Japanese relations within an EAC. See Efforts to build trust with Asian neighbors to test Hatoyama's fraternal diplomacy (23 September 2009). *Mainichi Daily News*.

[4] Hitherto, the regional economy was based on the "Flying Geese" model centered on Japan. By 2001, it became apparent that a new Asian production network has emerged with parts sourced from all over East Asia and final assembly in China for global exports. In this regard, China has become the factory of the world.

Regional institutions with the exception of Association of Southeast Asian Nations (ASEAN) are nascent and a common Asian identity is still inchoate. Culturally, the East Asia has been open to the diffusion of different values from within and outside the region. Multiculturalism should, therefore, be an asset and not an impediment to an EAC. Whether an EAC is just a pipe dream also depends on the wisdom and commitment of political leaders and an epistemological community in East Asia to promote this project and persevere amidst difficulties and obstacles in a long and arduous journey.[5] Indeed, closer economic ties are necessary but not a sufficient condition for an EAC.

This chapter is structured as follows. First is an examination of how order is maintained in the East Asia according to various models of international relations (IR). Following that is a brief explanation of the origins of the East Asian regionalism. Next is an analysis of the competing visions of an EAC. Indeed, the aphorism of "sharing the same bed but having different dreams" may be true. Finally is an examination of the obstacles and possibilities of an EAC in the long run.

My central argument is that the EAC should not mimic the European Union (EU) but must be based on "Asian" characteristics undergirded by the consent of both big and small nations in the region. This includes a "New Thinking" that moves beyond an obsolete and fatalistic Cold War mentality that conflict (including war) is often inevitable between rising and status quo powers. As an alternative, I suggest the "Hoi An" model based on regional history, mutual economic gain, multiculturalism, tolerance and cooperation as a "once and future" model for East Asia. In the 17th and 18th century, Hoi An was a bustling cosmopolitan port-city in central Vietnam which serviced merchants from Asia and beyond. I will explain Hoi An as a model and metaphor for East Asian cooperation in detail later in this chapter.

---

[5] An epistemological community can comprise scholars, intellectuals, journalists, artists and civil society activists who champion an EAC linked by geography, history, culture, economics, interests and imagination.

I. Maintaining East Asian Order: IR Models

1. *Balance of power: From hard to "soft" balancing*

A dominant IR paradigm is the school of "realism" which perceives that international affairs are predominantly driven by the national interests of sovereign states in an anarchical global system in which no authoritative global government exists to set the rules and maintain order. States engage in self-help and forge coalitions to balance a rising and threatening power. They may even go to war to maintain the balance of power to their own advantage. However, some weaker states may choose to bandwagon with a status quo great power or a rising great power in their perceptions of national interests.

According to the school of realism, rising great powers threaten preexisting great powers which enjoy the status quo (institutions, rules of the game and distribution of benefits) in the international system. Driven by the logic of "realism" and perhaps a Cold War mentality, the US apparently views the rise of China as a potential threat to American hegemony. To US strategists, order in the East Asia is maintained by a "hub and spokes" approach — with bilateral alliances radiating from the US core to the rims comprising Japan, South Korea, the Philippines, Thailand and Australia.[6]

While bilateral trade with China and Beijing's purchase of US treasury bonds and debts have become increasingly important, and expressions of engagement with China and the latter as an international stakeholder have been made by the US, it can be interpreted that the heart of American strategy towards China still is "hard" balancing underpinned by its preponderant military might and system of alliances. Arguably, the 2008–2009 American Financial Crisis has accentuated an odd characteristic of Sino–US relations: The US is increasingly indebted to China financially while China is a hostage to the US treasury bonds and the US dollars holding their value.

---

[6] See Cha, V (2010). Powerplay origins of the US alliance system in Asia. *International Security*, 34(3), 158–196. See also Park, JJ (2011). The US-led alliances in the Asia-Pacific: Hedge against potential threats or an undesirable multilateral security order? *Pacific Review*, 24(2), 137–158.

Indeed, the US approach can be interpreted as an "iron fist in a velvet glove". The velvet glove is diplomatic hedging while the iron fist is overwhelming military might. Despite its financial crisis, economic recession, high unemployment, fiscal debt and anti-Wall Street demonstrations in 2011, the American superpower spent around 42% of the world's total defense budget.[7] Simply put, while China and the US are economically and financially interdependent, they are also geo-political rivals.

Notwithstanding the demise of the Soviet Union and the end of the Cold War, the US continues to maintain 47,000 troops in many military bases in Japan especially Okinawa prefecture. The Hatoyama Administration from the new ruling Democratic Party of Japan (DPJ) tried to relocate the US marine base in Futenma, Okinawa out of that prefecture.[8] The aim was to relieve the pressure of the US military presence on Okinawa amidst resentment from the local population. But Prime Minister Hatoyama Yukio resigned after failing to fulfill his electoral promise made during the August 2009 Lower House Elections to shift the US marine base in Futenma out of Okinawa. After the 2010 incident in which a Chinese fishing craft collided with two Japanese Coast Guard vessels in the vicinity of the disputed Senkaku (Diaoyu) islands, many Japanese have become even more critical and suspicious of a rising China.[9]

After the Hatoyama Administration's initial flirtation to make the EAC the center piece in its foreign policy, improve relations with China and to lessen its dependence on the US, Japan has once again

---

[7] *SIPRI 2009 Yearbook: Armaments, Disarmaments and International Security* (2009), p. 183. Stockholm: SIPRI.

[8] Hitherto, the Liberal Democratic Party (LDP) was the perennial party-in-power which ruled for 54 years (1955–2009) except between 1993 and 1994. The LDP was a staunch supporter of the US–Japan alliance. The Japan Socialist Party (JSP), the number one opposition party during the Cold War years, supported unarmed neutrality as its security policy.

[9] Tokyo's suspicions of a rising and more assertive China are reflected in its annual White Paper, *The Defense of Japan: 2010*. Tokyo: Ministry of Defense. See also the 2010 National Defense Program Guidelines which are a blueprint for Japan's defense posture for the next decade.

placed itself firmly in the US camp by reiterating the US–Japan alliance.[10] Despite the fact that China has overtaken the US as Japan's number one economic partner, the habit of being the junior partner of the US, and the angst of being displaced as the second largest economy in the world by China in 2010 mean that many Japanese political elite and the media believe that balancing with the US against a rising China is the best approach for its own security and regional order. Simply put, the EAC was a dream which soon vanished from the Japanese public discourse after the departure of Prime Minister Hatoyama.

Ironically, the EAC concept was part of the DPJ's 2005 electoral manifesto and therefore official party policy and not just the personal preference of Hatoyama Yukio.[11] But there was no mention of an EAC in Japanese foreign policy after Kan Naoto succeeded Hatoyama as Prime Minister. Apparently, the prevailing mood in Japan during the Kan Administration is that the vision of cooperating with China within an EAC appears remote and naïve. Given Tokyo's territorial disputes with China, Russia and South Korea, the island country has no choice but to depend on the US for its security. This turnaround in Japanese sentiments from the proposal of an EAC to the reinforcement of the US–Japan Alliance is further cemented by the large deployment of US troops to assist Japan in the aftermath of the triple tragedies of earthquake, tsunami and nuclear accidents in

---

[10] In *Voice*, a Japanese magazine, Hatoyama Yukio argued that Japan is caught between two great powers — its US ally, a hegemonic power which practices "market fundamentalism", and China, a rising power. Implicit in his analysis is that Japan must find strategic space between the two great powers. Hatoyoma intimates that bilateral Sino–Japanese relations are problematic, in part, due to the history issue. To mitigate this, it is best to anchor Sino–Japanese relations within a larger regional framework especially an EAC. See Hatoyama, Y (2009). My political philosophy. *Voice*, September. See also Japanese Ministry of Foreign Affairs (2009). Address by H.E. Dr Yukio Hatoyama, Prime Minister of Japan. Japan's new commitment to Asia: Toward the realization of an East Asian community. 15 November, Singapore.

[11] Mulgan, AG (2009). Hatoyama's East Asia community and regional leadership rivalries. *East Asian Forum*, 13 October.

March 2011 — the greatest calamity faced by the country since the end of World War II. Despite the ambivalence of many Japanese towards the continual presence of the US troops in Okinawa after the end of the Cold War, there is also appreciation of the rapid deployment of the US troops to provide humanitarian assistance in the wake of the triple tragedies.

Unlike Japan, the ASEAN states do not balance militarily against a rising China. Presumably, they lack the intent and capability to do so. However, an argument can be made that they have adopted a more subtle "soft balancing" or hedging strategy by encouraging all great powers to remain engaged in Southeast Asia. This approach relies on diplomacy rather than military might to promote a political balance *among* great powers rather than against China *per se*. In this regard, besides the ASEAN Plus Three (APT), many ASEAN states have also supported the East Asian Summit (EAS) which includes the great powers of China, Japan, India, and Russia and the US superpower too. The assumption is that order in East Asia can be maintained by giving a stake in the region to all great powers. And if all great powers are engaged in the East Asia, it will be difficult for any one great power to dominate the region.

2. Power hierarchy: Hegemonic peace, middle kingdom, G2 or great power condominium

Another approach to maintain regional order is predicated on a power hierarchy in which states respect a regional pecking order by deferring to a preponderant power. Some US analysts assume that US hegemony is a good thing and that it provides "public goods" and "hegemonic peace" to the East Asia. Whether being a self-appointed US Marshall with a Deputy Sheriff like Australia or the perception that the US is the provider of oxygen to the security architecture of the East Asia is a good thing or not is debatable.

There is also the argument that China was the once and future dominant power in the East Asia which had and will underpin regional order. David Kang argues that historically a dominant China was a benevolent China.[12] Its traditional approach in international relations was based on trade and culture and not on military coercion. He opines that a China that has arisen will bring immense economic benefits to its neighbors and will be the great power which will underpin East Asian order. However, to the smaller East Asian states, there is no assurance that a China in the future will behave like a benevolent Middle Kingdom of the past. It is also hard for them to anticipate the intentions of China and other great powers in the future. Therefore, the ASEAN countries would prefer a "soft-balancing" approach among many great powers, and also to anchor China within multilateral processes.

Some contemporary Chinese scholars of international relations have found the classical idea of *All Under Heaven* (*Tianxia*: 天下) to be rather attractive.[13] They believe that there is a precedent for an

---

[12] Kang, D (2007). *China Rising: Peace, Power and Order in East Asia*. New York: Columbia University Press.

However, there are at least three other plausible reasons why the Middle Kingdom did not invade Korea, Japan and Southeast Asia. First, China was relatively self-sufficient and did not deem it necessary to occupy other lands. Second, the historical external threat to China was from the North including the nomadic tribes from Central Asia, Mongolia and Manchuria. Confronted by this perennial threat from the North for almost two millennia, there was little incentive for China to dissipate its strength by draining its exchequer, manpower and other resources to dominate the South. An exception was the armada of Admiral Cheng Ho during the Ming dynasty which sailed through the waters of Southeast Asia, the Indian Ocean and to the East of Africa. Third, historical China was often divided, ridden by rebellions and civil wars, and suffered from periodic dynastic decline. In this regard, it had limited capacity to dominate maritime East Asia.

[13] See, for example, Zhao, T (2009). A political world philosophy in terms of all-under-heaven (Tianxia). *Diogenes*, No.221 and Zhao, T (2006). Rethinking empire from a Chinese concept of all-under-heaven (Tianxia). *Social Identities*, 12(1), Janauary.

See also Zheng, Y (2010). From Tianxia (all-under-heaven) to modern international order. In *China and International Relations: The Chinese View and the Contributions of Wang Gungwu*, Zheng, Y (ed.). London: Routledge.

The Confucius Institute, the Department of East Asian Languages and Cultures, the Center for East Asian Studies, and the School of Humanities and Sciences at Stanford University hosted the *Tianxia Workshop: Culture, International Relations and World History* on 6–11 May 2011.

For a Western critique of the concept of *Tianxia*, see Callahan, WA (2008). Chinese visions of world order: Post-hegemonic or a new hegemony. *International Studies Review*, 10, 749–761.

East Asian order centered on China before the Age of Western Imperialism. However, it is debatable whether Japan and all Southeast Asian countries consented and abided by this regional order during the Ming and Ching dynasties. In the 21st century, Japan, Korea and Southeast Asia do not desire a new regional order in which they are merely satellites revolving around China.

To its neighbors, the proposition that China is a partner in an EAC is certainly more attractive than Chinese "hegemony". Apparently, Chinese scholars who consider *Tianxia* as the principle of a new East Asian order seem to forget the Chinese saying that one can obtain *Tianxia* only by winning the hearts of the people (*De minxin zhe de tianxia*: 得民心者得天下). In the same spirit, China's co-leadership role in the East Asia must be based on consent, cultural allure, and mutual respect and benefits and not propelled by great military might and nationalist pride. Rather than *Tianxia*, another Chinese aphorism which will go done very well as the philosophical underpinning of an EAC is: "Within Four Seas, All Men are Brothers" (*Shi hai yi jia*: 四海一家).

Some analysts have proposed a condominium of great powers to maintain order in East Asia. However, they may differ on the number of key players who would manage regional order. One idea is a G-2 comprising the US and China to manage not only regional but also world order.[14] The assumption is that instead of a Cold War bipolarity between the US and China, both superpowers should harmonize their relations and lead in an international order. The fundamental problem with this idea is that the US is unlikely to share co-leadership with China. Moreover, other countries and regions beyond East Asia would object to it. Why should they support a G-2 scheme which relegates them to the periphery? Conceivably, supporters of the G-2 can argue that it does not really matter what other smaller and weaker countries think whether the G-2 is desirable or not. They must simply accept the inevitability of a G-2.

But any regional order which is durable must be based on consent and not coercion. In this regard, the G-2 scheme is antithetical to the

---

[14]Brzezinski, Z (2009). The group of two that could change the world. *Financial Times*, 13 February.

spirit of an EAC based on partnership, cooperation and equality among nations big or small. Then Australian Prime Minister Kevin Rudd has proposed a condominium in East Asia beyond the US and China, but also includes countries like Japan, Indonesia and Australia.[15] However, such a scheme will be ignored and rejected by the ASEAN states who consider Australia to be merely a middle power at best. It appears that an EAC rather than a great power condominium is the preferred approach of most of the East Asian countries to maintain regional order.

3. *Liberal institutions: International and regional*

Proponents of a liberal institutional approach believe that regional and international organizations help to maintain order by making international relations rule-bound, predictable and reciprocal. Rather than a Hobbesian world based on a zero-sum game of "might is right", international relations governed by regional and international organizations can be a positive-sum game for big and small countries alike. Differences and disputes can be settled by international law, rules and norms rather than the strength and clash of arms.

In reality, the international organizations do reflect the relative weight of great powers. The US superpower remains a dominant player in the United Nations Security Council (UNSC) with veto powers, the International Monetary Fund and World Bank (with the largest voting rights). The G8 and G20 approaches to global governance also privilege the most powerful countries even though there are more than 190 members at the UN.

In Southeast Asia, a sub-region of the East Asia, there is ASEAN — a successful regional organization second only to the EU in the world. The year 2011 was considered as a significant year in which the flag of ASEAN symbolically flew besides the national flag in all ASEAN

---

[15] Rudd pushes for Asia Pacific community (2009). *Sydney Morning Herald*, 14 November. See also Frost, F (2009). Australia's proposal for an Asia Pacific Community: Issues and prospects. Parliament of Australia, Department of Parliamentary Services, Research Paper, No. 13, 1 December.

embassies abroad. Arguably, if the ASEAN Ten comprising of big, medium and small countries can co-exist and cooperate according to its norms of non-aggression and mutual tolerance based on habit and a new ASEAN Charter coupled with economic integration, then ASEAN can conceivably spearhead the EAC.

Certain ASEAN countries such as Singapore, Malaysia and Indonesia have also sought to resolve their territorial disputes by going to the International Court of Justice (ICJ) for adjudication. This is an approach which is not considered by the Northeast Asian countries of China, Japan and South Korea. Theoretically, ASEAN has the organizational framework to address intra-regional dispute through mediation and the good offices of third parties. But some ASEAN countries are still reluctant to embrace a regional approach to conflict resolution because of their insistence on national sovereignty. Case in point is the territorial dispute between Thailand and Cambodia over a disputed 900 year old Preah Vihear Hindu temple and its vicinity. Shots have been exchanged between their armies. At the time of writing, Thailand still is dragging its feet to accept the presence of Indonesian peace monitors while Cambodia is keen to draw in third parties into the bilateral conflict.

In theory, East Asia has an institution, the ASEAN Regional Forum (ARF), to discuss security measures. Interestingly, North Korea is also a member of this security forum. But the reality is that the ARF has yet to evolve beyond a talking shop and confidence building to conflict resolution. Nevertheless, this institution has launched the ARF–VDR (Voluntary Demonstration of Response) to promote a multilateral approach to address human security issues caused by natural disasters such as tsunami, typhoon and earthquake.

Since the post-Cold War era, more of the East Asians have perished in natural disasters than in man-made violence. Humanitarian assistance based on civil-military cooperation (including NGOs) is a promising approach to build institutions to address human security in East Asia. Perhaps an EAC can proceed along a multi-tracked approach by first concentrating on economic integration and a regional response to disaster relief coupled with cultural exchanges. More ambitious and difficult issues such as more open markets for labor migration, and greater political integration can be deferred according to the comfort level of regional states.

4. *Underpinning an EAC: Shared values and norms*

Conceivably, the "ASEAN Way" can provide the norms to a future EAC. While the "ASEAN Way" can be criticized as merely rhetorical and merely agreeing to disagree (by sweeping differences under the carpet), it is arguably a practicable way to secure the future together given the genuine differences among many East Asian states. The essence of the "ASEAN Way" is based on consensus among states big and small. Moreover, the ASEAN states have disavowed going to war with each other over territorial disputes. The ASEAN states have kept an open regionalism and are sensitive to the core interests of fellow member states and competing great powers too.

An amazing and unique feature of ASEAN is the composition of different regime-types among its members: Communist regimes (Vietnam and Laos), a military junta (Myanmar), an absolute monarchy (Brunei) and those with electoral competition (Cambodia, Indonesia, the Philippines, Thailand, Malaysia and Singapore). All ASEAN states are UN members and in theory must comply with the norms of human rights codified in the UN Charter. The Southeast Asian states have established an ASEAN Charter which does not ignore human rights and democracy. But given the disparate nature of the ASEAN states, it is impossible to demand that liberal democracy must be the operational norm for all Southeast Asian countries. The "ASEAN Way" should not be a legitimate fig leaf for brutal governments in Southeast Asia to avoid peer pressure to behave according to international norms of decency. However, the ASEAN states are relying on diplomatic peer pressure and not ostracism to nudge members especially the military junta in Myanmar to abide by international norms of behavior.

Hitherto, ASEAN has been an elite-driven, state centric approach to regional order. A challenge to the consolidation of ASEAN is: Can it harness the enthusiasm of civil society, citizens especially the young to identify themselves as ASEAN citizens? If the formation of an

ASEAN identity among citizens is difficult, it will be doubly hard for a bigger and broader entity like an EAC.

The next step towards the realization of an EAC is to tap the support of East Asian citizens to embrace each other as fellow East Asians. While the East Asia is enjoying increasing economic integration, its citizens have yet to base their identity as East Asians. Unless the East Asians perceive each other as friends rather than enemies, it will be difficult for an EAC to come into fruition. The onus must be on governments and the epistemological community to nurture the idea and identity of an East Asian regionalism over the next few decades before it comes into fruition. This idea can be reflected in the waiving of short-term visas for tourists among the East Asian countries, APT Games (sports), the EAC featured in postage stamps, exhibitions and festivals, youth exchanges, and the rewriting of history textbooks to avoid parochial nationalism. Simply put, order in East Asia need not be based purely on the balance of power or formal institutions, but also common and peaceable norms among states and their citizens.

II. East Asian Regionalism: Origins

The concept of "path dependency" will explain the present challenges and future trajectories of an EAC. Regional organizations do not start on a clean slate of ideas and ideals, but grounded in historical realities. Europe fought two World Wars (thereby sharing a common horror of total war and its futility among European states), and a common history and culture (from Rome to Christianity, the Renaissance and subsequently the scientific revolution and secularism). The royal houses of Europe also inter-married. In the post-Second World War era, Western Europe shared a common enemy in the Soviet Union and the Eastern bloc, and authoritarian states like Greece, Spain and Portugal eventually became democratic. France and Germany also provided co-leadership to the vision of a supranational political entity. In this regard, the East Asian countries cannot replicate the above factors to facilitate their own approach to regionalism.

Even though the conditions for regionalism in East Asia might not at first glance appear propitious like Western Europe, those conditions (or the lack of it) have not prevented various visionary proposals from being articulated for an Asian Community. Notable approaches include:

- The ASEAN experiment from five to ten countries under one Southeast Asian roof: Arguably the success of ASEAN has made it possible for a greater EAC to become conceivable. Simply put, if ASEAN had been a failure, an EAC would be impossible.
- Australia and Japan's envisaged Asia-Pacific Community in the 1970s: Then Prime Minister Malcolm Fraser and Prime Minister Ohira Masayoshi were associated with the idea. Being allies of Washington, they hope to include countries like the US and Canada into a community with Asia. But the idea to link three continents (East Asia, North America and Australia) was too ambitious and did not gain sufficient traction. However, the Asia-Pacific Economic Cooperation (APEC) can be regarded as the offspring of the Asia-Pacific Community concept. But APEC is simply too diverse for it to be more than a photo opportunity for leaders than a free trade community.
- Malaysian Prime Minister Mahathir's East Asian Economic Caucus (EAEC) in the 1990s: He envisaged an EAEC which comprised only Asian countries. Apparently, this idea was in response to the establishment of NAFTA (North America Free Trade Agreement) and EU. Japan did not support this idea after the US opposed it. With hindsight, Mahathir's EAEC will the forerunner to the APT framework. However, the East Asian countries have diplomatically couched the APT as open regionalism rather than targeting the US or the EU. The APT emerged from the Chiangmai Initiative launched in the aftermath of the 1997–1998 Asian Financial Crisis. It is conceivable that the 2008–2009 American Financial Crisis, 2011–2012 Eurozone Crisis and future financial and humanitarian crises and pandemics (which cannot be addressed by a single sovereign state) will cumulatively nudge the regional states to consider the EAC framework for their common good.

- Emergence of ASEAN-centric regionalism: Besides the APT, these include the ARF, EAS and the ASEAN Defense Ministers Meeting (ADMM) Plus. The East Asian countries have not put all their eggs in one institutional basket but have proceeded along parallel tracks to promote multilateral cooperation.

- Trilateral summits in Northeast Asia: Since the 2008 trilateral meeting in Fukuoka, these summits have taken place outside the sidelines of ASEAN meetings. There are at least two attractions to trilateral summits. First, the three Northeast Asian countries of South Korea, Japan and China comprise at least 90% of the APT's GDP. If these three can promote an FTA, then it will be a tremendous dynamo to the East Asian economy. Second, the three countries have been bedeviled by the burden of history. If they can adopt a future-oriented approach to their relations, then regional peace and stability will ensure.

- China's FTA with Southeast Asia and Japan's Economic Partnership Agreement (EPA) with Southeast Asia: China's FTA with Southeast Asia in 2001 was a catalyst to Japan's EPA with the same region. Presumably, if China had not offered an FTA with Southeast Asia, Japan would not have done likewise. In this regard, the competition between China and Japan to solidify their economic ties with Southeast Asia has benefited the latter. Even though China and Japan lack a bilateral FTA between themselves, the two Northeast Asian countries' economic arrangements with Southeast Asia may act as "Lego-like" building blocks of an incipient EAC.

- Second Track regionalism: Another feature of East Asian regionalism which runs parallel to the official first track is the informal second track which may comprise officials in their "personal" capacity, think-tanks, academics and "eminent" persons. Over the years, this second track comprises the epistemological community for East Asian regionalism. This include: The ASEAN-Institutes of Strategic and International Studies (ASEAN-ISIS), East Asian Vision Group (EAVG), East Asian Study Group (EASG) and Network of East Asian Think Tanks (NEAT). However, for the idea of an EAC to flourish, the third track comprising civil society, the media, ordinary citizens and the youth may be necessary to provide grassroots support for the process.

In summary, given the disparate sources of East Asian regionalism, the shape, roles, geographical scope and exact membership of an EAC is unclear at this juncture, but will be subjected to competition, tugs in different directions, negotiation and compromise in the years ahead. Whether the APT or the EAS will prevail will be a "Darwinian" process in which the institution which is more adaptable and relevant to the needs of East Asia will become the primary vehicle for regionalism.

III. Competing Visions: East Asia or Asia-Pacific?

There are at least two parallel tracks to East Asian regionalism today. The first is the APT while the second is the EAS which includes the US, India, Australia and Russia. China and Malaysia prefer the deepening rather than the broadening of regionalism. Others prefer to bring in extra-regional powers to balance the heft of a rising China. In reality, it is difficult for the EAS to be more than a talking shop given the diversity of its members and their competing interests.

The new DPJ government of Japan has also been ambiguous about an EAC. Then Prime Minister Hatoyama sidestepped the issue whether the US should or should not be a member of his envisaged EAC. One wonders whether Japan will resolutely join the EAC if the US is not a member and is opposed to it. However, there is a precedent: the United Kingdom joined the EU even though its American ally is not a member of that European grouping.

Another development is the formation of a Trans-Pacific Partnership (TPP) which is favored by the US. The members are: Brunei, Chile, New Zealand, Singapore, Australia, Malaysia, Peru, the US and Vietnam. Japan hopes to join the TPP but faces opposition from its agricultural lobby. China is not a member yet. Given its narrow scope as a multilateral free trade arrangement and the far-flung geographical spread of the TPP scheme, it is unlikely to pose a challenge to the APT as the main vehicle for East Asian regionalism.

IV. EAC: Obstacles and Possibilities

Conceivably, an attractive approach to order in East Asia is a future EAC because members who subscribe to the "friendship" paradigm are unlikely to go to war with each other. But there are a number of obstacles. First, the US superpower may be a potential spoiler who advocates a "spokes-and-hub" approach in security and may discipline its allies to tow the line. Second, parochial nationalism and domestic politics (especially narrow interest groups such as the agriculture lobby) may be another impediment to an EAC.

Insofar as China and Japan cannot play a pivotal and integrative role like France and Germany in the EU, an EAC is unlikely to happen. In this regard, both countries must manage their territorial disputes in the East China Sea and the Senkaku (Diaoyu) islands in a calm and peaceful manner. A problem with Sino–Japanese relations today is that their public has become less friendly towards each other. Even if the Chinese and Japanese top political elites were to patch up their relations, public opinion on both sides may not necessarily turn around easily. For an EAC to happen, it requires the support of the people in China, Japan and other East Asian countries.

Third, whether the EAC will be just an elusive dream or not depends in part, on the will and wisdom of political leaders and cannot be left to just markets and FTAs to bind the region together. As mentioned earlier, a pragmatic approach to an EAC is to take a multi-track approach by moving ahead with what is doable such as FTAs, humanitarian and disaster relief, environmental cooperation, anti-piracy measures and eradication of transnational crime, APT Games (sports) and cultural festivals and student exchanges. For an EAC to take hold, it must move beyond the First Track (state to state) and Second Track (academics, think-tanks etc) to the Third Track (civil society, NGOs, students etc) to embrace this regional enterprise.

V. Hoi An: A Model for EAC?

The past can inspire the future. In this regard, historical Hoi An may provide a model and metaphor for an EAC. Today, Hoi An is a small harbor town in Central Vietnam with a charming blend of traditional Chinese, Japanese and Vietnamese architecture giving a hint of its halcyon days of prosperity and cultural diversity. In the 16th and 17th century, Hoi An was one of the most cosmopolitan and busiest port in Southeast Asia attracting traders from China, Japan, Southeast Asia, India and Holland. In 1999, UNESCO declared Hoi An's old town as a World Heritage Site.

A river dissects and flows through the town. In historical Hoi An, Chinese and Japanese traders stayed on opposite banks of the river. They would place their wares in their boats and then row to the other shore to trade. Subsequently, the Japanese traders built a covered stone bridge across the river to facilitate trade with their Chinese counterparts. Today, it is known as the beautiful Japanese bridge of Hoi An. The Japanese and the Chinese traders then managed their own side of the bridge. There was a temple in the middle of the bridge patronized by both nationalities.[16]

Unfortunately, the Tokugawa Shogunate adopted the *sakoku* (national isolation) policy and the Japanese traders from Hoi An were ordered to return home. Subsequently, the Japanese traders abandoned the bridge they built and departed for Japan. The port-city of Hoi An went into gradual decline after the French were given permission by the Vietnamese authorities to build a rival port in Danang, central Vietnam. Apparently, Hoi An's harbor also suffered from the silting of its river. After being superseded by Danang, Hoi An became relatively obscure. The story of a bridge built by the Japanese and co-managed with the Chinese to facilitate regional trade was soon forgotten, but the tourists of Hoi An and local historians still remember it.

---

[16] My information about Hoi An was, in part, garnered from my Vietnamese tour guide. Gregory Rodgers writes: "The Hoi An Japanese Bridge remains a symbol of the significant impact that the Japanese had in the region. The bridge was originally constructed to connect the Japanese community with the Chinese quarter — separated by a small stream of water — as a symbolic gesture of peace. ... Roughly 40 years after the Hoi An Japanese Bridge was constructed, the Japanese were demanded by the Tokugawa Shogunate to return home to Japan under order of Sakoku — officially closing Japan to the rest of the world". See Rodgers, G. The Hoi An Japanese bridge: The history of Hoi An's star attraction in old town. *About.com, Southeast Asian Travel.* http://goseasia.about.com/od/hoi_an_vietnam/a/hoi-an-japanese-bridge.htm [accessed 30 May 2011].

Standing in front of the Japanese bridge in Hoi An in November 2007, I felt inspired by an era when Sino–Japanese relations were cordial. The Japanese traders did not mind taking the first step to build a bridge towards the Chinese side of the river bank, and the Chinese traders were happy to co-manage the bridge for mutual benefits. Until their repatriation to Tokugawa Japan, the Japanese traders cooperated with their Chinese counterparts to the benefit of all nationalities in Hoi An. The co-management of the bridge which linked both banks of Hoi An together is a precedent and a metaphor for the possibility of Sino–Japanese cooperation for an EAC. If the Chinese and Japanese of the past were wise enough to cooperate with each other and also with the Vietnamese, other Southeast Asians and European traders, surely East Asians today can also cooperate for their own enlightened self-interest.

VI. Conclusion

China, Japan, South Korea and ASEAN must build bridges in the region. The notion of an EAC may appear to be a "bridge too far" today. But so was ASEAN in 1967 and it has surely come a long way today. In a similar way, dreams will precede realities. To be sure, it is challenging to build a "bridge over troubled waters". A case in point is the territorial dispute in the South China Sea claimed by six parties (China, Taiwan, Vietnam, the Philippines, Malaysia and Brunei).

It is undeniable that systems of alliances, geo-strategic competition and parochial national interests are impediments to an EAC. But if leaders and the people of East Asia dare to dream, such challenges are not insurmountable if met with wisdom and goodwill. Greater economic interdependency and cooperation in natural disaster relief are necessary but not sufficient to create an East Asian regionalism. It demands political will on the part of leaders and opinion shapers to forge a common identity.

The French and Germans fought three devastating wars in three generations (1870 Franco–Prussian War, World War I, and World War II) but they have transcended their mutual hatred, bitterness and contempt, and are now friends. Perhaps the greatest challenge to an

EAC is whether the Chinese, Japanese, Koreans and Southeast Asians can view themselves as friends sharing a common identity and destiny.

Bibliography

Brzezinski, Z (2009). The group of two that could change the world. *Financial Times*, 13 February.

Callahan, WA (2008). Chinese visions of World order: Post-hegemonic or a new hegemony. *International Studies Review*, 10, 749–761.

Cha, V (2010). Powerplay origins of the US alliance system in Asia. *International Security*, 34(3), 158–196.

Frost, F (2009). Australia's proposal for an Asia Pacific community: Issues and prospects. Parliament of Australia, Department of Parliamentary Services, Research Paper, No. 13, 1 December.

Hatoyama, Y (2009). My political philosophy. *Voice*, September.

He, B (2004). East Asian ideas of regionalism: A normative critique. *Australian Journal of International Affairs*, 58(1), March.

Japan Ministry of Defense (2010). *The Defense of Japan: 2010.* Tokyo: Ministry of Defense.

Japanese Ministry of Foreign Affairs (2009). Address by H.E. Dr Yukio Hatoyama, Prime Minister of Japan. Japan's new commitment to Asia: Toward the realization of an East Asian community. 15 November, Singapore.

Kang, D (2007). *China Rising: Peace, Power and Order in East Asia.* New York: Columbia University Press.

Mulgan, GA (2009). Hatoyama's East Asia community and regional leadership rivalries. *East Asian Forum*, 13 October.

Park, JJ (2011). The US-led alliances in the Asia-Pacific: Hedge against potential threats or an undesirable multilateral security order? *Pacific Review*, 24(2), 137–158.

Rodgers, G. The Hoi An Japanese bridge: The history of Hoi An's star attraction in old town. *About.com, Southeast Asian Travel.* http://goseasia.about.com/od/hoi_an_vietnam/a/hoi-an-japanese-bridge.htm [accessed 30 May 2011].

SIPRI (2009). *2009 Yearbook: Armaments, Disarmaments and International Security.* Stockholm: SIPRI.

You, J (2006). East Asian community: A new platform for Sino–Japanese cooperation and contention. *Japanese Studies*, 26(1).

Zhao, T (2006). Rethinking empire from a Chinese concept of all-under-heaven (Tianxia). *Social Identities*, 12(1), Janauary.

Zhao, T (2009). A political world philosophy in terms of all-under-heaven (Tianxia). *Diogenes*, No. 221.

Zheng, Y (2010). From Tianxia (all-under-heaven) to modern international order. In *China and International Relations: The Chinese View and the Contributions of Wang Gungwu*, Zheng, Y (ed.). London: Routledge.

CHINA AND ITS NEIGHBORS

Chapter 8

WILL CHINA GIVE UP
NORTH KOREA?

CHEONG Young-Rok and SONG Mee Joo

With the inauguration of President Lee Myung-bak, many South Koreans complain that China's view toward the Korean peninsula has indeed changed. Some missed the good days of diplomatic normalization, when China was still struggling to invite foreign direct investment and was eager to learn from the Korean development model. In Beijing, South Korean diplomats were welcomed by their Chinese counterparts to share their views on speedy development of Korea. On the other hand, North Korea was downplayed, intentionally or unintentionally, by China.

The situation changed in 2008 when the American Financial Crisis erupted and hit global markets. Suddenly, many analysts speculated that China has become a component of the G2 alongside the US in the global hierarchy of power. Presumably China's huge foreign exchange reserves (especially US$) and purchases of US treasury bills underpinned its so-called G2 credentials. In the epoch of financial turbulence, "cash is king". Moreover, China surpassed Japan as the second largest economy in the world by the end of 2010.

Interestingly enough, China's attitude seems to be changing toward the Korean peninsula — becoming friendlier towards North Korea but sometimes neglecting South Korea. Two North Korean-initiated incidents in 2010 — the sinking of the Cheonan navy vessel and the barraging of Yeonpyeong island — highlighted the changes in Chinese attitude. South Korea had hoped for Chinese support in the allegations against North Korea based on its relative economic importance to China. For instance, it is estimated that South Korean FDI, 4% to 5% of total FDI ($1 trillion) into China, has generated 800,000 to a million jobs in China out of the total 17.5 million employed created through FDI. Moreover, South Korea's trade importance to China, when considering both exports and imports, was around 7% in 2010. However, China did not castigate North Korea for its aggression. Many analysts suspect that the reason China turned a blind eye to North Korean provocation was due to the former's seemingly changed attitude toward both South and North Korea. In this respect, this chapter addresses why China shows contradictory behavior.

When China adopted the open door policy in 1978, the criteria of an economically developed nation was a per capita income of US$10,000. Thus, it became a national goal to achieve this standard by 2050, the 100th anniversary of PRC, and finally turn into a developed nation. With the end of the Cold War, economic interdependence replaced ideology in its international relations, facilitating China's remarkable economic growth and rise. "Promoting sound and rapid development of the national economy" and "advancing the great cause of peaceful national unification" were core national interests underlined in the 17th National Congress of the Communist Party of China in October 2007. The unchanged factor with the passing of time is China's pursuit of these national interests. Consequently, Chinese foreign policies, creating the favorable environment which facilitates the fulfillment of national interest, are also reflections of well-known Chinese realist mechanisms. Similarly, maintaining status quo in the Korean peninsula is in line with Chinese national strategic interest as it creates regional stability, the prerequisite for continued speedy and designed development. Thus, in light of recent events on the Korean peninsula and fluctuating relationships, this chapter explores the possible change in value North Korea offers to China. In arguing that "as long as the Taiwan issue remains unresolved, China will not have the North Korean issue left unattended to", an analysis of North Korea's value to China will be conducted first at the bilateral level, through the assessment of the evolving Sino–North Korea Relations, and next at the regional level, through the assessment of the Taiwan issue.

I. Evolution of North Korea's Value to China: Bilateral Level

1. Sino–North Korean relations

It is common perception that China and North Korea share a long-standing alliance relations based historically first on mutual help in the early days of Communist Party activities in constructing critical mass support in each country during the 1920s and 1930s,[1] followed next by political and ideological similarities and strategic interest. However, the Sino–North Korean relationship has continuously evolved as a reflection of policies from changing bilateral perceptions and national interests.

1.1. China's One-Korea policy during the cold war

"Stable marriages" with key allies were characteristics of the Asian Cold War divide.[2] Mao Zedong's decision to enter the Korean War in 1950 on the side of Kim Il Sung bound the two nations into a special "life and blood" relationship, cementing close personal ties between the two socialist leaderships. The Sino–North Korean relations also held common fraternal ideological and revolutionary foundations that were borrowed from Soviet socialist organizational structures.[3] Under China's One-Korea Policy during the Cold War, China and North Korea signed the Sino–North Korean Mutual Aid

---

[1] The co-existence of both Chinese communists and Korean communists refer to Nym Wales (Helen Foster Snow) and Kim San (1941), *Song of Arirang: A Korean Communist in Chinese Revolution*. San Francisco: Ramparts Press.

[2] Dittmer, L (1981). The strategic triangle: An elementary game-theoretical analysis. *World Politics*, 33(4), 489.

[3] Armstrong, CK (2003). *The North Korean Revolution: 1945–1950*. Ithaca: Cornell University Press.

and Cooperation Friendship Treaty in 1961, whereby China pledged to immediately render military and other assistance by all means to its ally against any outside attack. Despite Sino–North Korean "blood ties" forged by common war experience against so-called US capitalist imperialism, the Sino–North Korean relationship was often strained by internal tensions which arose partly from Kim Il Sung's tactical efforts to play the Soviet Union and China against each other, and partly from Kim's innate direct suspicion of great power intentions toward Korea. However, the Sino–North Korean relationship remained largely intact.

1.2. *China's Two-Koreas policy: Formal equidistance*

The respective political experiences of the two regimes showed many parallels until China took a different path entailing economic reform under Deng Xiaoping, while North Korea adhered to its central planning mechanisms along the Juche ideology.[4] To support the ongoing reforms, Deng had determined the need for China to develop a healthy bilateral relationship with South Korea in order to benefit business and economic interests, and also to help South Korea terminate its relations with the Republic of China (hereinafter Taiwan).[5] However, the need for North Korean understanding and support in undertaking this transition from a pro-North Korea policy to a two-Koreas policy was equally necessary and important. Eventually, the potential benefits from Sino–South Korean economic cooperation, along with North Korea's stagnation, led to Sino–South Korean diplomatic normalization in 1992. Thus, the most significant implication for China's decision, despite strong objections from North Korea's

---

[4] A political thesis of Kim Il Sung that identifies the Korean masses as the masters of the country's development. It consists of a set of principles that the government uses to justify its policy decisions: independence from great powers, a strong military posture, and reliance on Korean national resources. According to Kim Il Sung, the Juche Idea is based on the belief that "man is the master of everything and decides everything".

[5] Qian, Q (2003). *Waijiao Shiji* [Ten Stories of China's Diplomacy], pp. 137–162. Beijing: Shijie Zhishi Chubanshe.

top leaders who saw normalization with South Korea as an act of betrayal, was a gradual shift in China's perception of its strategic interests toward the Korean peninsula from a framework that focused solely on North Korea as a strategic partner with a shared ideology, to one that viewed China's interests in the context of guarding China's economic development.[6]

Many factors facilitated Sino–South Korean bilateralism. First is China's implicit "disengagement" from Pyongyang. The absence of the Soviet Union as a strategic factor affecting the North East Asian security order also reduced considerably the strategic value of Pyongyang as a way of putting pressure on Moscow, and thus reduced the cost of China's political distancing from North Korea.[7] Another factor facilitating its decision to normalize relations with Seoul was China's need to strengthen relations with its neighbors to overcome its international isolation in the aftermath of the Tiananmen Square Incident.[8] The year 1992 was considered as an important year in China's history as it was struggling to maintain its target growth rate of over 8% in the midst of economic sanctions from the West as a result of the Tiananmen incident. Opportunities for official interaction through "hijack diplomacy", "torpedo diplomacy", and "sports diplomacy",[9] resulting from several events and episodes during the 1980s, permitted Chinese and South Korean diplomats to establish working relationships with each other that later became the foundation for closer contacts between Seoul and Beijing.[10]

---

[6] Liu, H (1993). The Sino–South Korean normalization: A triangular explanation. *Asian Survey*, 33(11), 1086–1088.

[7] Hakjoon, K (1991). China's policy since the Tiananmen square incident. Proceedings of the Academy of Political Science, 38(2), *The China Challenge: American Policies in East Asia* (1991), 107–114.

[8] Hao, J and Zhuang, Q (1992). China's policy toward the Korean peninsula. *Asian Survey*, 32(12), 1142.

[9] These refer to the subtle diplomacy such as Seoul's careful handling of incidents such as the 1983 hijacking of a Chinese airliner and China's participation in the 1986 Asian Games held in Seoul.

[10] Lee, C (1996). *China and Korea: Dynamic Relations*, pp. 106–112. Palo Alto, CA: Hoover Press.

1.3. *China's Two-Koreas policy: Regional stability*

Following the collapse of the Soviet Union, North Korea had lost a key patron and a source for considerable economic assistance including food and energy which were at the time in extreme shortage. This environment created an immediate and severe economic crisis in Pyongyang, simultaneously enhancing its economic dependence on China. On the contrary, China desired to lessen its aid burden by promoting greater market-based trade in its management of economic relations with North Korea, but Pyongyang was clearly unprepared to respond to such requests. As part of economic reforms, China also reformed its state-owned enterprises, which had formally worked as key vehicles of assistance to North Korea. Thus, the impact of Beijing's various efforts reinforced the political estrangement in Sino–North Korean relations that resulted from China's normalization of relations with South Korea.

With the possibility of China's strategic asset transforming into a strategic liability, China opted in favor of supporting regional stability rather than maintaining formal equidistance. Events such as the emergence of the first North Korean nuclear crisis and the ongoing political and security confrontation with the US (and South Korea), the death of Kim Il Sung on 8 July 1994, North Korea's political weakness and increased level of hostility in inter-Korean relations in the aftermath of Kim's death, North Korea's economic decline and the negative impact on China's national interests of instability on the Korean peninsula all led to an inevitable policy adjustment. North Korea's economic collapse would produce political instability, which in turn could create spill-over effects on China's northeastern provinces, which have historically been a source of uprisings leading to political instability. Thus, although China's priority on regional stability exposed political differences with North Korea to an unprecedented degree, these differences did not necessarily mean that China supported South Korean policies, mostly in relations to Korean reunification and especially if they produced greater instability on the Korean peninsula.

In this sense, China's post Cold-War "maxi–mini diplomacy" toward the Korean peninsula helped to maintain "geo-strategic ties" with North Korea while simultaneously pursuing "geo-economic ties" with the South.[11] Moreover, despite a transition in China's characterization of its relationship with North Korea from "special" to "normal", the latter's strategic location as a neighboring state on China's border ensures that it will continue to receive Chinese "strategic" economic assistance.

2. Assessing North Korea's value to China — liability or asset?

2.1. Economic value of North Korea to China

The overall trend of Sino–North Korean trade appears to serve as a measure of the relative health of political relations between the two nations. The economic relationship declined steadily, and correspondingly bilateral trade dropped from almost US$900 million in 1993 to US$550 million in 1996 following China's decision to normalize with South Korea.[12] As China sought to enhance its political influence on North Korea beginning in 2003, its share of North Korea's overall trade has continued to rise, though it remains at a marginal level of less than 1% of total Chinese trade.[13] Given concerns that withdrawal of Chinese assistance from North Korea might induce political instability or an economic collapse which would have a potential negative impact on China's economically lagging northeastern provinces, Chinese analysts justify assistance to North Korea. An estimated value of approximately 40% of China's overall development assistance in 2006 (up from an estimated 33% in 2002), "strategic" in nature, was handled through high-level leadership channels rather than through China's Ministry of Commerce, which is originally responsible for overseas development assistance.[14]

---

[11] Kim, SS (1994). The dialectics of China's North Korea policy. *Asian Perspective*, 18(2), 8.

[12] Bank of Korea. http://www.bok.or.kr/.

[13] In 2010, Sino–North Korean trade explains less than 1% in both export and import, remaining at US$2,278 million and US$1,188 million out of a total of US$1,576,817 and US$1,375,450 million respectively.

[14] Snyder, S (2009). *China's Rise and the Two Koreas: Politics, Economics, Security*, p. 112. Boulder and London: Lynn Rienner Publishers.

On the contrary, the level of Sino–South Korean bilateral trade has grown significantly: China's share of South Korea's total trade increased from 4% at the time of Sino–South Korean diplomatic normalization in 1992 to over 16% in 2004, ever since when China has become South Korea's largest trading partner.[15] Many South Koreans believe their economic future depends on the development of the Sino–South Korean relationship. The total size of GDP in 2009 of North Korea and South Korea are US$27.8 billion (China's 0.6%) and US$832.9 billion (China's 17.5%) respectively. Thus, though China has become North Korea's external lifeline and major source of economic exchange, the economic value of North Korea, apart from some value in regional balanced development projects, seems to be of marginal importance, especially when compared to South Korea's economic value to China.

2.2. *Socio-political value of North Korea to China*

China's recent support of North Korean leadership succession, compared to Mao's refusal to support the previous Kim succession, and overlooking North Korea's alleged sinking of the ROK Cheonan navy vessel and bombardment of Yeonpyeong, even amidst concern within China, can be mistook as some kind of increased importance in North Korea's political value to China, as a result of fortified political ties. On the contrary, even though relations have been repaired, beneath the surface, the two allies share very few common interests. In fact, North Korea and China can hardly agree to any matters between them, be it historical ties, ideological stance, political and economic development programs, economic assistance, diplomatic interactions, strategic differences in engagement versus isolation, or nuke and missile dilemma. There seems to be a gradual erosion of strategic ties. According to You Ji, the current troubles in the bilateral relations have deep historical roots that can be traced all the way back to the very beginning of North Korea.[16]

---

[15] Export–Import Bank of Korea. http://www.koreaexim.go.kr/index.jsp.
[16] Ji, Y (2007). China and North Korea: A fragile relationship of strategic convenience. *Journal of Strategic Studies*, 30(4/5), 585–608.

For China, economic instruments were always closely linked to the politics of managing its relationship with North Korea. However, the latter's increased economic dependency on the former, and greater levels of Sino–North Korean trade have not resulted in an enhancement of China's political leverage. Instead, North Korean policymakers seem to assume more and more that China's increasing aid, trade, and investment derive from the latter's own economic and political self-interest. This situation is likely to remain unchanged as long as North Korea continues to be perceived as a strategic asset rather than as a strategic liability. On the other hand, although China's core interest in maintaining a stable relationship with North Korea as a strategic security buffer has not changed, its views regarding the importance of the relationship underwent a profound change during the 1990s with the shift in focus to maintaining a peaceful strategic environment as an essential prerequisite for pursuing economic development. Thus, ever since China moved into a market economy, shared socialist ideologies, the only apparently shared link, have marginal importance.

2.3. *Diplomatic and strategic value of North Korea to China*

North Korea's core strategic value to China is that it provides a crucial buffer keeping US military presence away from Chinese border. Despite increased cooperation between the US and China over North Korea's nuclear proliferation and belligerence, both nations have differing interests on the Korean peninsula. The US welcomes Korean unification which entails South Korean advantage, as it values its military presence in South Korea because of geographical proximity to China. On the other hand, China benefits from the current division of the two Koreas: Two small Koreas are preferable compared to one large Korea, especially if it is allied with the US and results in continuous American military presence. Thus, Beijing's aid to Pyongyang is two-fold: It not only helps prevent regional instability, but also helps to perpetuate the current divide. As a result, North Korea serves as a buffer against China's encirclement by the US and its allies.[17] In its

---

[17] *Ibid.* pp. 585–608.

geo-strategic importance, North Korea still is a key chip with which China negotiates a workable relationship with the US.

China took on an active mediating role, through the six-party talks beginning in early 2003 as a result of the second North Korean nuclear crisis. The existence of relations with both Koreas created an opportunity for China not only to enhance its influence on the peninsula, but also play a diplomatic brokerage role among the participating parties, strengthening its regional and global influence and enhancing its stature on the global stage. However, also because of its special role and relationship with North Korea, China became North Korea's only regular channel of communication with the outside world. As a result, China was burdened with extra responsibilities and expectations especially in the eyes of the international community. Thus, with the risk of North Korean default, Chinese reputation of being a "responsible Great Power" could also be damaged. At the same time, the North Korean nuclear issue threatens Chinese and regional security. On the other hand, North Korea's "military-first politics" and its tactical tendencies toward brinkmanship at times worked in China's favor: For instance, by helping subdue China bashing, which was especially escalated since the 2008 global financial crisis; and divert international criticism directed towards China derived from threat perceptions of a rising China.

2.4. *North Korea — liability or asset?*

There has been a gradual improvement of the Sino–North Korean relations, in which China's importance to North Korea has moved from being a "patron" to "lifeline" in its economic sustainability and dependence. North Korea's economic stabilization, corresponding to the end of the "arduous march", and political stabilization, resulting in Kim Jong Il's chairmanship of the National Defense Commission in 1998, reflect the results of improvement in the Sino–North Korean political relationship. The level of China's compliance to support financially North Korea's economic recovery and the frequency of high-level political interactions between the two nations all demonstrate the degree of improved bilateral relations.[18]

The need to have high-level political contacts was directly catalyzed by the outbreak of the second North Korean nuclear crisis: China realized, on the one hand, the limits of its influence on North Korea as a result of estranged relations and, on the other hand, the risks that would accompany a military confrontation between the US and North Korea. As a part of its efforts to address the second nuclear crisis and possibly hedge further such crisis, China became the host and mediator for the six-party talks. This diplomatic move was twofold as it provided Beijing an additional excuse to maintain regular high-level contacts with North Korea, but also required additional use of economic instruments to secure Pyongyang's cooperation and participation in the talks.

The objective of maintaining stability on the Korean peninsula as a prerequisite for continued economic development became China's core objective which is still used in dealing with all kinds of North Korea issues, be it the North Korean nuclear crisis, or North Korea's power succession. Since 2005, China has increased investment in infrastructure projects along the Sino–North Korean border. China's stress on strengthening economic and trade cooperation based on an underlying principle of "mutual benefit" was evident during Premier Wen's visit to North Korea in October 2009, when he introduced the "Chang–Ji–Tu Development Plan". The plan, which aims to develop the Jilin and Tumen River region of the archaic industrial areas of China's three northeastern provinces, to be successful requires North Korean cooperation in securing access to the East Sea through a non-freezing sea port like Rajin.[19]

Then again North Korea has also contributed significant obstacles to China's pursuit of stability in the fulfillment of its core interests, creating core dilemmas in its conceptualization of policy toward North Korea. Such concerns are derived primarily from the gradual and

---

[18] Snyder, S, p. 124.
[19] IFES. DPRK–PRC summit and the outlook for bilateral economic cooperation. NK Brief No. 10-05-11-1.

continuous deterioration of North Korea's economic stability; North Korea's continued strategic isolation vis-à-vis the US and the rest of the world; Pyongyang's tactical tendencies toward brinkmanship and unilateral, uncompromising approaches to international issues; and the uncertain prospects for North Korea's long-term political stability given the current predominant role of Kim Jong Il. All of these North Korean developments run contrary to China's objective of maintaining regional stability and continued economic development. Thus, at the bilateral level North Korea's value to China are mixed and uncertain.

II. Regional Level Analysis

1. *Constraints in China's North East Asian regional strategy*

Historically China seemed to have been weak in formulating global strategies as China's interests was focused on the Asian continent apart from the exceptions of the Mongols in the 13th–14th centuries and Zheng He's navigation to Africa in 15th century Ming Dynasty. China maintained a Sino-centric perception of its surroundings as the "Middle Kingdom", with all other neighboring countries are considered subordinate to it. Furthermore, based on its perceived cultural superiority as a great civilization, China always transcended Asia in boundary definitions of its identity. The Qing dynasty that ruled just prior to the establishment of ROC and PRC was also really domestic oriented rather than having a global outreach. In the post-Mao period, even though China grew into a global political and economic actor, its foreign policy still concerned predominantly with Asia. [20] This was largely contributed by the need to ensure that hostile powers did not establish dominance around China's periphery. Thus, for reasons stemming from its differences in regional interests and global ambitions, China was characterized as "a regional power without a regional policy".[21]

---

[20] Sutter, R (2005). China's regional strategy and why it may not be good for America. In *Power Shift: China and Asia's New Dynamics*, D Shambaugh (ed.), p. 289. Berkeley: University of California Press.
[21] Levine, S (1984). China in Asia. In *China's Foreign Relations in the 1980s*, H Harding (ed.), pp. 109–114. New Haven, CT: Yale University Press.

With such historical and circumstantial drawbacks, Wang Yizhou devised three primary interests and needs that correspond to development, sovereignty, and responsibility as China faced the 21st century.[22] Moreover, with China's expanded capabilities and stature as a rising power, foreign policies have been adjusted to reflect its broadened interest in promoting regional stability. In a broader formulation of China's regional security priorities, Zhang Yunling and Tang Shiping identified six core ideas that are founded on the core principles of the new security concept: (1) seek comprehensive cooperation with regional states, (2) demonstrate benign intentions through the exercise of self-restraint, (3) demonstrate the ability to live with a US that does not threaten its core interests, (4) pursue its regional economic development strategy in an open way, (5) embrace regional multilateralism, and (6) shape the regional environment in ways that allow enhanced stature on the global stage.[23]

With the evolution of China's regional strategies, three features of contemporary China's North East Asian regional strategy can be distinguished. First, as a regional power with limited global interests, China's regional strategy corresponds largely with its grand strategy.[24] As development is viewed to be the most critical national interest, the grand strategy must serve the central purpose of nation building (mainly economic development) — ensure and shape a secure, economic, and political environment that is favorable to China concentrating on its economic, social, and political development. Thus, Chinese regional policy also is an extension of China's balanced development policy of local areas of Dongbei.

Second, China's Northeast Asian regional strategy reflects Chinese foreign policies: "great power diplomacy" (*daguo waijiao*), maintaining amicable relationships with its neighbors (*mulin youhao*,

---

[22] Wang, Y (1999). Chinese diplomacy oriented toward the 21st century: Pursuing and balancing three needs. *Zhanlue Yu Guanli* (Beijing), 30 December, 18–27. Accessed at http://www.opensource.gov, doc. No. CPP20000215000115.

[23] Zhang, Y and Tang, S (2005). China's regional strategy. In *Power Shift: China and Asia's New Dynamics*, D Shambaugh (ed.), pp. 48–49. Berkeley: University of California Press.

[24] *Ibid.*, pp. 48–49.

wending zhoubian), and active participation in multilateral economic institutions.[25] In accordance with its "great power" self-image, China has maintained great power diplomacy which is very much oriented towards the US as a recognition of the latter being the world's sole superpower. Beijing has also pursued a strategy for maintaining cordial relationships with its neighbors as a means to hedge against possible downturns in Sino–US relations. Also from an understanding that regional stability as the prerequisite of development, it engages, though limited, in multilateralism rather than in security institutions such as traditional military alliances.

Third, Beijing's Northeast Asian regional strategy is a circumstantial notion, in the sense that China recognizes the US, and not the regional actors, as the key to both the Taiwan and North Korea issues.[26] This perception reflects realist notions of power politics especially applicable in a region with the world's highest concentration of major power interaction. Northeast Asia is of vital strategic importance to China as it is also the only region in which all aspects of China's national interests — security, economic, and political — are present.

Accordingly, the most important goals of China's Northeast Asian regional strategy are to avoid direct military confrontation with the US, in North Korea and Taiwan, and prevent China from being isolated and encircled by the US and its allies by maintaining at least a workable relationship with all major powers in the region and maintaining a cordial relationship with regional states.

1.1. *The Taiwan issue*

As we assumed in the beginning, Chinese reunification is a core national interest. China does not recognize the legitimacy of Taiwan, and officially claims the latter to be a province of it. Furthermore, the Chinese Communist Party (CCP) asserts itself to be the sole

---

[25] Cho, YN (2008). *China's Politics in the Hu Jintao Era*, pp. 297–304. Seoul: Nanam.

[26] *Ibid.*, pp. 301–302.

legitimate government of China. Such cognition is the historical legacy of the domestic split between the CCP and Kuomintang (KMT). It is also the recognition of the need to clean up the vestiges of imperialism. Thus, China pursues reunification with Taiwan (including Penghu, Kinmen, and Matsu Islands) under the principle of "One Country, Two Systems", as has been done for both Hong Kong and Macau, as Taiwan remains as the only outstanding goal to be advocated for Chinese reunification.

Even though there has been recently a relaxation of former tensions with the change from independence-leaning Chen Shui-bian and the Democratic Progressive Party (DPP) administration to Ma Ying-jeou and KMT victories in 2008 in Taiwan, and Ma's definition of the relations between Taiwan and China as being "special", but "not that between two states", — meaning they are relations based on two areas of one state — unification can never be an option for China. The Anti-Secession Law (2005), which was adopted at the third conference of the 10th National People's Congress shows China's strong stand on the Taiwan issue. The legislation formalized the long-standing policy of China to use "non-peaceful means" against the "Taiwan independence movement" in the event of a declaration of Taiwan independence. Nonetheless, in actual unification, China's leaders would prefer never to have to use military capabilities — to win without fighting. The goal is to "keep the deterrence believable while doing all possible to draw bows without shooting and keeping the pressure on without actually fighting".[27] The hope is that as China grows militarily stronger and Taiwan becomes more economically dependent on China, this will eventually make reunification with Taiwan a natural outcome.

Another contemporary trend is the growing interdependence between the Island and the Mainland which has resulted in Taiwan being pulled into China's orbit economically and socially. When Deng Xiaoping opened China's door to the world economy in 1978, he also included Taiwan as a major source of both investment and trade.

---

[27] Shi, G (1999). Difficulties and options: Thoughts on the Taiwan matter. *Strategy and Management*, 1 October, FTS19991119000349.

Since then both China and Taiwan have offered special economic incentives and imperatives to attract Taiwan investment and trade into the Mainland which resulted in increased interactions and dramatically multiplied ties.

The movement of production by Taiwanese firms to the Mainland in search of cheaper land, facilities, and labor occurred in several waves.[28] The first was dominated by labor-intensive small and medium enterprises (SMEs). The second wave included larger firms such as the petrochemicals and food processing industries. The third wave gradually extended to large high-tech companies like Taiwan Semiconductor which is part of the dominant sector of the Taiwan economy. When the Taiwan information technology industry moved to China, it not only brought with it its entire network of supply and distribution infrastructure, but also significant exchanges in residents.

By the end of 2005, Taiwan's exports to China exceeded its exports to the US, Japan and Europe combined, making China as Taiwan's number one export market.[29] The trade volume increased to over 30% between the two in 2010. The signing of the Economic Cooperation Framework Agreement (ECFA), a preferential agreement between the governments of China and Taiwan that aims to reduce tariffs and commercial barriers between the two sides, shows the degree to which economic integration between the two has taken place. The pact, signed on 29 June 2010 in Chongqing, was seen as the most significant agreement between the two sides after the Chinese Civil War in 1949, the significance increased because the city was the last provisional capital of KMT.

The roots of the Chinese fixation on Taiwan are in part domestic and related to regime security.[30] Economic growth and nationalism are the two pillars that justify the CCP's dominant rule in China.[31]

---

[28] Bush, R (2005). Taiwan faces China: Attraction and repulsion. In *Power Shift: China and Asia's New Dynamics*, D Shambaugh (ed.), pp. 170–186. Berkeley: University of California Press.

[29] US–Taiwan Business Council (2005). Taiwan Business Topics. November.

[30] Shirk, SL (2008). *China: Fragile Superpower*, pp. 181–211. New York: Oxford University Press.

[31] Cho, YN, pp. 307–337.

State nationalism reinforced by the "century of humiliation" means history will not end until China is strong enough to achieve reunification. In this sense, China's stance on Taiwan is more about national honor than about territorial regain. The CCP's adherence to statist characteristics of Chinese nationalism and the need for reunification reflects its concerns about the innate dangers of internal fragmentation possibly created by cataclysmic ethno-national identity conflicts of China's numerous minorities. Moreover, because of the significance attributed to Taiwan's location, reunification can be seen as a strategic requirement for the development of Chinese sea power.[32]

Continued economic growth and political stability are widely acknowledged in China as the critical foundations for future power as measured by prosperity, influence, security, and status. Thus, to get there, China would also need to utilize its emerging capacities to ensure the safe and efficient transport of resources, especially oil and gas, and other commodities that are the indispensible for continued economic growth. All this reinforced the need to extend its capacity to operate as a maritime power, not just a continental power. Thus, Taiwan is a vital interest for the CCP, having become a litmus test of its nationalist credentials, which are again crucial to the regime's political survival.

Taiwan's location in the "imagined geography" of China has critical strategic significance. Power projection is inherently geo-political and concerns the continuation of certain long-term military trends in Beijing: Increased coordination between the US military and its Taiwanese counterpart; strengthening of the US–Japan alliance; the prospect of the introduction into the region of future upper-tier, theater-navy-wide ballistic missile defenses once these systems are fully developed, the fear of Taiwanese participation in the TMD system and revival of its independence movement.

Since the 1995–1996 Taiwan Strait Confrontation, China's strategists have given top priority to the possible need to use force in the Taiwan Strait — a scenario in which China anticipates facing

---

[32] Wachman, AM (2007). *Why Taiwan? Geostrategic Rationales For China's Territorial Integrity*, pp. 118–152. Stanford: Stanford University Press.

American intervention.[33] Besides, the other dimension of US encircle-ment as viewed by Chinese analysts is the ring of islands and island states, including Taiwan, with which Washington has cooperative security relations. Thereupon, as a response to these concerns, Beijing has been strengthening its military. The defense budget has been growing at an average rate of 16% between 1996 and 2007.[34] However, such increases in its military affairs are strictly limited in purpose: They serve only to improve China's coercive capacity against Taiwan and help to maintain the regional status quo and stability. Taiwan is not a visible test of the regime's ability to assert control over what it claims is national territory. For that reason, reunification is portrayed as a vital national interest without which the security and welfare of China will be in jeopardy.

1.2. *North Korea's value to China revisited*

Taiwan's symbolic importance for regime survival and for the need to clean up the vestiges of imperialism, and furthermore its strategic importance for national security and interest all reinforce China's stance on the Taiwan issue. Presumably, it motivates Beijing's imple-mentation of sustained military modernization: The primary near to mid-term focus is on the capabilities deemed necessary to coerce Taipei through decisive action, and thereby diminishing the possibil-ity of an American military intervention in the region. China's image of being a hegemonic power and destroyer of the regional status quo has to do mainly with its strong military stand towards Taiwan. Thus, continued hard-line policy towards Taiwan will also reinforce the China threat theory. If military tensions escalate in the Taiwan Strait, it will inevitably affect China's cordial relationships with regional states and hamper relationships with all major powers in the region. Moreover, it calls for US involvement in the Taiwan Strait.

---

[33] Ross, RS (2000). The 1995–1996 Taiwan strait confrontation. *International Security*, 25(2), 87–123.
[34] Office of the Secretary of Defense (2008). *Annual Report to Congress: Military Power of the PRC*, p. 31.

Thus far, China has not used force to unify Taiwan, and although Taiwan has made efforts to declare formal independence in the past, its leaders have thus far judged the risk to be too great. As a result, for effective deterrence to persist, all involved actors must value peace more than costly and forceful revisions of the status quo. Wherefore, the importance of North Korea's diplomatic and strategic value to China, especially as a strategic buffer, continues in China's pursuit of its core interests concerning Chinese unification and continued economic success. Peace in the Korean peninsula also requires mutual deterrence.

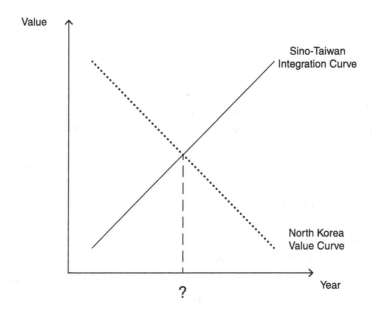

> ※ The Sino-Taiwan Integration Curve is derived by computing China's export and import dependence ratios from Taiwan. The export dependence ratio increased from 7.23% in 1992 to 42.11% in 2010. The import dependence ratio increased from 0.097% in 1992 to 11.79% in 2010. This trend is expected to continue, and manifest as deepened Sino-Taiwan integration with time.
> ※ The North Korean Value Curve shows the value of North Korea to China. The North Korean Value Curve, which is inclusive of diplomatic and strategic, socio-political and economic values, shows that North Korea's value to China will decrease with time.

Fig. 1. The value of North Korea to China in consideration of Sino-Taiwan integration.

Having two theaters, both serving as likely sources of war, divides attention of the US. Whereas the North Korean issue acts as a means to distract the US, the simmering of this issue without boiling over serves the strategic interest of China. By locking the US attention on the North Korean issue, the North Korea serves as a means of diverting the US attention from the Taiwan issue. As such, the North Korea still is a key chip with which China negotiates a workable relationship with the US. Moreover, China can focus its energy in implementing its grand strategy and pursuing its national interests. When the time is ripe, with its increased economic potentials that exceed that of US, China can fulfill its reunification with Taiwan.

III. Conclusion

Although the value of North Korea to China is marginal at the bilateral level, its value is immeasurable at the regional level especially when analyzed taking the Taiwan issue into account. As long as the Taiwan issue remains unresolved, China will not overlook the North Korea issue as it divides American attention into two different theaters, thus diffusing its power while simultaneously strengthening China's relative advantage. A favorable regional stability is conducive to China's economic growth which will act as a magnet to eventually integrate Taiwan into its orbit. Conceivably, if integration between both sides of the Taiwan Straits were to take place, the Korean peninsula may well diminish as a strategic bargaining chip for China. The reunification of China, therefore, may well facilitate the reunification of Korea.

It is possible to draw a graph which shows the "integration trend of Taiwan with China" versus the "value trend of North Korea" as shown in Fig. 1. We may derive at a point where those two lines meet. As of now, Sino–Taiwan integration is almost complete in the economic arena, judging from both the export dependence ratio and huge investment of Taiwan to the mainland. However, politics is far more complicated than economic issues. Cautiously, however, the time for reunification is approaching. Firstly, Taiwan's past history shows that once its economic security was ensured, the Island had a tendency to cooperate with the new power, as was the case when it was a colonial territory to the Dutch, a territory of the Qing, or a colonial territory to Japan. Secondly, stretching the argument, one can hypothesize the situation when China will assume the role of the regional stabilizer, a role formerly that of the US. This situation would arise in a future scenario that entails a need for the US to focus more on domestic issues, which would lead it to return to its isolationist policy, and thus, delegate this role to China. By 2020, China's GDP is estimated to equal if not overtake that of the US. If that comes to pass, it will be a milestone for Beijing. Moreover, China as the number one economic power will perhaps accelerate cross-Straits integration. Arguably, the year 2020 will be significant to the Korean peninsula as it implies the further decrease in North Korea's relative value to China in light of the Sino–Taiwan integration trend. Thus, with the maturation of time and circumstances, Korean unification may be a possibility as China distances itself from the North Korean issue as it approaches the year that makes domestic unification with Taiwan possible.

Bibliography

Armstrong, CK (2003). *The North Korean Revolution: 1945–1950*. Ithaca: Cornell University Press.

Bank of Korea. http://www.bok.or.kr/.

Bush, R (2005). Taiwan faces China: Attraction and repulsion. In *Power Shift: China and Asia's New Dynamics*, D Shambaugh (ed.), pp. 170–186. Berkeley: University of California Press.

Cho, YN (2008). *China's Politics in the Hu Jintao Era*. Seoul: Nanam.

Dittmer, L (1981). The strategic triangle: An elementary game-theoretical analysis. *World Politics*, 33(4), 485–519.

Export-Import Bank of Korea. http://www.koreaexim.go.kr/kr/index.jsp.

Hakjoon, K (1991). China's policy since the Tiananmen square incident. Proceedings of the Academy of Political Science, 38(2), *The China Challenge: American Policies in East Asia* (1991), 107–114.

Hao, J and Zhuang, Q (1992). China's policy toward the Korean peninsula. *Asian Survey*, 32(12), 1137–1156.

IFES. DPRK–PRC summit and the outlook for bilateral economic cooperation. NK Brief No. 10-05-11-1.

Ji, Y (2007). China and North Korea: A fragile relationship of strategic convenience. *Journal of Strategic Studies*, 30(4/5), 585–608.

Kim, SS (1994). The dialectics of China's North Korea policy. *Asian Perspective*, 18(2), 5–36.

Lee, C (1996). *China and Korea: Dynamic Relations*. Palo Alto, CA: Hoover Press.

Levine, S (1984). China in Asia. In *China's Foreign Relations in the 1980s*, H Harding (ed.). New Haven, CT: Yale University Press.

Liu, H (1993). The Sino–South Korean normalization: A triangular explanation. *Asian Survey*, 33(11), 1086–1088.

Office of the Secretary of Defense (2008). *Annual Report to Congress: Military Power of the PRC*, p. 31.

Qian, Q (2003). *Waijiao Shiji* [Ten Stories of China's Diplomacy]. Beijing: Shijie Zhishi Chubanshe.

Ross, RS (2000). The 1995–1996 Taiwan strait confrontation. *International Security*, 25(2), 87–123.

Shi, G (1999). Difficulties and options: Thoughts on the Taiwan matter. *Strategy and Management*, 1 October, FTS19991119000349.

Shirk, SL (2008). *China: Fragile Superpower*. New York: Oxford University Press.

Snyder, S (2009). *China's Rise and the Two Koreas: Politics, Economics, Security*. Boulder and London: Lynn Rienner Publishers.

Sutter, R (2005). China's regional strategy and why it may not be good for America. In *Power Shift: China and Asia's New Dynamics*, D Shambaugh (ed.). Berkeley: University of California Press.

US–Taiwan Business Council (2005). Taiwan Business Topics. November.

Wachman, AM (2007). *Why Taiwan? Geostrategic Rationales For China's Territorial Integrity*. Stanford: Stanford University Press.

Wales, N. (HF Snow) and Kim, S (1941). *Song of Arirang: A Korean Communist in Chinese Revolution*. San Francisco: Ramparts Press.

Wang, Y (1999). Chinese diplomacy oriented toward the 21st century: Pursuing and balancing three needs. *Zhanlue Yu Guanli* (Beijing),

30 December, 18–27. Accessed at http://www.opensource.gov, doc. No. CPP20000215000115.

Zhang, Y and Tang, S (2005). China's regional strategy. In *Power Shift: China and Asia's New Dynamics*, D Shambaugh (ed.), pp. 48–49. Berkeley: University of California Press.

Chapter 9

CHINA'S INVESTMENT IN SOUTHEAST ASIA: TRENDS AND PROSPECTS

YANG Mu and CHONG Siew Keng Catherine

The 1997 and 2008 financial crises were opportunities for China and Southeast Asia to widen and deepen their economic ties for mutual benefits. This provides a favorable background for China to diversify and increase its economic influence in the region. While the United States (US) and European Union (EU) economies were undergoing a slow recovery from the 2008 crisis, the China–ASEAN Free Trade Area (CAFTA) was realized on 1 January 2010. It has created the largest free-trade area (FTA) in terms of population (1.9 billion people), with a combined GDP close to US$6 trillion and total trade volume of US$4.5 trillion.[1] In terms of GDP, CAFTA is the third largest trading bloc after the EU and North American Free Trade Agreement region. In 2010, China–ASEAN bilateral trade reached US$292.8 billion with a year-on-year increase of 37.5%. The import volume by China from ASEAN totaled US$154.5 billion with an increase of 44.8%, while the export volume amounted to US$138.2 billion with an increase of 30.1%. China's investment in ASEAN reached US$1.96 billion from January to November in 2010 and the total amount has been accumulated to US$10.8 billion.

---

[1] ASEAN Foreign Ministers to experience ASEAN's multi-modal connectivity with China (2011). *ASEAN Website*, 21 January. http://www.aseansec.org/25792.htm.

I. Increasing Outbound Investment As One of China's Policy Priorities

With the world's rich countries recovering from the financial crisis, it is the emerging markets which offer a wealth of opportunities in trade, technology transfers and foreign direct investments. The global economy has realized that the emerging markets are now drivers of economic growth. Emerging markets are characterized by strong economic growth, resulting in rise in GDP and disposable income. Increasingly, machinery exporters, energy suppliers and raw material producers alike, look towards China and other fast-growing emerging countries to tap into their large, new customer bases, in an attempt to meet their "incremental demand". As such, there are two inevitable consequences.

First is a currency war. China, as well as the countries around the world, whether developed or developing, does not want their currency being over-appreciated. In the ASEAN plus Three meeting held on 29 October 2010 in Hanoi, leaders from Indonesia, Thailand and the Philippines all called for greater cooperation on currency policies in ASEAN. The Indonesian Foreign Minister urged ASEAN to develop a common perspective on the currency situation. He also noted that there should not be any inadvertent imbalances which are caused by some countries by artificially maintaining currencies at an exceptionally low level. The spokesman for the President of the Philippines called for better coordinated action rather than independent policies by individual country members. This was echoed by Thailand's Prime Minister then, Mr Abhisit who also suggested ASEAN's top financial officials to meet more often to coordinate policies.

Second, China, India, as well as other Southeast Asian countries, have become the target market for other countries' exports. Economically, the US never left ASEAN, and remains one of ASEAN's largest trade partners. In 2008, the US's export to ASEAN was almost as large as the US's export to China. In the first half of 2010, the growth in US exports to ASEAN almost doubled its total exports' growth. Total accumulated FDI from US into ASEAN is about US$150 billion. This is almost ten times of China's FDI in this region. The US wants to double its exports within the next five years. The Trans-Pacific

Partnership (TPP) is now one of US President Obama's main trade policies with ASEAN.[2] Malaysia could be the next to join the TPP, whereas Japan and South Korea also expressed interest in participating. The EU is one of ASEAN's largest trade partner and investor. Now the EU is also looking East for new export markets. On 6 October 2010, the EU signed a FTA with South Korea, sealing its first FTA in Asia. Talks are under way for next probable FTA deal with Singapore.

Faced with international pressure and world competition, the Chinese government insists that it will appreciate RMB slowly, but agrees to reduce its trade surplus. China's exports for the first two months of 2011 grew by 21.3% as compared to a year ago, while imports were up by 36% with a deficit in February 2011.[3] The Chinese government regards anti-inflation as its top priority in the domestic market. The Chinese government have been using active fiscal policy and stable monetary policy, coupled with the use of reserve requirement rate more than interest rate, to control M2. China's main strategies in recent years include, (1) higher consumption, (2) higher imports, (3) more investments abroad, and (4) innovation. With the huge foreign reserve and slow increase in the income level, more outbound investments could be a more effective strategy.

II. The Chinese Characteristics of China's Overseas Investment

In 2009, China's outward FDI reached US$43.3 billion, as compared to US$0.9 billion in 1990. China's investments cover 180 countries and span across different economies. In the first six months of 2010, China's investment in the US reached US$605 million, an increase of 260% as compared to the same period in 2009. China's investment in the Asian economies reached US$1.2 billion, an increase of 125.7% as compared to the same period a year before. China's investment in

---

[2] Within the ASEAN grouping, Brunei and Singapore have signed the TPP agreement on 3 June 2005. The TPP came into force on 28 May 2006. Malaysia as well as Vietnam are currently negotiating to join the group.

[3] *Wall Street Journal* (2011). 11–13 March, p. 1.

the EU reached US$406 million, an increase of 107.2%. China's investment in Russian alone reached US$264 million, an increased of 58.5%. By 2013, it is expected that China's overseas direct investment outflow will reach around US$100 billion.[4] China's "money" will play an important role in today's world.

In the past, the priority of China's overseas direct investment outflow was mainly gas and mineral resources, which are required to fuel its growing economic development. China's investment abroad is driven by its State Owned Enterprises (SOEs) and not private companies. This is unlike the FDI from the Western countries, Japan and ASEAN "Four Tigers" (namely Thailand, Malaysia, Indonesia and the Philippines). Even under tremendous pressure from the West to revalue its RMB, China is trying hard to remain competitive by adopting measures, such as slowly appreciating the RMB and raising its labor cost. Unlike Japan, South Korea, Taiwan and other Western economies which each has quite a number of domestic consumer electronics companies (for example, South Korea has LG, Japan has Hitachi and Sony, and Taiwan has Acer), China has very few big domestic consumer-electronics companies with the big names (like Haier) around the world. Consumer-electronics companies used to be the main driving forces in investing abroad in 1980s and 1990s. Most of the wealth in China is in the hands of the central and local governments and SOEs. In the past, China's demand for oil and raw materials was huge due to the need to fuel its economic growth. But in the coming years, Beijing will have new priorities and will be looking into new areas of growth, such as investments in infrastructures overseas.

III. Infrastructure as the Next Possible Priority for China's Investment in Southeast Asia

In 2007, FDI flowing into ASEAN was US$63 billion. Intra-ASEAN FDI only amounts to US$10 billion or about 15% of ASEAN's total FDI inflow. China's investment in ASEAN was even smaller. In 2007,

---

[4] China's overseas investments may reach US$100 billion in 2013 (2010). *China Daily*, 25 August. http://english.peopledaily.com.cn/90001/90778/90861/7117061.html.

China's investment in ASEAN only amounted to US$600 million, which was around 1% of ASEAN's total FDI inflow. In 2008, the amount increased to US$2.2 billion.[5]

In 2009, China established a US$10 billion ASEAN Cooperation Fund. China has the intention of establishing a US$15 billion loan to invest in ASEAN's infrastructure, energy, resources, information technology and telecommunication industries.[6] Lack of infrastructure is the first barrier in most developing ASEAN countries to further development. There is a huge need for transportation facilities, such as railways, highways, etc, to connect the various countries, especially the Greater-Mekong Sub-region. The proposed Kunming–Singapore railway will need to raise US$2 billion to complete a railway across eight countries, running from Singapore to Kunming, in China by 2015. Indonesia needs at least 1,400 trillion rupiah (US$160 billion) over the next five years for infrastructure building, which includes ports, roads and power plants. The state budget is capable of providing a maximum of 38% of the amount, so partnerships between the government and private investors are crucial.[7] On 21 September 2010, Malaysia unveiled an ambitious plan to attract US$444 billion worth of investments over the next ten years to fulfill its goal of becoming a high-income nation by 2020. About 60% of the total required investments would come from the private sector, and the rest will be from the government. The government has identified 131 projects, including a high-speed rail linking to Singapore and an integrated mass transit train system. If successful, the plan will create 3.3 million jobs, more than half of which will pay medium-to-high salaries. This will raise Malaysia's per capita income

---

[5] *ASEAN Investment Report 2007.* ASEAN website. http://www.aseansec.org/21406.pdf.
[6] ASEAN-China investment cooperation fund for infrastructure and energy launched (2009). ASEAN website, 24 October. http://www.aseansec.org/23633.htm.
[7] Indonesia to get benefit from ASEAN infrastructure funds (2010). philstar.com, 21 June. http://www.philstar.com/Article.aspx?articleId=586552&publicationSubCategoryId=200.

to at least US$15,000.[8] Malaysia also sees the solar energy industry as a bright spark for its economy. Between 2008 and 2010, this sector has attracted foreign investments totaling RM12.3 billion (S$5 billion) and created 10,000 new jobs.

On 27 September 2010, the World Bank released its new report: *The Day after Tomorrow: A Handbook for the Future of Economic Policy in the Developing World.* It was noted that investments in ASEAN, especially in the four middle income countries, declined in the decade after the Asian financial crisis. The report said rigidities in Malaysia labor market and entry barriers were Malaysia's main problems in discouraging private investors. Meanwhile, Indonesia's main challenge for development was in its public infrastructure. In Thailand, internal political strife has raised uncertainty. The Philippines' main challenge was a mixture of the challenges faced by countries mentioned earlier.[9]

China has promised to provide Indonesia with more than US$2 billion in loans to help Indonesia to finance its infrastructure development. The total amount of China's loans to the Philippines has reached US$8.4 billion. Two China-funded railway projects are already underway. There is also a plan to modernize the Laoag International Airport. For Malaysia, China had provided a US$800 million 20-year low interest loan for the construction of a 23 km-long bridge project in Penang, Malaysia. China also invested heavily in infrastructures in Cambodia, Laos, Myanmar and Indonesia. Highways from Nanning to Vietnam, from Kunming to Vietnam, Laos and Myanmar have been completed or are under construction. China has agreed to provide technical assistance to the Vietnam government's construction of two railways, one linking Cambodia (130 km) and

---

[8] This is the Economic Transformation Program, an initiative by the Malaysian government to turn Malaysia into a high income economy by the year of 2020. It is managed by the Performance and Delivery Unit (PEMANDU), an agency under the Prime Minister Department of Malaysia.

[9] The book can be downloaded at the World Bank website, http://web.worldbank.org/WBSITE/EXTERNAL/EXTABOUTUS/ORGANIZATION/EXTPREMNET/0,contentMDK:22708168~pagePK:64159605~piPK:64157667~theSitePK:489961,00.html.

another to Laos (119 km). The railways, which cost the Vietnam government US$525 million, will be completed in 2020.

On China's provincial level, Yunnan and Guangxi are two such provinces that have been taking advantage of their geographical location to call for sub-regional cooperation activities designed to optimize more economic benefits under the China–ASEAN framework. While Guangxi have been wooing ASEAN via its Nanning–Singapore Corridor, Kunming, on the other hand, is wooing ASEAN countries via its connecting them with roads, rails and bridges. This is in line with *ASEAN Connectivity,*[10] mooted by the ASEAN state leaders to enhance intra-regional connectivity within ASEAN and its sub-regional grouping via overland transport linkages. This would benefit all ASEAN Member States through enhanced trade, investment, tourism and development. Recently, a new bridge, with a cost of US$47.4 million, is near completion at the Mekong River. This will form a last link making, making it possible to drive 1,018 kilometers from Chiang Mai (in Northern Thailand) to Kunming (in Southern China), resulting in a near-seamless road traveling from Singapore to Kunming. Another project is a Thailand–China joint venture in high-speed rail which is expected to be completed in 2015.[11]

Guangxi, on the other hand, has linked up the logistics system between China and the ASEAN countries. Already 10 major ports in the region including Beihai, Fangchenggang and Qinzhou in China; Cai Lan, Hon Gai and Ho Chi Minh City in Vietnam; Sihanoukville

---

[10] The concept of "ASEAN Connectivity" was mooted by the ASEAN state leaders at the 15th ASEAN Summit in Cha-am Hua Hin, Thailand, on 24 October 2009. By enhancing intra-regional connectivity within ASEAN and its sub-regional grouping would benefit all ASEAN Member States through enhanced trade, investment, tourism and development. As all of the overland transport linkages will have to go through the mainland Southeast Asian countries of Cambodia, Laos, Vietnam and Myanmar, these countries stand to benefit the most through infrastructure development, and the opening up of remote inland and less-developed regions. All these efforts would significantly narrow the development gap within ASEAN. Also see ASEAN's Leaders' Statement on ASEAN Connectivity (2009). Association of Southeast Asian Nations website, 24 October. http://www.15thaseansummit-th. org/PDF/24-07ASEAN_Connectivity_with_Logo.pdf.

[11] ASEAN by road, rail and bridge (2011). *Straits Times,* 27 January.

in Cambodia; Bangkok in Thailand, and Port Klang and Penang in Malaysia are already in the network. With the improvement of the road and railway network, more ports will be able to integrate into the network, thus reducing the overall transportation costs, launch new routes, boost port storage, conduct training exchange and improve cargo transportation facilities. On one end of the N-S economic corridor, the Pan-Beibu ports will serve as distribution points for Guangxi, Yunnan, Sichuan, Guizhou and Chongqing; Singapore, on the other end, will serve as the distribution point for the ASEAN countries.[12]

IV. Other Opportunities for China's Overseas Direct Investment

Firstly, food supply will be a good opportunity for cooperation between Southeast Asia and China. With China's growing population and rapid industrialization and urbanization, there will be shortage in food supply in the years to come. The ASEAN nations are situated in tropical and sub-tropical regions with an annual rainfall of 1,500–2,000 mm. They have arable land of 153 million hectares with only 65% of its land resources utilized. Thailand, Vietnam and Myanmar are world renowned rice producing countries. ASEAN also has tropical produce, fruits, timbers and sea products. Primary industry contributes 12% of ASEAN's GDP, 13% of its exports and uses 45% of its labor.[13] With greater efficiency in agricultural technology, surplus labor can be transferred to manufacturing and service industries, in which Singapore has a leading edge.

China is rich with temperate produce and fruits but lacks water resources (especially in the Northern China) and arable land. China is a huge and stable market for ASEAN products. China is able to import tropical produce (such as fruits produce from the Philippines, rice from Vietnam, Thailand and Myanmar etc) while exporting

---

[12] Linking up the western route (2010). *The Star online*, 21 August. http://thestar.com.my/news/story.asp?sec=focus&file=/2010/8/21/focus/6892109.

[13] ASEAN statistical indicators, various years.

temperate produce and fruits. China also assisted ASEAN countries in agriculture output, by exporting its traditional industries where it has technical advantage, such as hybrid-rice production. China's Guangxi State-owned Farm Group has developed the cassava industries in Thailand, Myanmar and Laos, by expanding their sources of modified starch with better planting technology.[14] With the CAFTA in force, China and ASEAN's cooperation in food production will be a win–win arrangement for all.

Singapore and China have signed a Memorandum of Understanding to conduct a study to assess the commercial feasibility of jointly developing a modern agricultural and food zone in Jilin City, Jilin Province. This is a good start. This paves the way for other ASEAN member states, such as Indonesia, Myanmar and other countries, to jointly develop food supply bases. This is a win–win set-up for China and ASEAN states, as China will be able to ease some of its demand for food, and ASEAN states would secure a stable market for their products.

Secondly, energy security is another area of cooperation. China, the world's second largest oil consumer, sees the use of oil pipelines as a way to get around the "Straits of Malacca dilemma".[15] Bringing the energy through Myanmar via pipeline is a good way to bypass the Straits of Malacca, as it expands the effort to diversify its supply routes. On 21 December 2009, China National Petroleum Corp (CNPC) signed an agreement with Myanmar's Energy Ministry to receive exclu-

---

[14] Beijing keen to unlock ASEAN Investment doors. *Asia Times* Website, China Business. *http://www.atimes.com/atimes/China_Business/HK02cb01.html.*

[15] China's Malacca dilemma is a product of Beijing's growing anxiety over energy security, particularly oil supply security. China relies on an uninterrupted supply of crude oil and natural gas imports to sustain its double-digit economic growth. The Chinese government is concerned that any disruption to its energy imports would result in an economic slowdown or even derailment in its economic development. The locus of China's concern is the Malacca Strait, the 900-kilometer long narrow body of water separating Indonesia and Malaysia, with Singapore located at its Southern tip. The strait is the quickest passage between the Indian and Pacific oceans, with more than 65,000 vessels transiting through it each year carrying more than one third of global trade and half of the world's energy supplies.

sive rights to build and operate the China–Myanmar crude oil and gas pipeline. The construction formally began when Premier Wen Jiabao visited Myanmar on 3 June 2010. It was reported that this oil–gas pipeline can deliver 22 million tons of oil, approximately 400,000 barrels a day, and 12 billion of cubic meters of gas to China every year.[16]

China and Vietnam have been working on oil and gas exploration and extraction in border waters of the Beibu Gulf, and also signed agreements on economic and technological cooperation, as well as Chinese loans for the construction of a coal-fired power plant in Northern Vietnam, which got its official approval in 2010. The project, the Wing Hing power plant, developed under the build-operate-transfer (BOT) model, will include two sets of 600-million-kilowatt coal-fired sub-critical thermal power units in Binh Thuan, a province in Southern Vietnam, and will be fueled by local blind coal. It will support the electricity consumption in the South Vietnam. This has been the largest project invested by Chinese companies in Vietnam, and is expected to start operation in 2014.[17]

Since December 2010, China and Brunei have been discussing possible areas of cooperation which include refinery, downstream and joint exploration of oil and gas. Petroleum BRUNEI may cooperate with one of China's oil giants, China National Offshore Oil Corporation Ltd (CNOOC), which is also very keen to establish a logistics base in Brunei. And Brunei is also looking for opportunities to cooperate with China on green energy as it is one of the biggest green energy producers.[18]

On top of that, China has been exporting electricity to Vietnam. Since 2004, three 110-kilovolt lines have been in operation to supply electricity to Vietnam by way of Yunnan Province and Guangxi Zhuang

---

[16] Qin guang rong pei tong wen jia bao zong li fang mian hui kun shi biao shi dian mian he zuo qian jing guang kuo (2010). Xinlang net, 6 May. http://news.sina.com.cn/c/2010-06-05/080617613917s.shtml.

[17] Zhongguo zai Yuenan zuida tuozi xiangmu houpi (2010). Caijing.com, 27 August. http://www.caijing.com.cn/2010-08-27/110506620.html.

[18] Brunei open to joint oil exploration with China (2011). Brudirect.com, 3 February. http://www.brudirect.com/index.php/2011020238882/Third-Stories/brunei-open-to-joint-oil-exploration-with-china.html.

Autonomous Region. In September 2006, the first 220-kilovolt power transmission line between China and Vietnam was inaugurated in Kunming, capital of Yunnan Province. By the end of March 2007, the four existing lines had transmitted 1.84 billion kilowatt hours, worth US$80.76 million to Vietnam. The China Southern Power Grid Company has enhanced the power transmission capacity to Vietnam by inaugurating a second 220-kilovolt line linking Wenshan in Southwest China's Yunnan Province with Ha Giang in Vietnam.[19]

Thirdly, since the FTA implementation in January 2010, most goods traded between China and ASEAN countries have been subject to zero or very low tariffs, thus allowing a freer flow of capital, resources, technology and talent. Tapping on this, Ashima Yunnan Cultural Industry Group from Yunnan Province is building a 104,000 square-meter China City complex costing 45 billion baht (S$1.9 billion) on the outskirts of Bangkok. The trade center alone is expected to create 70,000 new jobs and 45 to 50 billion baht worth of intra-ASEAN trade annually.[20] This acts as a springboard for Chinese goods not only to ASEAN countries, but also to third-party countries within ASEAN community, thus enhancing closer cooperation. There are also talks that investors from Wenzhou, Zhejiang province in China, will be setting up a "China City" wholesale complex in Malaysia. With a cost of RMB100 million (about US$14.6 million), this wholesale center can accommodate 300 wholesalers, thus creating a trading place for Chinese goods in Malaysia.[21] Singapore has been considering setting up a trading hub for Chinese products. In view of Singapore's strong connection with Guangdong, Zhejiang and Jiangsu, strong trade connections and a number of FTAs in force with other countries, such a project is feasible.

---

[19] China to Export 2.5-bln-kwh Electricity to Vietnam (2007). China.org, 29 April. http://www.china.org.cn/english/environment/209678.htm.
[20] China to Build Massive trading complex in Bangkok (2011). *Thailand Business News*, 6 January. http://thailand-business-news.com/news/top-stories/28129-china-to-build-massive-trading-complex-in-bangkok.
[21] Zhongguo wai bin gou touzi xincelu (2010). *yazhou zoukan*, 28 March.

Bibliography

China's Statistics Yearbook (2011). Beijing: China's Statistics Publishing House.

Direction of Trade Statistics Year Book 2010 (2011). New York: International Monetary Fund.

Li, MJ and Kwa, CG (eds.) (2011). *China-ASEAN Sub-Regional Cooperation: Progress, Problems and Prospects.* Singapore: World Scientific.

Yeoh, EK-K *et al.* (eds.) (2009). *China-ASEAN Relations: Economic Engagement and Policy Reform.* Malaysia: Institute of China Study, University of Malaya.

Chapter 10

DEFENDING ASEAN'S "CENTRALITY": INDONESIA AND THE POLITICS OF EAST ASIAN REGIONAL ARCHITECTURE IN THE POST-AMERICAN FINANCIAL CRISIS ERA

Syamsul HADI

The idea of an East Asian regional framework gained further attention after then Australian Prime Minister Kevin Rudd proposed a regional architecture for the wider Asia Pacific region. He argued that there is a need for strong and effective regional institutions to "underpin an open, peaceful, stable, prosperous and sustainable region". He stressed the importance of regional institutions in addressing collective challenges that no country can address alone.[1] Rudd envisaged a regionalism in which the US and other non-Asian countries, including Australia, can be influential insiders.[2]

During his Asian visit in November 2010, President Barack Obama also mentioned about intention of the US to be more actively involved in the East Asia's regional architecture including

---

[1] Soesastro, H (2008). Kevin Rudd's architecture for the Asia Pacific. http://www.eastasiaforum.org/2008/06/09/kevin-rudds-architecture-for-the-asia-pacific/.

[2] Milner, A (2010). From Asia-Pacific to Asia? http://www.eastasiaforum.org/06/03/from-asia-pacific-to-asia/.

the East Asia Summit (EAS). Presumably, Obama wishes India, a rising regional power, to be more active in regional politics to balance a rising China. Obama has hailed India's rise as world power, days ahead of a visit to the country, calling the South Asian nation a "cornerstone" of US engagement in Asia.[3] The India–US joint statement envisages greater cooperation between India and the US in Southeast Asia, East Asia and the larger pursuit of evolving an Asian architecture. A bigger role of India in East Asia would widely be interpreted as a counterbalance to perceived Chinese assertiveness in the region.[4]

In his visit to Indonesia, Obama sought greater support for US active involvement in the East Asian regional dynamics. In this context, Obama voiced his backing for Indonesia's "strategic role" in ASEAN, especially when the country would be the chairman of ASEAN in 2011. As the chairman, Indonesia would automatically become the chairman of East Asia Summit, which would be attended by Obama in 2011.[5]

Obama's visit to India and Indonesia could be seen as a part of US "diplomatic offensive" to be more actively in East Asia. For this purpose, the US membership in EAS would provide a relatively strong institutional base. Moreover, Obama's positive image as a president of the US in contrast to his predecessor George W. Bush (who initiated US-led wars against Iraq and Afghanistan), won approval from President Yudhoyono to strengthen Indonesia–US relations. This was explicitly mentioned by Yudhoyono in a speech in November 2008, in which he called a "strategic partnership" between Indonesia and the US.[6]

This chapter seeks to analyze Indonesia's position in the East Asian regional dynamics, which has developed into the discourse on the East Asia regional architecture, especially after the global financial crisis in 2008. How would Indonesia respond to the growing international and

---

[3] India would be a cornerstone of US engagement in Asia. http://www.tnsela.org/news/obama-hails-India-as- cornerstone-of-us-engagement-in-asia.html
[4] *Ibid.*
[5] Saya Optimis Melihat Negeri Ini (2010). *Kompas,* 10 November.
[6] Murphy, AM (2009). Toward a US–Indonesia comprehensive partnership. *Indonesian Quarterly,* 79(3), 271.

regional dynamics? What kind of regional architecture does Indonesia want to pursue, and what are the prospects of Indonesia's position in this architecture formation? I would argue that Indonesian responses to the issue of an East Asian architecture are consonant to the country's perspective of the importance to maintain ASEAN centrality — a hallmark of Jakarta's foreign policy. For Indonesia, the increasing complex challenges for the East Asian region in the aftermath of the 2008–2009 American Financial Crisis only confirm the importance of ASEAN to be resilient and to preserve the peace and stability in East Asia, by avoiding the domination of big powers with competing interests in the region.

I. The Issue of Regional Architecture in East Asia and the Dynamics of Indonesian Foreign Policy

Australia has promoted an Asia Pacific framework for decades — going back to Asia Pacific Economic Cooperation (APEC), which commenced in 1989. It is the first regional institution to bring the leaders and the economies of the Asia-Pacific in one forum. The original group comprised 12 countries: Six ASEAN countries, Japan, South Korea, Australia, New Zealand, and the US.[7]

The establishment of APEC was based on a growing anxiety of the failure of multilateral trade negotiation in GATT and the emergence of Europe as a new economic bloc (the European Union). Australia as the leading initiator of APEC envisaged the forum to be its gate to the East Asia region, which is the location of ASEAN and the newly industrialized countries — the next major source and markets of global growth. At first, Australia's proposal did not include the US. Nevertheless, Japan proposed that the US and Canada be granted membership in APEC. Japan then was subjected to American pressure for its yawning trade deficit with the US.[8] For Tokyo, APEC is

---

[7] McIntyre, A (1997). Southeast Asia and the political economy of APEC. In *The Political Economy of South-East Asia: An Introduction*, G Rodan, K Hewison and R Robison (eds.), p. 227. Melbourne: Oxford University Press.

[8] Hadi, S (2009a). Dinamika Asia Pasifik. *Kompas*, 23 November.

expected to address US protectionism by channeling it into a multilateral framework.[9]

In December 1990, the Malaysian Prime Minister, Dr Mahathir Mohamad, proposed an alternative regional organization for Asians only: The East Asian Economic Group (EAEG). In the context of the apparent slide towards protectionism and defensive regionalism in Europe and North America at that time, this move was alarming to some Western countries which feared a discriminatory Asian trading block centered on Japan. Much attention has been given to Washington's hostility and Japan's lukewarm response. Less well noted was Indonesia's unusually blunt rejection to the idea, together with opposition of Singapore and South Korea.[10]

Indonesia was particularly upset that Mahathir failed to consult its ASEAN partners before proposing the EAEG, which might dilute ASEAN's standing in a wider forum.[11] In October 1991, after consulting with ASEAN members, Malaysia agreed to rename the forum the East Asian Economic Caucus (EAEC), following Indonesian suggestion. The ministers also clarified that EAEC would be presented a meeting with "ASEAN dialogue partners" to maintain ASEAN centrality.

The discourse of the East Asia economic integration reappeared after the Asian Financial Crisis 1997–1998. The crisis was a stark reminder of the interdependency in Southeast and Northeast Asia for the better or the worse. The crisis also gave momentum to ASEAN to widen its cooperation with Northeast Asian countries, especially Japan, China, and South Korea. On December 1997, the First ASEAN+3 Summit was held in Kuala Lumpur. It was expected that the cooperation would strengthen East Asia's economic resiliency in encountering various economic turmoil.[12]

---

[9] Munakata, N (2006). *Transforming East Asia: the Evolution of Regional Economic Integration.* Washington, DC: Brooking Institution Press.

[10] McIntyre. *Op. cit.*, p. 230.

[11] Munakata. *Op. cit.*, p. 72.

[12] Rahardjo, S (2004). Indonesia dan Integrasi Asia Timur: Suatu Perspektif. A paper in *East Asian Experts Meeting Related to the Idea of East Asian Community*, Yogyakarta, 24 December, p. 1.

In ASEAN+3 Summit 1998, President Kim Dae Jung of South Korea proposed an East Asian Vision Group (EAVG) to spearhead an incipient East Asian Community (EAC). In its 2001 report titled "Towards an East Asian Community: Region of Peace, Prosperity and Progress", the EAVG recommended that evolution of ASEAN+3 annual meetings into an EAS which will, in turn, facilitate an EAC. Moreover, President Kim also proposed an East Asian Study Group (EASG) to review all EAVG recommendations and promote concrete cooperation to bring this vision into fruition. The final report of EASG delivered on ASEAN+3 Summit in Pnom Penh, Cambodia in November 2002, recommended a pragmatic step-by-step approach and careful consideration of the modalities of regionalism before coming into force in Malaysia on 2005.[13]

Interestingly, China and Malaysia seemed to be the most enthusiastic ones in realizing the idea of transforming ASEAN+3 to become an EAC. Apparently, China saw the East Asian regionalism as a good platform to play a more prominent role in the region. On the other hand, Malaysia considered the EAC idea as a reincarnation of Mahathir Mohammad's thought in December 1990 about the establishment of EAEG that flopped due to US opposition. China's serious commitment was proven in its willingness to sponsor the second-track Network of East Asian Think Tank (NEAT), which was expected to hatch progressive ideas about the East Asian regional integration for the ASEAN+3 governments. Malaysia's intention to realize the idea, on the other hand, was shown by its seriousness in hosting the first EAS in December 2005.[14]

Initially, Indonesia was relatively passive towards the advent of East Asian regionalism and gave an impression that it would not block the transformation of the ASEAN+3 to the EAS. However, Indonesia soon realized the danger of translating this idea into an institutional

---

[13] Hadi, S (2005). Integrasi ekonomi Asia timur dalam agenda politik luar negeri Indonesia. dalam *Quo Vadis Indonesia*, Jakarta: IPS.
[14] Hadi, S (2009b). Indonesia–China relations in the post-new order era. In *East Asia's Relations with the Rising China*, Lam, PE, Narayan, G and C Durkop (eds.), p. 231. Singapore: Konrad Adenaur Stiftung.

form, which would possibly threaten to displace ASEAN's role as the only advanced regional organization in East Asia. Indeed, since its establishment in 1967, ASEAN as a regional organization has become the main vehicle for Indonesia to play its role in regional and international level.[15]

The formation of an EAC, a goal of the EAS in the first place, means that the significance of ASEAN would concomitantly decline because an EAC is bigger and more prestigious, as its membership would include ASEAN members as well as the rich "+3" countries. Cognizant of this, Jakarta decided to rein back the process of regionalism proceeding too quick for comfort.[16] Based on the arguments of open regionalism, Indonesia suggested that Australia and New Zealand, which are geographically located outside Asia, should be invited as EAS participants. The Philippines also supported the candidacy of India for the EAS. Indonesia also proposed the principle of ASEAN as *the driving force* to any forms of cooperation in East Asia. The principle of ASEAN as the driving force meant that the status of the EAS is merely *a part of* ASEAN Summit. Therefore, non-ASEAN or "+3" countries have no right to host the summit. This principle was a snub to China which openly offered to host the second EAS.

Indonesia's proposal gained firm support from Japan which would not be happy to have China dominating EAS. In the first EAS in Kuala Lumpur, December 2005, Japan supported Indonesia to position ASEAN as the driving force for cooperation in East Asia. Hence, the EAS is only part of the dialogue process in ASEAN Summit. Simply put, the EAS means only ASEAN+6.

The Japanese support for the Indonesian position was clearly based on its political rivalry with China, which peaked during the

---

[15] *Ibid.*

[16] In regard to the official respond of Indonesian government to the *East Asia Summit* idea, read R.M. Marty M. Natalegawa, ASEAN+3 versus the East Asia Summit, in *Duta Indonesia and the World*, April 2005. Marty stated: "Indonesia does not find it appealing that ASEAN 3 Summit should simply be duplicated by an East Asia Summit with the same participants and essentially the same agenda, each coexisting with the other. This would be inefficient and cannot possibly be sustainable in the long run" (page 3).

Koizumi period (2001–2006). Under Prime Minister Koizumi, it was clear that Tokyo did not want Beijing to use the ASEAN+3 to play a dominant role in the East Asia region. Indeed, Japan preferred to bring in additional countries such as Australia, India and the US in a larger regional grouping especially the EAS to dilute the influence of a rising China. With the principle of "ASEAN as the driving force" in all forum of cooperation in East Asia, only the ASEAN member countries that have right to become a host of East Asia Summit.

As the next host of the ASEAN Summit, the Philippines, the United States' traditional ally which would certainly more supportive to the political agenda of Indonesia and Japan rather than that of China.[17] In fact, the discourse of the EAC faded away in the next ASEAN Summit hold in Cebu, the Philippines in January 2007. At the ASEAN Summit, President Gloria Macapagal Arroyo of the Philippines viewed China and India as serious competitors for ASEAN in attracting global investment. She also advocated the acceleration of the ASEAN Community from 2020 to 2015 to strengthen ASEAN competitiveness against China and India.

However, in September 2009, Japanese Prime Minister, Yukio Hatoyama Yukio, raised again the idea of an EAC. He envisages the community as potentially consisting of Japan, China, South Korea, Australia, New Zealand, India, and 10 members of ASEAN. Although details remained sketchy, Hatoyama's vision could see greater cooperation in the areas of trade, counterterrorism, environment, and disaster relief operations.[18] Many observers see this proposal as Hatoyama's grand strategy to reengage with Asia and strike a more independent role in Japan's relationship with the US — a vision that he proposed during his political campaign to challenge the then ruling Liberal Democratic Party responsible for Japanese dependence on the US in security and foreign relations.

---

[17] Hadi, S (2009). Indonesia–China relations in the post-new order era. *Op. cit.*
[18] Australia ponders place in Japan's East Asian community. http://www.japantoday.com/category/commentary/view/australia-ponders-place-in-japans-east-asian-community.

Interestingly, Hatoyama's idea was welcomed especially by Australian Prime Minister Kevin Rudd who had earlier proposed the idea of Asia Pacific Community (APC). Both Hatoyama and Rudd advocated greater regional cooperation across a range of economic, political and security issues, but their proposals differed in membership. Potential members of APC would include Japan, China, Russia, India, South Korea, Australia, New Zealand, the 10 ASEAN members and the three South American members of APEC — Chile, Mexico, and Peru.[19] While the key difference between the two proposals is the absence of the US, both leaders agreed that the community needs to be more comprehensive and inclusive to cope with future challenges.

II. Preserving the "Dynamic Equilibrium": Indonesia and Regional Architecture after the Global Financial Crisis 2008

Due to its large territory and huge population, Indonesia sees itself as the most important member of ASEAN. Apparently, Indonesia views itself as a *de facto* leader of ASEAN. That the ASEAN Secretariat is located in Jakarta, the country's capital, is symbolic of Indonesia being a key driver of ASEAN. Bantarto Bandoro, the editor of *Indonesian Quarterly*, wrote:

> Indonesia burst forth as a strategic regional player more than 40 years ago when the region saw the establishment of ASEAN. Our influence touched almost every aspect of the region. Southeast Asia was and continued to be on the radar of the Indonesian foreign policy. ASEAN was seen as the main venue where Indonesia articulated its foreign policy interests.[20]

ASEAN's importance for Indonesia's foreign policy is reflected, for example, in the explicit inclusion of ASEAN into the Medium-term National Development Plan 2004–2009 (mostly known as

---

[19] *Ibid.*

[20] Bandoro, B (2007). Indonesian foreign policy 2008 and beyond. *The Indonesian Quarterly*, 35(4), 327.

RPJMN 2004–2009[21]), the document of which becomes the formal guidance for the development activities of Indonesian government in the period of 2004–2009. The document states that actualizing international cooperation is needed to optimize the country's positive potentials in various arena of international cooperation. The document also underlines some main agendas to be followed:

1. To establish understanding and more coordination between ministries and government institutions, such as the Ministry of Defense, Coordinating Ministry of Politics, Law, and Security, the Indonesian National Army (*Tentara Nasional Indonesia/TNI*), Police, and Intelligent Community in order to cooperate more with bilateral, regional, and international partners. Such cooperation is needed to maintain peace, territorial integrity, and national resources security.
2. To formulate a more effective framework to establish the ASEAN Security/Economic/Socio-cultural Community.
3. To resolve international cooperation in economic, trade, social, and cultural field so that it will support the attainment of socio-economic development goals, including the Millennium Development Goals (MDGs).
4. To facilitate cultural and educational diplomacy based on people's initiatives.
5. To facilitate efforts aimed to widen and increase "Sister City" projects between cities and provinces in Indonesia with advanced and developing cities, provinces, and districts abroad.

By explicitly mentioned ASEAN in such a formal and important document, it is no doubt that the Indonesian government (still) positions ASEAN as the main focal point for Indonesia's foreign policy. Politically, ASEAN is considered to be important to ensure security and political stability in Southeast Asia, which is the nearest regional circle of the country. Accordingly, strengthening the level of cooperation and

---

[21] RPJMN is an acronym of Rencana Pembangunan Jangka Menengah Nasional (The Mid Term National Development Plan).

institutional arrangement within ASEAN are expected to prevent negative consequences of the emergence of great powers in Southeast Asia.

Economically, more cooperation in ASEAN is seen as further step in various leading cooperation such as the AFTA and ASEAN Community, which established in ASEAN with the Indonesian active participation. In 2004–2009, various active roles played by Indonesia to improve institutional arrangement and to strengthen ASEAN, can be seen. One of the most important points to be pursued in this context is to ensure ASEAN as the driving force on various regional cooperation in East Asia.

As mentioned earlier, Indonesia has struggled for "ASEAN centrality" when there was an idea to transform ASEAN+3 into an EAC. The idea, which was strongly supported by Malaysia and China, has a big potential to diminish ASEAN as the most important driving force of the East Asia regional arrangement. Indonesia gained success in convincing its fellow countries in preserving ASEAN as the central pillar of regional cooperation. The EAS, previously was designated to gradually transform ASEAN+3 into an EAC, is now an integral part of the ASEAN Summit — an "ASEAN+6" formula to include Japan, China, South Korea, India, Australia, and New Zealand.

The "ASEAN centrality" has been included as an ASEAN principle, among other principles, which mentioned explicitly in the ASEAN Charter. Article 2 point 2 (m) of the Charter states that the ASEAN and its member states should follow the principle of "the centrality of ASEAN in external political, economic, social and cultural relations while remaining actively engaged, outward-looking, inclusive and non-discriminatory".[22] The existence of the Charter, which has been ratified by all member states in 2007, indicates its members' intention to transform ASEAN from a mere informal and consensus-based association to a legal-based organization with binding commitments.

Domestically, Indonesia's economic recovery from a long period of crisis has been proven by the country's success in maintaining positive

---

[22] Association of Southeast Asian Nations (2007). *The ASEAN Charter*, p. 7. Jakarta: ASEAN Secretariat.

Table 1. Growth performance of selected countries in 2009.

Country	2009	GDP growth projection
Malaysia	4.8	0.2
Thailand	4.5	2
Australia	2.2	1.7
Indonesia	6	4.5
USA	0.1	–0.8
UK	–0.1	–1.3
Singapore	3.5	–5
Japan	0.5	–0.2
South Korea	3.5	2.5
India	6.9	6
China	9.3	8

Source: CEIC Database.

economic performance during the global financial crisis 2008–2009, in which most developed countries' economies suffered.[23] Along with China and India, Indonesia stood out as only few economic powers that performing well during the global crisis. In 2009, China enjoyed the highest economic growth, reaching 8.7%, while India in the second position with 7.2%, and Indonesia in the third place with 4.5% (See Table 1). This rate was above that of Singapore (–5%), Japan (–0.2%), Malaysia (0.2%) and even South Korea (2.5%), as shown in Table 1.

The success of Indonesia's democratic consolidation process coupled with socio-political stability since the collapse of Suharto's dictatorial rule triggered by the 1997–1998 Asian Financial Crisis have boosted the confidence among the country's political elite to strengthen Indonesia's role in various existing of international cooperation's. Indeed, Indonesia's membership in the G20 (an institution which resulted from the 2008–2009 Global Financial Crisis) reflects the country's larger role in

---

[23] Siregar, R and W Wiranto (2009). In the midst of global financial slowdown: The Indonesian experience. *The Indonesian Quarterly*, 37(4), 399.

international relations. Although the G20 is a loose multilateral organization, it influences greatly the agenda and directions of international financial organizations such as IMF and the World Bank.

In the domestic context, Indonesia's membership in G20 has raised various debates on whether Indonesia should maintain ASEAN as the cornerstone of its foreign policy. Some critical observers say that Indonesia should reduce its diplomatic focus on ASEAN and play a larger role globally. Indonesia's commitment to ASEAN is seen to come at a cost. For example, the ASEAN–China Free Trade Area (ACFTA) impacted negatively on many domestic manufacturing industries due to the "invasion" of Chinese cheap products. Only four months after the implementation of ACFTA, China's export to Indonesia increased to 952% in toy sector and 215% in textile sector.[24]

Responding to this debate, both President Yudhoyono and Foreign Minister Marty Natalegawa have explicitly reassured that Indonesia would continue to maintain ASEAN as the main instrument of Indonesian foreign policy. Indonesian leaders, as always, are mostly very proud with their claim about Indonesia's success in leading ASEAN. The perception that "Indonesia as the leader of ASEAN" has continuingly influencing the country's behavior in international relations, in bilateral, regional and multilateral levels.

Indonesia's desire to preserve its leadership in ASEAN has continually influenced and restrained its behavior. A good example is the incident when three Indonesian civilian officers were detained by Malaysian personnel's around Bintan Island in September 2010. Instead of playing "hardball" like what China did to Japan in the similar incident around the Senkaku (Diaoyu) Islands, Indonesia responded mildly to Malaysia by only delivering diplomatic protest notes. In the midst of parliament's disappointment and public anger, Foreign Minister Marty Natalegawa stated that Indonesia's position as chairman of ASEAN in 2011 obliged his country to deal with the dispute diplomatically and peacefully. President Yudhoyono also stated that as the leader of ASEAN, Indonesia should set a good example for other ASEAN countries to deal with disputes.[25]

---

[24] *Investor Daily*, 23 July 2010.
[25] *Kompas*, 3 September 2010.

The principle of ASEAN Centrality is at the heart of so-called "Natalegawa Doctrine", an Indonesian perspective of foreign policy introduced by Foreign Affairs Minister Marty Natalegawa. According to him, it is an undoubted fact that the geo-political trend in the foreseeable future projects the rising prominence of East Asia. According to Natalegawa,[26] the concept of *dynamic equilibrium* is marked by the absence of domination of any single great power. Moreover, dynamic equilibrium exists when countries engage with one another in a mutually beneficial and peaceful way. Amidst this backdrop of the East Asia rising, regional states should pursue regionalism with ASEAN at its core. Natalegawa noted:

> We must not be diverted away from the ASEAN Community track, because any future of APC must have as a constituent element the ASEAN community. It is a prerequisite. So, first and foremost we must continue to integrate ourselves into ASEAN Community building efforts by 2015.[27]

Natalegawa also defined the recent situation in the Asia-Pacific as a "cold peace". Residual forces from the Cold War still exist, but new forces have also arisen in its aftermath. For example, China and India are emerging forces in regional and even international economies. Relations between these forces are not hostile like in the Cold War era, but more competitive, dynamic and non-political.[28] According to Natalegawa, the paradigm of international security today must shift in line with the plurality of actors. Increasing economic cooperation among ASEAN member countries and in the Asia-Pacific is necessary to respond to this new reality of rising Asian powers.[29]

Amidst Obama's visit to Indonesia in November 2010, there was a growing concern whether Indonesia would move closer to the US in regional politics. It is no doubt that Indonesia has substantial interest to

---

[26] Budianto, L (2010). ASEAN presence a prerequisite in any future Asia Pacific community. *Jakarta Post*, 1 May.

[27] *Ibid.*

[28] Umar, ARM (2010). Leading to global South. *The Jakarta Post*, 7 January.

[29] *Ibid.*

promote good relations with the superpower, especially to increase the capability of its military and to secure military equipment — many of the equipments were supplied by the US. Increasing "strategic relations" between Indonesia and the US also would strengthen the country's strategic position in the new "fragmented political power" in Asia Pacific region.[30]

However, according to the "Natalegawa Doctrine", Indonesia would seek to maintain its identity as the "main pillar" of ASEAN in regional politics of Southeast Asia, East Asia and Asia Pacific. Indonesia has an interest to support US and Russia's involvement in the politics and security architecture of the East Asian region in order to counter-balance China's assertiveness which is too powerful to be faced by Indonesia and ASEAN countries alone. The US presence is needed as a balancing power against China with a burgeoning economy and territorial claims in the South China Sea.

However, on the other hand, Indonesia does not want to lose its identity by becoming too close to the US. Consequently, Indonesia will maintain its distance between great powers in East Asia, a position that enables the country to be an "intermediary power". In this context, it is understandable when President Yudhoyono declared that Indonesia rejects hegemony by any countries in the new regional architecture in East Asia. Responding to Australia's proposal on the APC, Japan's EAC proposal, and China's preference for an ASEAN+3 format, President Yudhoyono stated that the new architecture should preserve "ASEAN centrality". According to him, if ASEAN can maintain peace and stability in its region, then it would make a meaningful contribution to the world peace and security.[31]

Amidst the debates on the new configuration in East Asia, Chinese Prime Minister, Wen Ji Bao, visited Indonesia and some other ASEAN countries in April 2011. In Jakarta, Wen revealed the Chinese intention to increase its role in ASEAN development. He reminded that in 2010 China became the biggest ASEAN trading partner, and that both economies have targeted that their trade would be valued at US$500 billion in 2015. Prime Minister Wen also highlighted Chinese

---

[30] *Ibid.*
[31] *Era Baru News*, 10 April 2010.

commitment to help the construction of land transportation, accelerate the development of infrastructure, train and electrical through credit programs in ASEAN.[32] Wen's statements that focused in the economic aspects of China–ASEAN relations could be perceived as China's intention to shift the attention from the "hard" political issues such as territory disputes towards the "lower" ones such as cooperation in the infrastructure building. Hence China does not voice its objection towards Indonesian stance in the newest dynamics of East Asia and avoid discussing such issues in a "direct way".

In the case of territorial conflict between Cambodia and Thailand, as the chairman of ASEAN, Indonesia has endeavored to mediate the conflict through diplomatic efforts within the ASEAN framework. However, it has been proven that such efforts were not truly easy. Cambodia has shown its willingness to put the settlement within the ASEAN framework (as proposed by Indonesia), while Thailand seems to avoid regional and multilateral arrangement. Thailand prefers bilateral ways rather than ASEAN framework.[33] In fact, Indonesian eagerness to mediate the conflict had been stroke by the broken of military crash between Thailand and Cambodia in 22 April 2011, only two weeks after the meeting of Joint Border Committee (JBC) held in Bogor in attempt to find a peaceful solution. As if becoming more realistic with the situation, after the bilateral meeting with PM Thailand, Yingluck Sinawatra in Jakarta, 12 September 2011, President Yudoyono said that the Thailand-Cambodia conflict "could be settled through *bilateral* as well as ASEAN channels".[34]

As mentioned earlier, it is clear that Indonesia would subordinate itself to any hegemonic or dominant power in the region. This is basically in line with the fundamental jargon of Indonesian foreign

---

[32] China ingin Tingkatkan Peran Pragmatis di ASEAN. http://www.bbc.co.uk/indonesia/dunia/2011/04/110439_pmwenspeech.shtml.

[33] Ikfal, SN. Menanti diplomasi tingkat tinggi Indonesia dalam konflik Thailand–Kamboja. dalam.http://www.politik.lipi.go.id/index.php/en/ens/columns/politik-internasional/451-menanti-diplomasi-tingkat-tinggi-indonesia-dalam-konflik-thailand-kamboja.

[34] SBY: Thailand–Kamboja dapat selesaikan konflik. http://nasional.kompas.com/read/2011/09/12.

policy, namely the politics of "neutral and active" (*politik bebas aktif*) declared by the first country's vice president, Mohamad Hatta, in 1946. Although during Soekarno era (1945–1965), Indonesia had been closer to the communist bloc, and being closer to Western block during Soeharto era (1965–1998), the country's leaders always tried to maintain the country's autonomy. This has been the reason why Indonesia has continually active in the Non-Aligned Movement (NAM), which declared its neutrality during the long period of Cold War era.

Indonesian active involvement in the Organization of Islamic Conference (OIC) in the last two decades also does not provide a sensible reason for the country to base its foreign policy on religion identity rather than regional identity. When the OIC Charter launched in 1971, Indonesia even refused to sign it, based on the argument that, according to 1945 Constitution, Indonesia is not an Islamic country.[35] Indonesian government only started to involve in OIC in 1991, when Soeharto started to exercise the "politics of accommodation" towards the Muslim groups in the country. However, Indonesia realizes that political difference amongst OIC members has caused it to lose its effectiveness in dealing with the issues in Islamic World. In addition to this, the dominant role of Arabic countries in the organization also a fact that one could not neglect. While in ASEAN Indonesia could play a strategic role as the biggest country in Southeast Asia, in OIC Indonesia would only position itself under the shadow of Saudi Arabia, Turkey, or Egypt.

III. Conclusion

The 2008–2009 American Financial Crisis has raised the question about the appropriate East Asia regional architecture to withstand such turbulence. In fact, the idea of East Asian integration had been widely discussed in aftermath of the 1997–1998 Asian Financial

---

[35] Ghafur, MF. Revitalisasi Peran Indonesia di OKI. http://www.politik.lipi.go.id/index.php/en/columns/politik-internasional/443-revitalisasi-peran-indonesia-di-organisasi-konferensi-islam-oki.

Crisis, which reflected an increasing awareness on the high degree of economic interdependence amongst countries in East Asia. The initial notion had been focused on how to achieve regional economic integration as a collective self-help against external economic turmoil, especially related to negative effects stemming from the rapid trans-border financial inflows and outflows.

Indonesia, views itself as the main defender of the idea of ASEAN as the "driving force" of all regional process of cooperation in East Asia. In fact, this was notably in line with the Indonesian elite's perception on the necessity to defend the country's leadership in ASEAN as its political leverage in regional and international affairs.

The discourse of East Asian regional architecture has reappeared in the wake of global financial crisis 2008–2009, which has been mostly dominated by political aspects instead of economic ones. In relations with this dynamics, Indonesia has positioned itself exactly in the same way like the one in the EAC debate after the Asian Financial Crisis 1997–1998. In both cases, Indonesia defended the principle of "ASEAN centrality" and reminded fellow neighboring countries on ASEAN's longstanding contribution in preserving peace and stability in Southeast Asia. Indonesia's consistency to the idea of "ASEAN centrality" is also related to the political elite perception on necessity of preserving Indonesia's leadership in ASEAN, including against a new "threat" coming from the discourse of East Asian regional architecture-building that may diminish ASEAN's centrality in an expanded regionalism.

The so-called "Natalegawa Doctrine" (which defines the Indonesian mission to seek a strategic position in the *dynamic equilibrium* in the Asia-Pacific) emphasizes an "ASEAN Centrality" against a backdrop where no single great power can dominate East Asia. For Indonesia, ASEAN is not only an instrument, but also its inseparable identity in regional as well as global diplomacy. Consequently, as long as the Indonesian elite still perceives ASEAN as an important card for the country in playing its role in regional and global level, the principle of ASEAN centrality would be defended by the government at all cost.

Bibliography

Association of Southeast Asian Nations (2007). *The ASEAN Charter*. Jakarta: ASEAN Secretariat.

Bandoro, B (2007). Indonesian foreign policy 2008 and beyond. *The Indonesian Quarterly*, 35(4), 327–334.

Budianto, L (2010). ASEAN presence a prerequisite in any future Asia Pacific community. *Jakarta Post*, 1 May.

Era Baru News, 10 April 2010.

Hadi, S (2005). Integrasi ekonomi Asia timur dalam agenda politik luar negeri Indonesia. dalam *Quo Vadis Indonesia*. Jakarta: IPS.

Hadi, S (2009a). Dinamika Asia Pasifik. *Kompas*, 23 November.

Hadi, S (2009b). Indonesia–China relations in the post-new order era. In *East Asia's Relations with the Rising China*, Lam, PE, Narayan, G and C Durkop (eds.). Singapore: Konrad Adenaur Stiftung.

Investor Daily, 23 July 2010.

Kompas, 3 September 2010.

Milner, A. (2010) From Asia-Pacific to Asia? http://www.eastasiaforum.org/06/03/from-asia-pacific-to-asia/.

McIntyre, A (1997). Southeast Asia and the political economy of APEC. In *The Political Economy of South-East Asia: An Introduction*, G Rodan, K Hewison and R Robison (eds.). Melbourne: Oxford University Press.

Munakata, N (2006). *Transforming East Asia: The Evolution of Regional Economic Integration*. Washington, DC: Brooking Institution Press.

Murphy, AM (2009). Toward a US-Indonesia comprehensive partnership. *Indonesian Quarterly*, 79(3), 265–282.

Rahardjo, S (2004). Indonesia dan Integrasi Asia Timur: Suatu Perspektif. A paper in *East Asian Experts Meeting Related to the Idea of East Asian Community*, Yogyakarta, 24 December.

Natalegawa, RMMM (2005). ASEAN+3 versus the East Asia Summit. *Duta Indonesia and the World*, April.

Saya Optimis Melihat Negeri Ini (2010). *Kompas*, 10 November.

Siregar, R and W Wiranto (2004). In the midst of global financial slowdown: The Indonesian experience. *The Indonesian Quarterly*, 37(4), 399–421.

Soesastro, H (2008). Kevin Rudd's architecture for the Asia Pacific. http://www.eastasiaforum.org/2008/06/09/kevin-rudds-architecture-for-the-asia-pacific/.

Umar, ARM (2010). Leading to global South. *The Jakarta Post*, 7 January.

Chapter 11

TWENTY YEARS OF SINO–SINGAPORE DIPLOMATIC TIES: AN ASSESSMENT

LYE Liang Fook

China–Singapore relations are strong and substantive due to painstaking efforts by the leaders of the two countries in order to value and nurture this relationship over the past two decades. Today, in addition to the good rapport of the leaders, there is a high-level institutional mechanism in place to drive cooperation. Flagship projects like the Suzhou Industrial Park and the Sino–Singapore Tianjin Eco-city further add substance to bilateral ties. It is important for both sides to constantly review the state of relations and suggest new areas to cooperate in. Such a proactive approach will help to sustain the momentum in the bilateral relationship. In the midst of the global economic uncertainty, it will be even more important for the two countries to maintain a stable and mutually beneficial relationship.

I. Overview

Singapore's relations with China today are deep and broad. The two countries interact and cooperate in many fields ranging from politics, economics, business, the arts, culture and education to the environment. Their relationship is also manifested at many levels ranging from government-to-government ties involving the top leaders to people-to-people exchanges of tourists and students. Over the years, bilateral relations has not only deepened, but has also broadened into new areas.

A review of the state of bilateral relations between Singapore and China is timely for two reasons. First, the two countries marked the 20th anniversary of the establishment of their diplomatic relations on 3 October 2010. It is, therefore, useful to review how far their relationship has progressed over the past 20 years. Second, and from a broader perspective, the shift in the world's center of gravity towards the Asia-Pacific is likely to hasten in view of the current economic difficulties confronting the US and European countries. This shift, and the hastening of it, will have implications for Singapore's relations with China and vice versa.

This chapter argues that a strong and stable relationship, especially economic ties, between Singapore and China will become even more important with Europe saddled with its debt crisis and the US struggling with unemployment and spending issues. With Europe and the US preoccupied with their internal problems, it is even more in the interests of Singapore and China to maintain the momentum of their mutually beneficial relationship. On Singapore's part, this will help to ensure continued economic growth and prosperity by riding on the opportunities that China's rise can offer. On China's part, further building on ties with Singapore will reinforce its pledge to peaceful development, demonstrating that Beijing is prepared to jointly prosper with regional countries regardless of their size on the basis of mutual respect for each other's sovereignty and territorial integrity.

To be sure, Singapore's relations with China before the latter's open door and reform policy in 1978 were dogged by ideological differences and threats to national security. Then, governments in Southeast Asia, Singapore included, had to grapple with communist insurgents who were supported by Beijing. Yet, despite their differences then, both countries displayed considerable pragmatism that allowed their economic relationship to proceed ahead of political differences.

The pragmatism embraced by the Deng Xiaoping reformist leadership further spurred relations between the two countries. In particular, Singapore seized the opportunity to expand its economic ties with China, especially after Deng's tour of South China in early 1992. Therefore by the end of 2010, Singapore was China's eighth largest trading partner and the seventh largest investor. The Singapore–China Free Trade Agreement which came into force in January 2009 has further spurred growth in bilateral trade and investments.

Most notably, the Suzhou Industrial Park (SIP) which the two countries had embarked on in 1994 celebrated its 15th Anniversary in May 2009. Building on the foundation of the SIP, the two countries have since opened up another new front of cooperation in the form of the Sino–Singapore Tianjin Eco-city that seeks to balance the objectives of environmental protection, economic growth, and social harmony. There are many other commercial projects, undertaken by the private sectors of the two countries.

At the political level, China and Singapore relations are warm and productive, buttressed by regular high level exchanges of visits. Augmenting the warm personal ties between the leaders of the two countries is an overarching institutional mechanism in the form of the Joint Council of Bilateral Cooperation and other bilateral cooperation bodies under this council that oversee the various areas of cooperation between the two countries. These bodies provide useful platforms for both sides to not only engage but also to continually explore mutually beneficial areas of cooperation. This will in turn strengthen the foundation of the bilateral relationship.

To further examine the state of Singapore–China relations in detail, the chapter is divided into the following section. It will first provide an overview of bilateral ties especially in its early years where there was a difficult period to give readers a sense of how far the relationship has come. Second, it will highlight key aspects of the current bilateral relationship to show how broad-based ties have become. Singapore's good relations with Taiwan will also be mentioned in this section to demonstrate the leeway that China has accorded to Singapore under the "One China" policy. Third, besides the multifaceted ties between the two countries, there is a high-level mechanism that proactively oversees bilateral cooperation between the two countries. It is relatively unusual for China to have such a mechanism with a small country like Singapore, indicating the level of importance China attaches to its ties with Singapore. Fourth, the chapter will share some recent downturns or hiccups in the bilateral relationship to demonstrate the need for both sides to constantly work to keep their ties on track. Finally, the concluding section will underscore the importance for Singapore to build on its existing ties, especially its economic linkages, with China with Europe and the US mired in their own domestic challenges. For China, it can secure greater political mileage if it can strike a relationship based on the principles of mutual respect, fairness and win–win outcomes even though its counterpart is a small country.

II. The Two-Way Relationship in Perspective

Singapore has geographically and historically been an integral part of Southeast Asia. Its interactions with China, in the past and at present, can be viewed not only within a bilateral context but also as part of a wider region. Today, Singapore enjoys a strong and substantive relationship with China. It ties with China, like with many other countries, are guided by a high sense of pragmatism, not ideological correctness. A large part of Singapore's "core interests" are trade, investments and economic growth. Singapore welcomes China's growing engagement in the region as this provides ample opportunities for it to participate in China's development, both to help China as well as to ride on China's growth.

Singapore–China relations go back a long way, well before the establishment of diplomatic relations on 3 October 1990. Even before the founding of the People's Republic of China (PRC) in 1949, China's relations with Southeast Asia, traditionally called *Nanyang* or South Sea by the Chinese (and of which Singapore is a part of), are extensive and deep-rooted on account of history, geography and migration.

Geographically, Singapore was part of the "Pan-Malayan lands". Historically, trade between China and Pan-Malaya can be traced back to the early centuries. A fair amount of trade was recorded as early as the Tang Dynasty (618–907). The early trade activities were often mixed with tribute-bearing missions, a peculiar Chinese way of conducting diplomacy with smaller states in *Nanyang*. But regular and steady growth in trade started only after the second part of the 19th century, with the increased influx of Chinese immigrant labor into British Malaya.

In fact, the Chinese had frequented the Malay lands long before the Portuguese conquered Malacca in 1511. In 1349, a Chinese trader gave a vivid account of life in Temasek, the name of old Singapore. In 1409, Admiral Zheng He led an expedition to Malacca and made it one of China's tributary states. However, it was not until 1819 when the British East India Company established a settlement in Singapore that sizeable Chinese communities began to grow.

By 1860, ethnic Chinese constituted 60% of Singapore's total population of 82,000, 15% of Malacca's 67,000, and nearly 30% of Penang's 67,000. Most Chinese, mainly from Fujian and Guangdong, migrated into Malaya under the contract-labor system. But they soon became traders and craftsman, and they eventually dominated the economic life of the Straits Settlements.

After the founding of the PRC in 1949, however, China's relations with Southeast Asia assumed new dimensions, with complex ideological and geo-political forces coming into play. China lent moral and material support to communist insurgency movements in Southeast Asia that threatened to overthrow the post-colonial governments in these countries. Singapore was particularly concerned given its vulnerability following its separation from Malaysia in 1965 and the intractable challenges of economic growth and nation-building. During this period, China also supported the communist government in North Vietnam against the capitalist South Vietnam. When the North overran the South in 1975, there were fears that other countries in Southeast Asia would soon fall under communism.

Despite such ideological differences and threats to its national security, Singapore adopted a pragmatic approach and maintained its ties with China. When Malaysia's relations with China deteriorated during the period when Singapore was a part of Malaysia in 1963–1965, the Singapore government came under intense pressure from the Malaysian government to close the Bank of China branch in Singapore.

However, the Singapore government resisted such a pressure and kept the branch open. Bilateral trade was also conducted in the absence of diplomatic ties. For the most part of the 1970s for instance, bilateral trade between Singapore and China hovered around S$700 million to S$800 million, with the balance of trade in China's favor.

When Deng Xiaoping embarked on economic reform and the open door policy in 1979, China's approach to foreign relations was also characterized by pragmatism. For its internal economic development, China required a conducive external environment. China was opposed to Vietnam's 1978 invasion of Cambodia and wanted the help of other Southeast Asian countries to form a united front with China against Vietnam's aggression. Deng was reportedly receptive to Singapore Prime Minister Lee Kuan Yew's suggestion (when they met in November 1978) that China stopped communist radio broadcasts from Hunan that were directed at the Southeast Asian countries in return for improved relations with China and for support for the Khmer Rouge cause.[1] Sometime in June 1981, the broadcasting station in Hunan was shut down.[2]

This positive action by China provided a good basis for the improvement of relations between China and Southeast Asia (or ASEAN) in general, and China and Singapore in particular. Out of respect for the sensitivities of its neighbors, Singapore was the last country in ASEAN to formalize relations with China. Thus, Singapore only set up a Trade Office in Beijing in 1981, and it waited until October 1990 to formalize diplomatic ties with China, shortly after Indonesia did so in August 1990. This move was intended to send an unequivocal message to its neighbors that Singapore was an independent and sovereign actor on the international stage, and was not an agent of another state, i.e., not a "Third China". On hindsight, this move laid a good basis for Singapore's ties with China to develop.

---

[1] Lee, KY (2000). *From Third World to First: The Singapore Story 1965–2000*, pp. 665–667. Singapore: Singapore Press Holdings.
[2] Chin, P (2003). *My Side of History*, pp. 457–460. Singapore: Media Masters Pte Ltd.

China–Singapore ties received a further boost when Deng mentioned Singapore during his Southern Tour or *Nanxun* in 1992. Thereafter, numerous official "observation groups" came to Singapore to study Singapore's development experiences. In 1992 alone, Singapore received over 400 delegations from China keen to study various aspects of Singapore's development experience.[3] This culminated in the joint development of the two countries' first flagship project in Suzhou in 1994, which eventually took off after overcoming initial hurdles.

III. A Broad-based and Substantive Relationship

Today, China and Singapore enjoy a multifaceted relationship with cooperation and interactions on many fronts. One of the important anchors is their ever expanding and deepening trade and investment ties. In 2010, China was Singapore's third largest trading partner with total trade amounting to S$95.3 billion, a jump of 26% from the previous year figure of S$75.7.[4] Since 2001, after China's entry into the World Trade Organization (WTO), the bilateral trade volume expanded more than threefold from S$22.4 billion in 2001 to S$95.3 billion in 2010, averaging an annual growth rate of more than 15% (see Fig. 1). In 2010, Singapore was China's eight largest trading partner.

The China–Singapore Free Trade Agreement (CSFTA) that came into force on 1 January 2009 has brought notable benefits to both countries as indicated by the above figures. This was also the view shared by Singapore and Chinese officials when they met for their first review of the CSFTA in April 2010. To ensure its continued relevance, the CSFTA will need to continually evolve to meet the needs of the Singapore and China's business communities.

Since 1997, China overtook Malaysia as the most important destination for Singapore's foreign direct investment in cumulative

---

[3] Speech by Senior Minister Mr Lee Kuan Yew at the "International Conference on National Boundaries and Cultural Configurations", at the 10th Anniversary Celebration of the Center for Chinese Language and Culture, Nanyang Technological University, Wednesday, 23 June 2004.

[4] Singapore, China witness strong bilateral trade growth (2011). *China Daily*, 5 February.

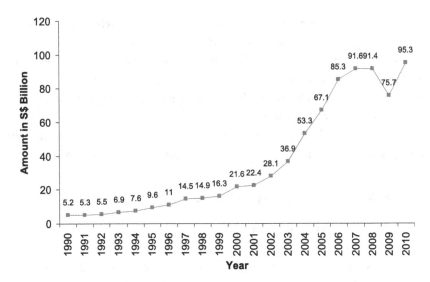

Fig. 1.   Singapore's trade with China (1990–2010).

Sources: Singapore Statistics and IE Singapore Statistics.

terms. In 2010, Singapore's cumulative direct investment in China reached S$58.1 billion, an increase of more than 12% from S$51.6 billion in 2009 (see Fig. 2). Singapore's investments in China are predominantly in manufacturing and real estate, rental and leasing. In 2010, Singapore was China's seventh largest investor.

Many Chinese companies have also chosen Singapore as a springboard into the region and the Singapore Exchange as a fund-raising platform. Apart from accessing global capital, a listing on the Singapore Exchange helps these companies generate overseas brand awareness and broaden shareholder base. In the past five years, China listings have grown from 85 in 2005 to some 154 in 2010. Till the end of April 2011, Chinese companies make up around 7% of market capitalization of listings on the Singapore Exchange Mainboard.[5]

However, there appears to be an increasing trend of China firms on the Singapore Exchange seeking dual listings elsewhere in Taiwan, Hong Kong and even Seoul. These Chinese firms are now looking beyond the Singapore Exchange in search of higher valuations and

---

[5] Singapore Exchange Statistical Report April 2011.

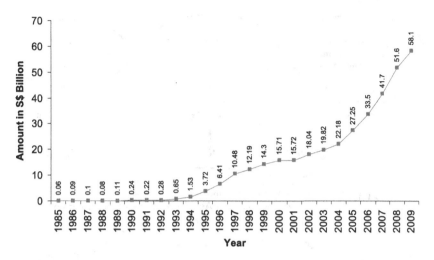

Fig. 2. Singapore's cumulative direct investment in China (1985–2009).

Source: Singapore Statistics.

bigger trading volumes which translates into higher liquidity and higher profiles for these companies.

On its part, the dynamism and resilience of the Chinese economy is making a significant positive impact in the region and the rest of the world. This is especially evident after the 2008 financial contagion that engulfed the major economies of the world. Bucking the trend, China achieved a stellar GDP growth of 9.1 and 10.3 in 2009 and 2010 respectively, becoming an ever more important economic driver. In Asia, China–ASEAN trade volume reached US$235.4 billion in the first 10 months of 2010, upto 42% year-on-year, retaining ASEAN's position as China's fourth biggest trading partner.[6] Indeed, China's economic relations with ASEAN have been much boosted by the China–ASEAN Free Trade Area (CAFTA) which went into effect on 1 January 2010.

In fact, China has continued to run substantial trade deficits with its neighbors from Japan, Korea, Taiwan, Australia and the ASEAN countries of Malaysia, Thailand and the Philippines. By opening up its vast market for their exports, China has become a critical engine for their economic growth. More significantly, by importing

---

[6] China ASEAN trade soars on China's deficit (2010). *China Daily*, 9 December.

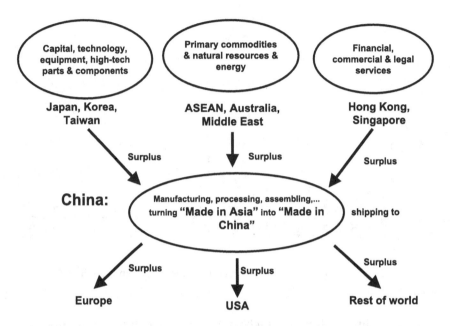

Fig. 3.   China at the center of global and regional production networks.

Source: Chart provided by Prof John Wong, Professorial Fellow, EAI.

raw materials, intermediate products, machinery and equipment, and services from different Asian economies, Singapore included, and then re-exporting the finished products to different markets in the region and beyond, China operates as an important integrator of regional and global manufacturing activities (see Fig. 3).

At the financial level, the two countries have sought ways to strengthen their economic resilience and financial stability. In July 2010, the People's Bank of China and the Monetary Authority of Singapore announced the setting up of a bilateral currency swap arrangement that will provide Chinese *Yuan* liquidity of up to RMB150 billion and Singapore dollar liquidity of up to S$30 billion. The two countries are reportedly also in talks to explore the possibility of Singapore as a second offshore *yuan* trading hub after Hong Kong.

On tourism, or people-to-people relations, China is Singapore's second largest visitor-generating market with 1,171 million Chinese tourist arrivals after Indonesia at 2,305 million in 2010 (see Fig. 4). Over the years, the size of China tourists gradually crept upwards to

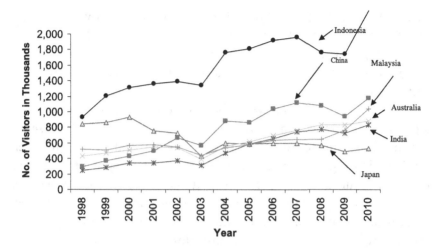

Fig. 4.   Top six visitor generating markets for Singapore (1998–2010).
Source: Singapore Tourism Board Statistics.

seventh position in 1998, third position in 2002 (over-taking Malaysia and Australia) and second position in 2003 (over-taking Japan). In 2008, China overtook India to become the second top Total Expenditure of Visitors (TEV) generator.

In the field of education, Singapore is an important destination for Chinese overseas students. In 2008, there were an estimated 97,000 foreign students in Singapore, a 13% increase from the 86,000 figure in 2007. The students coming to Singapore are mainly from China, India, Indonesia, Malaysia, Myanmar, South Korea, and Vietnam.[7] Furthermore, there is also extensive education collaboration between the two countries. Most recently, in November 2010, Singapore's renowned National University of Singapore and Nanyang Technological University signed separate agreements with the local municipal authorities in China to set up institutes in the Sino–Singapore

---

[7] Speech by Mr Lee Yi Shyan, Minister of State for Trade and Industry at the "Singapore Education Awards 2009", 19 March 2009 at http://app.mti.gov.sg/default. asp?id=148&articleID=17921. According to an unofficial figure, the number of Chinese students in Singapore comprises around 42% of the total number of foreign students.

Tianjin Eco-city and the Suzhou Industrial Park respectively.[8] In June 2010, Hwa Chong Institution (also a famous high school in Singapore) signed an MOU to have exchanges and mutual learning programs with a top local school in the Sino–Singapore Knowledge City in Guangzhou.[9]

Cultural exchanges between the two countries also cover various aspects. For instance, the *Little Nonya* (小娘惹), a television series produced in Singapore, was aired in China and was quite well received. During a trip by Singapore's Media Development Authority to China in July 2010, a total of nine agreements were signed that will pave the way for television audiences in China and Singapore to view more programs co-produced by the two countries.[10] Separately, but in the same month, the China–Singapore Film Co-production Agreement was signed that covers cooperation in the areas of theatrical films, telemovies, across live-action, animation and documentaries. This agreement will facilitate greater cinematic cross-pollination between the two countries in technical and creative know-how.

At the political level, the two countries have kept up the momentum of high-level exchanges. In 2010, Singapore leaders like Prime Minister Lee Hsien Loong, President S R Nathan, Deputy Prime Minister Wong Kan Seng, Deputy Prime Minister and Minister for Defense Teo Chee Hean, MM Lee Kuan Yew, Senior Minister Goh Chok Tong and Foreign Minister George Yeo have visited China. In November of the same year, Vice President Xi Jinping visited Singapore to commemorate the 20th anniversary of the establishment of diplomatic relations between the two countries. During Xi's visit, a bronze bust of Deng Xiaoping was unveiled, indicating the recognition by Singapore and China of Deng's contribution to the nurturing and building of the bilateral relationship. Xi also officiated at the ground-breaking ceremony of the China Cultural Center in Singapore.

---

[8] NUS, NTU to open research institutes in China (2010). *Straits Times*, 16 November.

[9] In 2007, Hwa Chong Institution became the first Singapore school to set up the Hwa Chong-Beijing Satellite Campus. It scored another first with the latest MOU to establish a Singapore presence in Guangzhou.

[10] This will cover telemovies, documentaries and concerts produced by each country.

A lesser known facet of Singapore's relations with China is Singapore's ties with Taiwan. Singapore subscribes to the "One-China" policy. Yet under this framework of "One China", Singapore has been accorded a certain degree of leeway by China to maintain relatively good ties with Taiwan. The October 1990 communiqué establishing diplomatic relations between Singapore and China contains only a short one paragraph that states that bilateral relations are to be built on the basis of the Five Principles of Peaceful Coexistence and the principles enshrined in the United Nations Charter, but it makes no mention of Taiwan. In contrast, in separate communiqués that China signed with Malaysia (in May 1974), the Philippines (in June 1975) and Thailand (in July 1975), specific references were made to the People's Republic of China as the "sole legal government of China" and that Taiwan is an "integral" or "inalienable" part of Chinese territory.

Singapore has also been able to send its soldiers to Taiwan to be trained under the "Starlight Project". This process started in 1975 before Singapore and China established formal relations. When Chinese Premier Li Peng visited Singapore in August 1990, he reportedly observed that China understood Singapore's need to set up a credible defense force and would not be unduly disturbed by its continued use of military training facilities in Taiwan. Two months after this, diplomatic relations were established.[11] To date, Singapore has continued to send its soldiers to Taiwan for military training. To avoid ruffling China's feathers, Singapore has kept a low profile on this issue with Taiwan.

IV. Effective High-level Collaborative Mechanism

The development of China–Singapore ties is overseen by a high-level institutional mechanism known as the Joint Council for Bilateral Cooperation (JCBC) that meets on a regular basis. The JCBC was launched by then Prime Minister Goh Chok Tong and Premier Wen Jiabao in

---

[11] Lee, LT (2001). China's relations with ASEAN: Partners in the 21st Century? *Pacific Review*, 13(1), 63–64.

November 2003. This mechanism has enabled both sides to periodi-
cally review the state of bilateral ties and proactively suggest ways to
improve existing cooperation or identify new areas to work on. The
JCBC also provides a useful platform for political leaders and officials
as well as businessmen from both sides to get to know each other better by collaborating on joint projects. This network of interactions has
helped to lay the groundwork for stronger political and economic ties.

Maintaining the momentum of the bilateral relationship, the
JCBC held its 7th meeting in Beijing chaired by Vice Premier Wang
Qishan and Deputy Prime Minister Wong Kan Seng in July 2010.
Under the JCBC are two Joint Steering Councils (JSCs), also headed
by Vice Premier Wang and DPM Wong, that oversee policy-related
issues on the Suzhou Industrial Park and the Sino–Singapore Tianjin
Eco-city. The collaboration on the industrial park and now the eco-
city provides vivid examples of how the two countries are constantly
finding ways to stay relevant and benefit from each other's growth.
The success of these two flagship projects have strengthened and will
add substance to bilateral ties.

Below the JCBC framework are seven other key bilateral cooperation councils that Singapore has with Shandong (1993), Sichuan
(1996), Liaoning (2003), Zhejiang (2003), Tianjin (2007), Jiangsu
(2007) and Guangdong (2009).

Singapore-Shandong Business Council (1993);
Singapore-Sichuan Trade & Investment Committee (1996);
Singapore-Liaoning Economic & Trade Council (2003);
Singapore-Zheiiang Economic & Trade Council (2003);
Singapore-Tianjin Economic & Trade Council (2007);
Singapore-Jiangsu Cooperation Council (2007);
Singapore-Guangdong Collaboration Council (2009).

They provide additional avenues for Singapore to explore meaningful collaboration with the respective Chinese provinces based on
their comparative strengths. Some of these projects include the Sino–
Singapore Guangzhou Knowledge City (that held its groundbreaking
ceremony in June 2010) and the Sino–Singapore Nanjing Eco High-
Tech Island (officially launched in May 2009). Singapore companies

are also taking the lead in the Jilin Food Zone that fits into Singapore's food diversification strategy.

V. Rough Patches

It is normal for bilateral relations, such as relation between Singapore and China, to encounter difficulties from time to time. Most notably, China reacted strongly to the visit by Deputy Prime Minister Lee Hsien Loong (DPM Lee) to Taiwan in July 2004 before he became Prime Minister a month later. China regarded the visit as a departure from Singapore's "One China" policy that would embolden the pro-independence forces in Taiwan to move further away from the mainland.

From Singapore's perspective, the purpose of the visit was for DPM Lee to obtain an update on the current situation and to understand how the Taiwanese saw things, in order to assess how the situation may evolve.[12] A conflict across the strait would have dire consequences not just for the involved parties, but the entire region (Singapore included), and for many years.[13]

Interestingly, Singapore had informed China of the visit before DPM Lee left for Taiwan "as a matter of courtesy" and China had asked that the visit be cancelled. Singapore reportedly gave China's representation a careful consideration but did not agree. A key reason cited was that to call off the trip at China's request would have undermined Singapore's right to make independent decisions, and damaged its international standing. As a small country, this is a vital consideration in its dealings with other countries.[14] An over-riding aspect of the conduct of Singapore's foreign policy has been a determined insistence that

---

[12] The Singapore Ministry of Foreign Affairs Media Resource Center, Transcript of questions and answers with DPM Lee Hsien Loong on his visit to Taiwan on 19 July 2004. http://app.mfa.gov.sg/2006/lowRes/press/view_press.asp?post_id=1098.

[13] *Ibid.*

[14] *Ibid.* For further details of the visit please refer to Prime Minister Lee Hsien Loong's National Day Rally 2004 Speech dated Sunday 22 August 2004, at the University Cultural Center (National University of Singapore) at http://www.gov.sg/nd/ ND04.htm.

it should not be pressured by larger powers.[15] Singapore wants to be seen as making its decision based on a hard-nosed calculation of what its national interests are. It regards itself as a long-time friend of both China and Taiwan and would like to conduct its relations with both in a way that is consistent with its "One China" policy.

In fact, under the "One China" policy, Singapore has attempted to value add to the development of stable cross-strait relations. In April 1993, Singapore momentarily played a bridging role by hosting the historic meeting between Wang Daohan (from China) and Koo Chenfu (from Taiwan), who headed unofficial organizations from both sides. It was subsequently told to stay out of China's internal matter when cross-strait relations deteriorated.[16] As mentioned above, Singapore, at the acquiescence of China, has also continued to send its troops to get trained in Taiwan due to a lack of training space in Singapore. These instances show how Singapore has attempted to position itself to be helpful to both China and Taiwan.

Even more recently, there had been unhappiness particularly on the part of Chinese netizens in response to remarks made by Singapore's Minister Mentor Lee Kuan Yew (MM Lee) on the need for the US to balance China. At a dinner hosted by the US–ASEAN Business Council in October 2009, MM Lee reportedly told his audience that "the size of China makes it impossible for the rest of Asia, including Japan and India, to match it in weight and capacity in about 20 to 30 years. So we need America to strike a balance".[17]

In response to the use of the word "balance", comments from Chinese netizens came fast and furious particularly after *Global Times*, a state-owned newspaper, and other Chinese media channels gave it

---

[15] Way back in October 1968, the Singapore government went ahead with the execution of two Indonesian marines who had bombed the MacDonald House killing innocent people despite the personal intervention of President Suharto. Writing on this episode, Leifer was of the view that this execution was a deliberate act of policy to demonstrate Singapore's determination to defend its independence in every way. See Leifer, M (1974). *The Foreign Relations of the New States*, p. 67. Hong Kong: Dai Nippon Printing Co.

[16] Lee, KY. *From Third World to First*, pp. 629–631.

[17] MM calls on US to retain key role in East Asia (2009). *Straits Times*, 29 October.

prominent coverage. More specifically, the word "balance" was carried in *Global Times* and other media channels to mean that the US should "counteract" China's rise or the US should be involved in Asian affairs as a "check against" China or worse, even to "contain" China. Comments by Chinese netizens range from the mild such as "Singapore trusting the US more than it trusts China", that MM Lee had treated the Chinese as outsiders although they had treated Singaporeans as "among their own" to the highly critical view that "Singapore is America's beachhead in containing China".[18]

It is the author's view that MM Lee had used the word "balance" in a factual and non-antagonistic sense to refer to the US as the only country that was able to establish some form of equilibrium vis-à-vis China. This was needed so that smaller countries like Singapore could have the political and economic space to maneuver. He had never intended to use the word "balance" in a negative way of containing China. Also, it is important to bear in mind the context in which MM Lee's remarks were made. It appears that he had also intended to stress to an American audience of the importance for the US to stay engaged in the Asia-Pacific region, at a time when the Americans were becoming inward looking in the wake of the 2008 financial crisis. Fortunately, at the Chinese official level, cooler heads prevailed. They seemed to have understood where MM Lee was coming from. Consequently, bilateral relations were not affected.[19]

Nevertheless, this episode raises a point that bears watching for others and especially for a small country like Singapore. China, with its rise in stature, will most likely be increasingly more sensitive to perceived slights or unfair criticisms of various aspects related to the country. In particular, its response to matters that it regards as its core

---

[18] Li Guangyao de yanlun baolu Xinjiapo shi Meiguo weidu Zhongguo de qiaotoubao (Lee Kuan Yew's Remarks Reveals that Singapore is America's Beachhead in Containing China) (2009). *Zhonghuawang luntan*, 4 November. http://military. china.com/zh_cn/critical3/27/20091104/15689477.html. See also MM's speech in US draws flak online in China (2009). *Straits Times*, 2 November.

[19] Beijing plays down controversy over MM Lee's remarks (2009). *Straits Times*, 7 November.

interests can be expected to be even stronger and more intense. The spat between China and Japan over the Senkaku or Diaoyutai Islands in September 2010 is one such example. On this matter, China showed not only the regional countries (Singapore included) but the rest of the world the leverage that it could bring to bear on Japan when an issue impinges on its core interests.

VI. Looking Forward

China and Singapore have a substantive relationship that extends into many areas. This has been made possible by the committed and visionary leadership on both sides, and at various levels, to constantly add value to the relationship. Such strong leadership will remain a key factor in sustaining the momentum of bilateral ties.

To sustain the momentum of bilateral ties, the two countries will need to constantly explore ways and means to be relevant to each other. In this way, they can expand common grounds and benefit from each other's growth. Already, the China Cultural Center is scheduled to be completed in Singapore in 2011, providing yet another avenue for furthering cultural relations between the two countries. In April 2012, the tripartite partnership among the newly-opened Singapore University of Technology and Design (SUTD, Singapore's fourth university), Zhejiang University and the Massachusetts Institute of Technology will kick in when SUTD admits its inaugural cohort of undergraduate students.

On a lighter but no less significant note, is the feverish preparation being made by the Singapore Zoo to receive two pandas from China in 2012. Already, in March 2011, a judging panel has selected the names of "Kai Kai" (凯凯 which means "successful") and "Jia Jia" (嘉嘉 which means "beautiful and fine") for these two pandas in a nation-wide competition held in Singapore.

While working on new areas, the two sides ought to work even more closely together to ensure the success of existing collaborative projects such as the Suzhou Industrial Park and Sino–Singapore Tianjin Eco-city so that they can generate greater synergies, and further enhance bilateral ties.

From time to time, differences may arise that affect relations between the two countries. This is unavoidable as China and Singapore are two different countries. What is more important is for both sides to respect each others' interests and properly manage these differences as they surface so as not to lose sight of the bigger strategic benefits of working together.

As a small and export-oriented country, Singapore would like to continue to see a stable, prosperous and responsible China. This will provide Singapore with the necessary economic and political space to grow, and to ride on China's growth. With the US and Europe preoccupied with their own domestic challenges, Singapore's ties with China, especially its economic linkages, will become even more important.

For China, a giant in many ways, the building of a more comprehensive relationship with Singapore on the continued basis of mutual respect and mutual benefit will underscore China's pledge to peaceful development. With its rising international clout, it is even more important for China to be cognizant of this. China can make a more lasting impression regionally and on the rest of the world if it can subscribe less to the conventional practice of might is right and appeal more to principles of mutual respect, fairness and win-win outcomes.

With realistic expectations and building on the basis of what has been achieved so far, there are good prospects for China–Singapore relations to grow from strength to strength.

Bibliography

Chin, P (2003). *My Side of History*. Singapore: Media Masters Pte Ltd.

Lee, KY (2000). *From Third World to First: The Singapore Story 1965–2000.* Singapore: Singapore Press Holdings.

Lee, LT (2001). China's relations with ASEAN: Partners in the 21st century? *Pacific Review*, 13(1), 63–64.

Leifer, M (1974). *The Foreign Relations of the New States.* Hong Kong: Dai Nippon Printing Co.

Chapter 12

VIETNAM–CHINA ECONOMIC RELATIONS: 2009–2010

DO Tien Sam and HA Thi Hong Van

Vietnam–China relations have improved since bilateral relations were normalized in 1991. The principles codified in their joint communiqués of *Friendly neighborhood, comprehensive cooperation, durable stability and future-oriented outlook* in 1999, *good neighbors, good comrades, good partners* in 2002 and *Comprehensive strategic cooperation partnership* in 2008 have reinforced mutual trust and built a good foundation for economic cooperation between two countries. This chapter examines Vietnam–China economic relations in the post-2008 financial crisis and identifies the achievements and limitations of bilateral economic relations. In addition, the paper assesses the challenges and opportunities toward greater Vietnam–China economic relations in the foreseeable future.

I. Context of Vietnam–China Relations and Vietnam's Economic Situation

1. *Vietnam's economic situation post-financial crisis*

The 2008–2009 Financial Crisis impacted negatively on Vietnam's economic growth. Indeed, the Vietnamese economy registered only 3.1% in the first quarter of 2008 — the lowest GDP growth between 2009 and 2010. Nevertheless, the country staged a recovery and its economic growth has been fairly high since — thanks to the government's stimulus package.[1] In 2009, the total investment capital in Vietnam increased 15.3% over the previous year and accounted for 42.8% of its GDP. Indeed, government investment capital comprised 21.8% of total investment in Vietnam. Investment capital from the private sector increased 13.9% while FDI decreased by 5.8%.[2] Despite the Financial Crisis, Vietnam enjoyed a moderately high economic growth, about 5.3% in 2009 and around 6.5% in 2010.[3]

The Financial Crisis also impacted on Vietnam's foreign trade. Exports are important to Vietnam's economy since it contributes to around 70% of the country's GDP. Up to November 2009, total export values decreased by 13.8% compared to the same period in the previous year.[4] Export values in 2009 decreased by US$5.5 billion compared to the year before.[5] In 2010, Vietnam's exports rebounded with US$69.82 million. This was an increase by 27.8% compared to the data obtained in 2009 (US$54.6 billion).[6] Imports suffered heavily from the Financial Crisis in 2009.Total import values of Vietnam in 2009 was US$69.45 billion decreased US$8.86 billion comparing with year 2008. However, in 2010, Vietnam's import values went up sharply with values of US$83.36 billion.[7]

---

[1] Le, QH (2010). Tổng quan kinh tế Việt Nam năm 2010 và khuyến nghị cho năm 2011. http://www.neu.edu.vn/?page=news_detail&portal=news&news_id=1291 [accessed in December 2010].

[2] Nhat, M and Ngoc, C (2009). "Kinh tế Việt Nam tăng trưởng 5.3%. http://vnexpress.net/gl/kinh-doanh/2009/12/3ba1744a/ [accessed in December 2010].

[3] Cap nhat tinh hinh phat trien kinh te Vietnam nam 2010 (2010). World Bank Report, September.

[4] Cap nhat tinh hinh kinh te Vietnam nam 2009 (2009). World Bank Report, December.

[5] General Statistics Office of Vietnam. http://www.gso.gov.vn/default.aspx?tabid= 217 [accessed in January 2010].

[6] Bao cao tinh hinh san xuat hoat dong cong nghiep, thuong mai Vietnam 9 thang dau nam 2010. Ministry of Industry and Commerce of Vietnam.

[7] General Statistic Office of Vietnam and calculated by the Author.

2. *Vietnam–China political relations*

The year 2010 was considered as a significant year which marked many important events for Vietnam–China friendship relations. That year was the 60th anniversary of establishing diplomatic relations between the two neighbors. Vietnam–China relations have achieved new progress. Many high-ranking visits and exchanges are made in recent years. Within the first eight months of 2010, there were 176 official bilateral visits.[8]

The leaders of both countries earmarked 2010 as Vietnam–China Friendship Year. Along with many important activities and events, Vietnam–China Youth Festival was successfully organized. This festival held in August 2010 at Guangxi, China attracting thousands of participants. Besides, the Protocol of Land Border Demarcation and Landmark Planting, Documents on Border Management and Documents on Border Gates and Vietnam–China Inland Border Gate Management in 14 July 2010 are important legal framework for building stable, friendship and peaceful border, and creating favorable conditions to build trans-border cooperation zones between two countries.

II. Trade Relations

Although Vietnam's foreign trade suffered heavily at the outset of the Financial Crisis, Vietnam–China trade relations further developed. In 2003, China surpassed Japan to become Vietnam's largest trading partner. In 2009, bilateral trade valued at US$21.05 billion accounted for 16.97% of total trade value of Vietnam. Vietnam's exports to China worth US$4.75 billion, accounted for 8.4% of total Vietnam export values. China is the third largest importer of importing Vietnamese goods, just behind the US and Japan. Vietnamese imports from China valued at US$16.3 billion accounted for 14.5% of total import values of Vietnam. Indeed, China is the largest importing partner of Vietnam.

---

[8] Ambassador Sun Guo Xiang's speech at the reception on the occasion of the 61st year of establishing the People Republic of China. *Chinese Studies Review*, 10. Hanoi, Vietnam.

In 2010, total bilateral trade values between two countries was US$27.37 billion accounted for 17.4% total trade values of Vietnam. Vietnam exports to China US$7.3 billion, accounted for 10.4% of total exporting values of Vietnam. Vietnam imports from China: US$27.37 billion, account for 24% of total import values of Vietnam. Total bilateral trade values in 2010 surpassed the target of US$25 billion in 2010 set by two countries leaders.

1. *Trade balance*

Table 1 reveals that bilateral trade between Vietnam and China expanded dramatically since 2000 but is rather unbalanced to China's advantage. Indeed, Vietnam's trade deficit with China has risen over the past decade. Vietnam's trade deficit with China in 2003 was US$1.7 billion compared to US$12.7 billion deficit in 2010 with China taking a big portion of Vietnam's total trade deficit. In 2009, Vietnam's trade deficit with China was a whopping 97% of Vietnam's total trade deficit. The deficit value in trading with China did not decrease much in 2010, and it comprised 94% of the total Vietnam's trade deficit with the world.

2. *Structure of export–import goods between two countries*

Generally, Vietnam's export goods to China comprise mostly raw material, food and consumer products. In the period 2000–2009, Vietnam's exports to China included four main categories:

- Raw materials (e.g., coal, oil, rubber, iron ore).
- Agricultural products (e.g., tea, vegetables, cashew nuts).
- Fresh and frozen sea food (e.g., shrimp, crab, fish).
- Consumer goods (e.g., handicrafts, fine arts, shoes, high quality household products).

Looking at the composition of export goods from Vietnam to China in the Table 2, we can see that raw materials and agriculture are the main exports. In 2009, coal exports alone accounted for 23.8% of

Table 1. Situation of bilateral trade between Vietnam and China.

Year	2000	2001	2002	2003	2004	2005	2006	2007	2008	2009	2010
Export–Import Values	2,957.2	3,047.2	3,654.3	4,870	7,192	8,739.5	10,420.9	16,356.1	20,187.8	21,046	27,376.6
Export Values	1,534.0	1,418.1	1,495.5	1,747.7	2,735.5	2,961	3,030	3,646.1	4535.7	4,746	7,308.8
Import Values	1,423.2	1,629.1	2,158.8	3,122.3	4,456.5	5,778.9	7,390.9	12,710	15,652.1	16,300	20,018.8
Trading Balances	110.8	211	663.3	−1,734.6	−1,721.1	2,817.9	−4,360.9	−9063.9	−11,116.4	−11,554	−12,710

Sources: Vietnam Ministry of Industry and Commerce and General Statistic Office of Vietnam.

Table 2.   Structure of export–import goods in 2009.

SITC	Import commodities	Import values	SITC	Export commodities	Export values US$ million
65	Textile yarn. Fabrics. Made-up articles. n.e.s. and related products	2.225.03	32	Coal. Coke and briquettes	1129.632
76	Telecommunications and sound-recording and reproducing apparatus and equipment	1.455.29	05	Vegetables and fruit	336.63
33	Petroleum. Petroleum products and related materials (Petroleum)	1.252.69	33	Petroleum. Petroleum products and related materials (crude oil)	667.50
74	General industrial machinery and equipment. n.e.s	983.85	65	Textile yarn. Fabrics. Made-up articles. n.e.s. and related products	138.83
67	Iron and steel	935.81	76	Telecommunications and sound-recording and reproducing apparatus and equipment	157.93
84	Articles of apparel and clothing accessories	884.93	77	Electrical machinery. Apparatus and appliances. n.e.s.	129.85
77	Electrical machinery. Apparatus and appliances. n.e.s.	860.07	28	Metalliferous ores and metal scrap	262.02
71	Power generating. Machines	690.09	24	Cork and wood	166.79
78	Road vehicles	642.34	75	Office machines and automatic data-processing machines	284.10
72	Machinery specialized for particular industries	610.80	85	Footwear	153.50

Source: Ha, THV (2011). Intermediate goods trade between Vietnam and China. In *Intra-regional Intermediate Goods Trade in the ASEAN and MRBCs*, M Kagami (ed.). Bangkok Research Center-IDE JETRO.

Vietnam's total export value to China. Crude oil comprised 14% in total export values. Raw materials export values comprised 43.3% in total export value to China in 2009. This pattern of export commodities to China has not changed much since 2000. Values of export products with codes 75, 76 and 77 (machinery and components for office and telecommunication etc) occupied 13.3% in the total of Vietnam's export goods values in 2009. Recently, these products have been exported to China due to the supply chains of Japanese Companies such as Canon, Sumiden and Hitachi etc. These companies invested in Northern Vietnam to supplement for their production networks in Huanan, China.[9] Although these products comprise only a small portion of the total exports to China, they appear to be a harbinger of change to the old pattern of exports predominantly based on raw material and agricultural goods. Products from Japanese supply chain in Vietnam may herald the trend of an Asian production network with components sourced from all over East Asia with final assembly in Chinese factories. Presumably, this will help underpin an insipient East Asian Community.

The composition of imported Chinese goods to Vietnam is very diverse. There were more than 200 kinds of products including four main product groups:

- Materials for footwear, textile and garments and chemicals.
- Machinery and equipment: Mechanical machinery, transport vehicles, health equipment, knitting and agricultural machinery, electric components etc.
- Gasoline and materials for constructions and agricultural cultivation (e.g., cement, iron, pesticides and fertilizer).
- Consumer products such as medicines, electronic products, textile fabrics and toys.

The composition of imported Chinese goods has changed considerably since the two countries normalized relations. Between

---

[9]Tran, VT (2010). Việt Nam trước dòng thác công nghiệp của Trung Quốc. http://www.tinkinhte.com/viet-nam/phan-tich-du-bao/gs-tran-van-tho-viet-nam-truoc-dong-thac-cong-nghiep-cua-trung-quoc.nd5-dt.133219.113121.html [accessed on 7 August 2010].

1991 and 1995, Vietnam imported mainly consumer goods from China such as traditional medicine, cotton, knitwear, clothes, soft drink etc. In the period 1996–2000, the composition of imported Chinese goods was more diversified. They are mainly consumer goods, equipment and materials for production. However, between 2000 and 2009, consumer goods were not the biggest category in terms of value. In 2009 alone, materials for textile and garment industry were the import category with the highest import values. Different kind of machinery imports also had high value to Vietnam. This trading pattern can be explained by the fact that the Vietnam's economic development level is lower than China's. Moreover, China has both the ability to compete at two levels — low skill products with other countries and participating well in global economic chains with developed countries. The pattern of export–import goods between Vietnam and China is illustrated a "north–south" trade relation, vertical trade relation.[10]

To reiterate, even though the Vietnamese economy was affected by financial crisis, Vietnam–China's trade relations grew unabatedly. However, the trading pattern is unbalanced and skewed to China's advantage, and Vietnam's trade deficit with China is soaring. It is apparent that the pattern of their bilateral trade illustrates a "north–south" (developed–developing) trade relation — a reflection of the fact that the two countries are at different stages and levels of their economic development. Moreover, Vietnam's enterprises still lack a strategy to improve their competitiveness. Therefore, Vietnamese manufactured products have difficulties in expanding in the Chinese market.

III. China's FDI in Vietnam

1. *China's FDI: 1991–2010*

China's FDI to Vietnam started to flow shortly after both countries normalized their relations in 1991. However, in the period 1991–1999, China's FDI activities in Vietnam were still modest. There were only 79 Chinese projects with registered capital amount of US$120 billion

---

[10] *Ibid.*

and China then ranked 20th place among 60 FDI investors in Vietnam. The growth rate of investment capital was slow and the average investment capital per project was small averaging US$1.5 million per project. Moreover, the investment duration for a project was short, around 15 years per project. Investment sectors were mainly hotels, restaurant, light industries and consumer good producing with low and medium technologies level and small amount of investment capital.

Between 2000 and 2009, China's FDI to Vietnam increased considerably. By 2009, accumulate FDI projects numbered 657 with registered capital worth US$2.67 billion. China ranked 14th place among 43 countries and territories which invested in Vietnam. In 2009, there were 48 China FDI projects with investment capital of US$180.4 million in Vietnam. The number of China's FDI projects was a half of number projects in 2008 and total registered capital was about one-third comparing with year 2008. Decreasing number of FDI projects illustrated the consequences of global financial crisis happened in 2008. By December 2010, China ranked 11th place out of 55 countries and territories invested in Vietnam (see Table 3).

2. Characteristics of China's FDI in Vietnam

There was a shift in investment sectors in the period 2000–2009. As stated earlier, the Chinese invested mainly in hotels, restaurants and light industries. Presently, investment sectors have expanded and are more diversified with 17 major sectors. Processing and manufacturing industry attracted the largest number of projects and investment capital (547 projects accounted for 73% of total investment projects and amount of investment capital of US$2.195 billion). Real estate sector is one of the most attractive investment sectors in Vietnam today. Cumulative Chinese investment capital is valued at US$382 million. Vietnam is undergoing industrialization and modernization, and demand for building housing and infrastructure is very high. Not surprisingly, the third sector which attracts Chinese investors is construction with investment capital amount of US$ 237 million (see Table 4).

Chinese investment capital per project is still small with an average of US$2 million per project while the average FDI capital/project in

Table 3. List of large FDI partners of Vietnam in 2010.

Order	Partners	New licensed projects	New registered investment capital (million US$)
1	Singapore	88	4,350.2
2	South Korea	256	2,038.8
3	Netherlands	14	2,364.0
4	Japan	114	2,040.1
5	United States	52	1,833.4
6	Taiwan	95	1,180.6
7	British Virgin Islands	23	726.3
8	Malaysia	19	412.6
9	Cayman Islands	5	500.7
10	British West Indies	1	475.9
11	People's Republic of China	84	172.8
12	Sweden	3	285.2
13	Hong Kong	43	154.0
14	Thailand	16	131.9
15	Russia	5	139.3
55	**Total**	**969**	**17,229.6**

Source: Foreign Investment Agency, Ministry of Planning and Investment of Vietnam. http://www.mpi.gov.vn/portal/page/portal/bkhdt/dtttnn(fdi)/sltk.

Vietnam is US$17 million in 2010. Apparently, large Chinese companies are still hesitant to invest in Vietnam. Nevertheless, in comparison with Chinese investments in the previous period, Chinese FDI in Vietnam has improved in the scale of investment projects. There are indeed bigger investment projects such as some outstanding projects below:

- Building Hai Phong Industrial Zone: US$175 million
- Building Tien Giang Industrial Zone: US$100 million
- Dong Nai Shoes Factory: US$60 million
- Thai Binh Steel Factory: US$33 million
- Building Hoang Dong Urban Center in Lang Son Province: US$27.75 million

Table 4. Investment sectors.

Order	Sectors	Number of projects	Total capital (US$)	Percentage in total number of projects
1	Processing and Manufacturing Industry	547	2,195,465,732	73.62
2	Real Estate	11	382,807,380	1.48
3	Construction	46	237,049,771	6.19
4	Agriculture, Forestry and Aquatic Sector	24	72,264,461	3.23
5	Hotels and Restaurants	15	71,101,700	2.02
6	Mineral Exploring	6	41,259,467	0.81
7	Retail and Wholesale	30	29,913,473	4.04
8	Producing and Distributing Electricity, Gas and Air-conditioning	1	28,437,000	0.13
9	Information and Communication	7	28,305,600	0.94
10	Science and Technology Contracts	24	23,914,560	3.23
11	Art and Entertainment	6	19,771,536	0.81
12	Finance, Banking and Insurance	2	15,300,000	0.27
13	Transportation and Warehouse Services	11	15,234,000	1.48
14	Other Services	4	8,222,505	0.54
15	Medical Care and Social Assistance	6	3,571,400	0.81
16	Administrative and Supporting Services	2	1,650,000	0.27
17	Water Supply and Waste Disposal	1	600,000	0.13
Total		**743**	**3,174,868,585**	**100.00**

Source: Foreign Investment Agency, Ministry of Planning and Investment of Vietnam. http://www.mpi.gov.vn/portal/page/portal/bkhdt/dtttnn(fdi)/sltk.

- Project of producing starch Wolfram in Quang Ninh: US$20 million
- Project of producing electronic component in Da Nang: US$18 million

Chinese investors in Vietnam come mainly from the Southern provinces of China. The provincial sources are: Guangdong — 44 projects with total investment capital US$560 million; Guangxi: 50 projects valued at US$520 million; Yun Nan: 47 projects at US$52 million. Yunnan and Guangxi are two Chinese provinces bordering Vietnam. Therefore, it is convenient for investors in these two provinces to invest in Vietnam. Their investment projects are located mainly in the Northern border provinces of Vietnam of Lang Son, Lao Cai and Lai Chau. Many investors from Guangdong province are also investing in Vietnam. Between 2008 and 2009, Guangdong province and Vietnam organized Guangdong–Vietnam Economic and Trade Cooperation Forum which attracted many Guangdong entrepreneurs.[11]

Chinese investments are present in 52 provinces and cities of Vietnam. However, investment projects are unevenly distributed among provinces. Cities and provinces which have good infrastructure and convenient transportation networks have received large number of projects and investment capital such as Hai Phong, Binh Duong, Ba Ria-Vung Tau, Ho Chi Minh, Ha Noi, Quang Ninh, and Dong Nai. This pattern is similar to other FDI partners who have invested in Vietnam (see Table 5). A significantly difference is that China investment also concentrated in the Northern border provinces of Vietnam as Lao Cai, Lang Son, Cao Bang, and Lai Chau. However, these provinces' development level is still low with undeveloped infrastructure. Nevertheless, economic cooperation between Yunnan, Guangxi (China) and Northern Border Provinces of Vietnam has further developed.

---

[11] Nguyen, PH (2010). Dau tu Trung Quoc tai Vietnam 10 nam qua. *Chinese Studies Review*, 1. Hanoi, Vietnam.

Table 5. 10 Major cities and provinces.

Order	Provinces and cities	Number of projects	Total registered investment capital (US$)
1	Lao Cai	24	469,609,547
2	Hai Phong	41	331,464,226
3	Tien Giang	9	195,080,000
4	Binh Dương	58	192,125,737
5	Ba Rịa-Vung Tau	7	189,845,720
6	TP Ho Chi Minh	72	187,618,509
7	Ha Noi	135	164,720,778
8	Quang Ninh	36	155,203,448
9	Bac Giang	29	134,902,000
10	Đong Nai	24	125,305,666
Total of 52 provinces and cities		**743**	**3,174,868,585**

Source: Foreign Investment Agency, Ministry of Planning and Investment of Vietnam. http://www.mpi.gov.vn/portal/page/portal/bkhdt/dtttnn(fdi)/sltk.

In summary, China is now ranked 11th out of 55 countries and territories which have invested in Vietnam but may well break into the top ten soon.

IV. Opportunities and Challenges for the Development of Vietnam

1. *Opportunities*

About global situation: The Financial Crisis has stimulated the reorganizing of the global economy. Having weathered the Crisis better than the US and the EU, it is probable that East Asia (including China and Vietnam) will play a larger role in global economy.

Regional situation: From 1 January 2010, the ASEAN–China Free Trade Area (ACFTA) officially started with ASEAN-6 (with ASEAN-4 in 2015). This free trade area will unite a big market of 1.9 billion consumers with GDP worth around US$2 trillion.

China situation: China is entering a new phase of economic development based more on domestic demand in response to the slowdown of its exports caused by the Global Financial Crisis. This is an opportunity for Vietnam enterprises to take advantage of a booming Chinese domestic market.

2. *Challenges*

At the time of writing, the US, EU and Japan are still mired in economic difficulties. Global stock markets and foreign exchange markets have been volatile. Therefore, the present global economy is neither stable nor predictable and may well impact on the Chinese and Vietnamese economies reliant on foreign trade. ACFTA has been established but the benefits gained for each member is not similar due to their different levels of development. Vietnam will face a big challenge when participating fully in this free trade area in 2015. At that time, Vietnam's trade deficit with China might well increase. Moreover, Vietnam is still faced with undeveloped infrastructure and a lack of trained human resources.

V. Conclusion

Notwithstanding territorial disputes in the South China Sea, Vietnam–China economic relations between 2009 and 2010 have indeed been enhanced. Bilateral trade values between two countries increased even though Vietnam's total foreign trade value has decreased in 2009. In 2010, China's FDI projects have increased 1.5 times compare to the year before. Efforts to strengthen friendship between the two countries have played an important role to stimulate economic cooperation. Some suggestions to further enhance economic relations between Vietnam and China are: Mutual respect and trust with a win–win mentality, comprehensive cooperation, development together, expanding new fields of trade, and to reduce the considerable bilateral trade deficit.

Bibliography

Ambassador Sun Guo Xiang's speech at the reception on the occasion of the 61st year of establishing the People Republic of China (2010). *Chinese Studies Review*, 10. Hanoi, Vietnam.

Bao cao tinh hinh san xuat hoat dong cong nghiep, thuong mai Vietnam 9 thang dau nam 2010. Ministry of Industry and Commerce of Vietnam.

Cap nhat tinh hinh kinh te Vietnam nam 2009 (2009). World Bank Report, December.

Cap nhat tinh hinh phat trien kinh te Vietnam nam 2010 (2010). World Bank Report, September.

General Statistics Office of Vietnam. http://www.gso.gov.vn

Ha, THV (2011). Intermediate goods trade between Vietnam and China. In *Intra-regional Intermediate Goods Trade in the ASEAN and MRBCs*, M Kagami (ed.). Bangkok Research Center-IDE JETRO.

Le, QH (2010). Tổng quan kinh tế Việt Nam năm 2010 và khuyến nghị cho năm 2011. http://www.neu.edu.vn/?page=news_detail&portal=news&news_id=1291 [accessed in December 2010].

Nguyen, PH (2010). Dau tu Trung Quoc tai Vietnam 10 nam qua. *Chinese Studies Review*, 1, 60–67, Hanoi, Vietnam.

Nhat, M and Ngoc, C. (2009) (2010). Kinh tế Việt Nam tăng trưởng 5.3%. http://vnexpress.net/gl/kinh-doanh/2009/12/3ba1744a/. [accessed in December 2010]

Tran, VT (2010). Việt Nam trước dòng thác công nghiệp của Trung Quốc. http://www.tinkinhte.com/viet-nam/phan-tich-du-bao/gs-tran-van-tho-viet-nam-truoc-dong-thac-cong-nghiep-cua-trung-quoc.nd5-dt.133219.113121.html [accessed on 7 August 2010].

Chapter 13

MALAYSIA–CHINA ECONOMIC RELATIONS: 2000–2010

LEE Kam Hing

This chapter examines the exponential rise in Malaysia–China economic ties after the 1997–1998 Asian Financial Crisis. Indeed, the growth in bilateral trade and investments since that crisis has been quite remarkable. The compounded growth rate of bilateral trade has been estimated at 25.6% over eight years from 1997 to 2004 while investments have grown steadily. This chapter also analyzes the rate and changing pattern in trade, the nature of investments made, and the significance of these changes for their overall bilateral ties. Trading and investment ties are poised for further growth especially when underpinned by China's economic rise as the world's second largest economy by 2010 and its strong and sustained demand for Malaysian commodities. Although the 2008–2009 American Financial Crisis and its aftermath have impacted on China and Malaysia in a globalized world, both countries have fared better economically than the US, EU, and Japan. Economic relations between Malaysia and China are anticipated to deepen and broaden notwithstanding the 2008–2009 Financial Crisis.

Malaysia is China's largest trading partner in the ASEAN region with almost a quarter of China's trade with the region in 2009. China is also the seventh largest investor in Malaysia. Strong ties between Malaysia and China were built on Kuala Lumpur's initiative as the first ASEAN country to establish diplomatic relations with Beijing. Despite allegations that China had supported a communist-led insurgency in Malaysia during which there were no diplomatic ties between the two countries, Tun Abdul Razak, Malaysia's second Prime Minister, visited China in 1974. Apparently, Tun Razak sought to normalize relations with Beijing in order to secure the electoral support of the ethnic Chinese minorities in Malaysia. Other countries in ASEAN followed suit. When Tun Razak's son Dato Seri Najib Tun Razak became Prime Minister in April 2009, one of his first official trips abroad was to China.[1]

Nevertheless, it was Dr Mahathir Mohamad, Malaysia's fourth Prime Minister, who expanded trade and travel between both countries in the 1990s. Mahathir engaged with Beijing more closely and declared that China is not a threat to the region. Hence, when Mahathir proposed an East Asia Economic Caucus (EAEC) in 1990, China gave strong support despite the hesitations of other Asian countries. It was Mahathir who mooted the idea of ASEAN + 3 (China, Japan, and South Korea) which would connect China to ASEAN through a multilateral institution.[2]

Bilateral ties were further consolidated during Najib's visit in June 2009 to China which led to the signing of 16 MOUs and other important agreements.[3] Witnessed by Najib and Chinese Prime Minister Wen Jiabao, the first agreement was the "Malaysia–China Joint Action Plan on Strategic Cooperation." The second was the "Abolition of Visa Agreement" which covers travel of holders of diplomatic and official or service passports. Personnel under these categories no longer require visas for travel to China or Malaysia. The third document signed was the "Marine Science and Technology Cooperation Agreement". The final MOU was the "Malaysia–China Postal Agreement". There had been, in addition to these, the Avoidance of Double Taxation Agreement, Maritime Transport Agreement, Bilateral Trade Agreement, Investment Guarantee Agreement, Air Services Agreement, Agreement on Co-operation in

---

[1] Lim, TS (2009). Renewing 35 years of Malaysia–China relations: Najib's visit to China. *EAI Background Brief*, No. 460, East Asia Institute, National University of Singapore, 23 June.

[2] Liow, JCY (2000). Malaysia–China relations in the 1990s: The maturing of a partnership. *Asian Survey*, XL(4), July/August, 672–690.

[3] More Malaysia–China MOUs taking off (2009). *The Edge*, 11 November.

Science and Technology, and Sports Agreement, all of which have been in force since 2002.[4]

Malaysia–China economic ties in the 2000 to 2010 period strengthened against a background of the 1997–1998 Asian Financial Crisis and its aftermath. However, the Chinese economy escaped relatively unscathed from the crisis in contrast to many other Asian economies. The crisis gave China an opportunity to establish a stronger presence in the region by offering financial assistance to several badly-affected countries in the region. More importantly, Beijing did not devalue its currency which could have led to a vicious cycle of competitive devaluation among the Asian countries. Recovery from the crisis was, in part, due to growing trade between China and Southeast Asia.

While trade and economic issues are important, regional geopolitical concerns are equally paramount in Malaysia–China relations. Beijing seeks good relations with the ASEAN states as evidence of its foreign policy strategy of "peaceful rise". Moreover, closer ties and integration with Southeast Asia are attractive to China especially when the Northeast Asian states of China, South Korea and Japan are lacking in institutionalization like ASEAN. Furthermore, by achieving a free trade agreement with ASEAN under the China–Asean Free Trade Agreement, China expects to play a more influential role in the ASEAN + 3 framework.[5]

However, Malaysia remains wary of a rising China but perceives that this concern is vastly outweighed by mutual economic benefits through increased trade and economic cooperation. According to Kuik Cheng-chwee, Malaysia's strategy towards China is based on a "limited bandwagoning" — a kind of hedging between balancing and full "bandwagoning".[6] Pure balancing (by aligning Malaysia with

---

[4] Malaysia approves 80 investments from Chinese companies (2002). *AsiaPulse News*, 17 May.

[5] Ku, SCY (2006). China's changing political economy with Malaysia: A regional perspective. In *China and Malaysia in a Globalizing World: Bilateral Relations, Regional Imperatives and Domestic Challenges*, EK-K Yeoh and HK Chung (eds.), pp. 29–44. Kuala Lumpur: Institute of China Studies, University of Malaya.

[6] Kuik, C-C (2008). The essence of hedging: Malaysia and Singapore's response to a rising China. *Contemporary Southeast Asia: A Journal of International and Strategic Affairs*, 30(2), 159–185.

other great powers against a rising China) will alienate Beijing and is a risky strategy for a small country. But pure "bandwagoning" with China will offend the US superpower and is unacceptable in the context of Malaysian domestic politics predicated on Malay ethnic dominance. (Malaysian Chinese as immigrants and ethnic minorities are obliged to accept Malay political dominance).

Notwithstanding Malaysian domestic ethnic politics and geo-strategic concerns, it is prudent for Kuala Lumpur to establish close relations with Beijing to boost its own economic growth. Furthermore, according to Kuik, closer Malaysia–China ties may boost Malaysia's agenda for a new East Asian economic order and consequently enhance its regional and international standing. Indeed, Malaysia hopes to leverage on China to promote its conception of the East Asian regionalism. Simply put, Malaysia's ambitious goal of East Asian multilateralism will not come into fruition without China's consent and cooperation.

I. Growing Trade and Investments

1. *Trade*

The growth in bilateral trade between Malaysia and China has been most remarkable. In the last 10 years from 2000 to 2009, compound growth rate of this trade has been estimated at 25.6%. The trade figures obtained in 2009 show that China has become Malaysia's number one trading partner. In that year China was Malaysia' second export market and since 2008 is the top country for Malaysia's imports. Significantly, between 2002 and 2009, Malaysia had continuous trade deficits with China. There has also been a changing pattern in this growing trade largely arising from the expanding Asian production network (with components sourced from all over East Asia with final assembly in Chinese factories) which China and ASEAN countries are part of. Within this production network of largely multi-national corporations, there is considerable inter and intra-regional trade.

Figures in the following tables (Tables 1–14) illustrate this inter and intra-regional trade. The early trade flow between Malaysia and

Table 1.   Bilateral trade between Malaysia and China (RM billion).

Year	Total exports	Total imports	Total trade	Balance of trade
1994	5.06	3.58	8.64	1.48
1995	4.90	4.30	9.20	0.60
1996	4.80	4.72	9.52	0.08
1997	5.26	6.27	11.53	−1.01
1998	7.77	7.26	15.03	0.51
1999	8.80	8.15	16.96	0.65
2000	11.51	12.32	23.83	−0.81
2001	14.68	14.47	29.16	0.21
2002	20.01	23.33	43.34	−3.32
2003	25.79	27.63	53.42	−1.84
2004	32.15	39.29	71.44	−7.14
2005	35.22	49.88	85.10	−14.66
2006	42.66	58.23	100.89	−15.57
2007	53.04	64.90	11794	−11.86
2008	63.44	66.85	130.29	−3.41
2009	67.24	60.66	127.90	6.58

Source: Kwek, K-T and Tham, S-Y (2007). Trade between Malaysia and China: Opportunities and challenges for growth. In *Emerging Trading Nation in an Integrating World: Global Impacts and Domestic Challenges of China's Economic Reform*, EK-K Yeoh and E Devadason (eds.), p.124. Kuala Lumpur: Institute of China Studies, University of Malaya.

Table 2.   Top ten tourist receipts, 2008–2010.

Country of residence	Tourist Receipts (RM Million)		
	2008	2009	2010
Singapore	22,990.7	27,499.2	28,417.4
Indonesia	4,570.7	4,478.5	4,758.7
China	2,469.0	2,783.5	3,129.6
Brunei	2,545.7	2,496.3	2,624.8
Australia	1,697.5	2,139.8	2,388.4
India	1,496.1	1,601.8	1,807.1
United Kingdom	1,407.4	1,690.4	1,647.4
Thailand	1,686.0	1,468.7	1,480.9
Japan	1,136.0	1,033.0	1,144.1
Philippines	745.2	753.1	913.1

Source: Tourism Malaysia: www.tourism.gov.my [accessed 16 June 2012].

Table 3. Performance of Chinese tourist arrivals.

Year	Tourist arrivals	Tourist receipts (RM mil)	Average per capita (RM)	Average per diem (RM)	Average length of stay (night)
1993	81,874	170.9	2090.0	321.5	6.5
1994	95,789	180.7	1912.0	261.9	7.3
1995	103,130	171.9	1666.7	276.1	6.0
1996	135,743	305.0	2247.0	387.4	5.8
1997	158,679	294.1	1863.7	300.5	6.1
1998	159,852	363.8	2276.0	490.6	4.6
1999	190,851	531.2	2783.5	568.1	4.9
2000	425,246	1226.4	2884.0	565.5	5.1
2001	453,246	1270.0	2802.2	438.5	6.4
2002	557,647	1487.5	2667.5	459.9	5.8
2003	350,597	903.8	2578.0	477.4	5.4

Source: Departing Visitor Survey Unit, Planning & Research Division of Tourism Malaysia.

China was dominated by the export of raw materials from Malaysia, mainly rubber in the 1980s and later by palm oil. China was the largest market for Malaysia's rubber and palm oil. In 1994, palm oil comprised some 37% of Malaysia–China trade while Electrical and Electronic (E and E) products were only 3.3%. However in 2004, palm oil had dropped to 16.5% while E and E products had risen to 39.5% and chemicals and chemical products to 12.2%. In 2006, E and E products were a large component of Malaysia's export to China. The top four export of Malaysia to China are E.E. products, palm oil and products, chemical products and mineral oil.[7]

---

[7] Li, Y (2006). An analysis of recent Sino–Malaysian trade relations. In *China and Malaysia in a Globalizing World: Bilateral Relations, Regional Imperatives and Domestic Challenges*, EK-K Yeoh and HK Chung (eds.), pp. 127–136. Kuala Lumpur: Institute of China Studies, University of Malaya.

Table 4. Malaysia's top ten trading partners (%).

2006		2007		2008		2009	
USA	16.0	USA	13.4	Singapore	13.0	China	12.9
Singapore	13.7	Singapore	13.2	USA	11.7	Singapore	12.7
Japan	10.8	Japan	10.9	Japan	11.5	USA	11.1
China	9.4	China	10.6	China	11.0	Japan	11.0
Thailand	5.4	Thailand	5.1	Thailand	5.1	Thailand	5.7
Republic of Korea	4.4	Republic of Korea	4.3	Republic of Korea	4.3	Republic of Korea	4.2
Taiwan	4.0	Taiwan	4.1	Indonesia	3.8	Indonesia	4.1
HK	3.9	HK	3.8	Taiwan	3.6	HK	4.0
Germany	3.2	Indonesia	3.5	HK	3.5	Germany	3.3
Indonesia	3.1	Germany	3.4	Germany	3.2	Taiwan	3.3
Others	26.2	Others	27.5	Others	29.2	Others	27.7
Total	**100.0**		**100.0**		**100.0**		**100.0**

Sources: Malaysia External Trade Development Corporation (Matrade), Kuala Lumpur, various years. http://www.matrade.gov.my/ [accessed 30 November 2010 and 1 March 2011].

Table 5. Malaysia's top ten trading partners (RM billions).

2006		2007		2008		2009	
USA	170.80	USA	149.21	Singapore	154.07	China	127.90
Singapore	146.94	Singapore	146.46	USA	138.84	Singapore	125.31
Japan	115.78	Japan	120.78	Japan	135.57	USA	109.22
China	100.89	China	117.94	China	130.29	Japan	108.71
Thailand	57.45	Thailand	56.99	Thailand	60.78	Thailand	56.16
Republic of Korea	47.20	Republic of Korea	47.97	Republic of Korea	51.18	Republic of Korea	41.23
Taiwan	42.26	Taiwan	45.17	Indonesia	44.88	Indonesia	40.32
HK	41.79	HK	42.65	Taiwan	41.96	HK	39.66
Germany	33.84	Indonesia	39.13	HK	41.74	Germany	33.25
Indonesia	33.08	Germany	38.25	Germany	37.80	Taiwan	32.90
Others	279.70	Others	305.42	Others	345.71	Others	273.58
Total Trade	**1,069.74**		**1,109.97**		**1,182.82**		**988.24**

Sources: Malaysia External Trade Development Corporation (Matrade), Kuala Lumpur, various years. http://www.matrade.gov.my/ [accessed 30 November 2010 and 1 March 2011].

Table 6. China's top trade partners 2009 ($ billions).

	Country	Volume
1	United States	298.3
2	Japan	228.9
3	Hong Kong	174.9
4	South Korea	156.2
5	Taiwan	106.2
6	Germany	105.7
7	Australia	60.1
8	Malaysia	52.0
9	Singapore	47.9
10	India	43.2

Source: PRC General Administration of Customs, China's Customs Statistics.

Table 7. Top ten countries China exports to (US$ billions).

Countries	2005	Countries	2008	Countries	2009
United States	162.9	United States	252.3	United States	220.8
Hong Kong	124.5	Hong Kong	190.7	Hong Kong	166.2
Japan	84	Japan	116.0	Japan	97.9
South Korea	35.1	South Korea	74.0	South Korea	53.7
Germany	32.5	Germany	59.2	Germany	49.9
Netherlands	25.9	Netherlands	46.0	Netherlands	36.7
United Kingdom	19	United Kingdom	36.1	United Kingdom	32.3
Singapore	16.6	Russia	33.0	Singapore	30.1
Taiwan	16.6	Singapore	32.3	India	29.7
Russia	13.2	India	31.5	Australia	20.6

Sources: 2005 — http://www.suite101.com/content/chinas-top-trading-partners-a3413, 2008 — PRC General Administration of Customs, China's Customs Statistics, 2009 — http://www.uschina.org/statistics/tradetable.html.

Table 8. Top ten countries China imports from (US$ billions).

Countries	2005	Countries	2008	Countries	2009
Japan	100.5	Japan	150.7	Japan	130.9
South Korea	76.8	South Korea	112.2	South Korea	102.6
Taiwan	74.7	Taiwan	103.3	Taiwan	85.7
United States	48.7	United States	81.4	United States	77.4
Germany	30.7	Germany	55.8	Germany	55.8
Malaysia	20.1	Australia	37.4	Australia	39.4
Singapore	16.5	Malaysia	32.0	Malaysia	32.3
Australia	16.2	Saudi Arabia	31.0	Brazil	28.3
Russia	15.9	Brazil	29.7	Thailand	24.9
Thailand	14.0	Thailand	25.6	Saudi Arabia	23.6

Sources: 2005 — http://www.suite101.com/content/chinas-top-trading-partners-a3413, 2008 — PRC General Administration of Customs, China's Customs Statistics, 2009 — http://www. uschina.org/statistics/tradetable.html.

Table 9. Malaysia's top ten export markets (%).

2006		2007		2008		2009	
USA	18.8	USA	15.6	Singapore	14.6	Singapore	14.0
Singapore	15.4	Singapore	14.6	USA	12.5	China	12.2
Japan	8.9	Japan	9.1	Japan	10.7	USA	11.0
China	7.2	China	8.8	China	9.6	Japan	9.8
Thailand	5.3	Thailand	5.0	Thailand	4.8	Thailand	5.4
Hong Kong	4.9	Hong Kong	4.6	Hong Kong	4.3	Hong Kong	5.2
Netherlands	3.6	Netherlands	3.9	Republic of Korea	4.1	Republic of Korea	3.8
Republic of Korea	3.6	Republic of Korea	3.8	India	3.7	Australia	3.6
India	3.2	Australia	3.4	Australia	3.7	Netherlands	3.3
Australia	2.8	India	3.3	Netherlands	3.5	Indonesia	3.1
Others	26.3	Others	27.9	Others	28.6	Others	28.6
Total	**100.0**		**100.0**		**100.0**		**100.0**

Sources: Malaysia External Trade Development Corporation (Matrade), Kuala Lumpur, various years. http://www.matrade.gov.my/ [accessed 30 November 2010 and 1 March 2011].

Table 10. Malaysia's top ten export markets (RM billion).

2006		2007		2008		2009	
USA	110.59	USA	94.52	Singapore	97.02	Singapore	77.20
Singapore	90.75	Singapore	88.51	USA	82.70	China	67.24
Japan	52.21	Japan	55.24	Japan	70.69	USA	60.58
China	42.66	China	53.04	China	63.44	Japan	54.42
Thailand	31.18	Thailand	29.98	Thailand	31.63	Thailand	29.85
Hong Kong	29.14	Hong Kong	27.97	Hong Kong	28.21	Hong Kong	28.85
Netherlands	21.43	Netherlands	23.60	Republic of Korea	26.96	Republic of Korea	21.10
Republic of Korea	21.29	Republic of Korea	23.03	India	24.73	Australia	20.00
India	18.78	Australia	20.40	Australia	24.36	Netherlands	18.42
Australia	16.71	India	20.20	Netherlands	23.44	Indonesia	17.29
Others	154.22	Others	168.66	Others	189.85	Others	158.34
Total	**588.97**	**Total**	**605.15**	**Total**	**663.01**	**Total**	**553.3**

Sources: Malaysia External Trade Development Corporation (Matrade), Kuala Lumpur, various years. http://www.matrade.gov.my/ [accessed 30 November 2010 and 1 March 2011].

Table 11.　Malaysia's top ten import origins (%).

2006		2007		2008		2009	
Japan	13.2	Japan	13.0	China	12.9	China	14.0
USA	12.5	China	12.9	Japan	12.5	Japan	12.5
China	12.1	Singapore	11.5	Singapore	11.0	USA	11.2
Singapore	11.7	USA	10.8	USA	10.8	Singapore	11.1
Thailand	5.5	Taiwan	5.7	Thailand	5.6	Thailand	6.1
Taiwan	5.5	Thailand	5.3	Taiwan	4.8	Indonesia	5.3
Republic of Korea	5.4	Republic of Korea	4.9	Republic of Korea	4.7	Republic of Korea	4.6
Germany	4.4	Germany	4.6	Indonesia	4.7	Taiwan	4.3
Indonesia	3.8	Indonesia	4.2	Germany	4.3	Germany	4.2
Philippines	2.6	Hong Kong	2.9	Hong Kong	2.6	Hong Kong	2.5
Others	23.4	Others	24.1	Others	26.2	Others	24.4
Total	**100.0**		**100.0**		**100.0**		**100.0**

Sources: Malaysia External Trade Development Corporation (Matrade), Kuala Lumpur, various years. http://www.matrade.gov.my/ [accessed 30 November 2010 and 1 March 2011].

Table 12.　Malaysia's top ten import origins (RM billion).

2006		2007		2008		2009	
Japan	63.57	Japan	65.54	China	66.85	China	60.66
USA	60.21	China	64.90	Japan	64.88	Japan	54.29
China	58.23	Singapore	57.96	Singapore	57.06	USA	48.64
Singapore	56.19	USA	54.69	USA	56.13	Singapore	48.12
Thailand	26.28	Taiwan	28.71	Thailand	29.15	Thailand	26.31
Taiwan	26.22	Thailand	27.01	Taiwan	25.09	Indonesia	23.03
Republic of Korea	25.91	Republic of Korea	24.93	Republic of Korea	24.23	Republic of Korea	20.12
Germany	21.06	Germany	23.42	Indonesia	24.18	Taiwan	18.47
Indonesia	18.17	Indonesia	21.38	Germany	22.45	Germany	18.42
Philippines	12.65	Hong Kong	14.68	Hong Kong	13.53	Hong Kong	10.81
Others	112.3	Others	121.60	Others	136.25	Others	106.08
Total	**480.77**		**504.81**		**519.8**		**434.94**

Sources: Malaysia External Trade Development Corporation (Matrade), Kuala Lumpur, various years. http://www.matrade.gov.my/ [accessed 30 November 2010 and 1 March 2011].

Table 13. Malaysia: Exports of top ten products to China, 2005–2006.

Products	2005 RM million	2005 Share (%)	2006 RM million	2006 Share (%)	Changes (%)
Manufactured goods	25,501.3	4.8	30,863.0	5.2	21.0
Agricultural goods	7,809.3	1.5	9,941.2	1.7	27.3
Mining goods	1,423.3	0.3	1,367.9	0.2	−3.9
Total	**35,221.0**	**6.6**	**42,660.4**	**7 .2**	**21.1**
Electrical & electronic products	15,292.0	2.9	19,171.5	3.3	25.4
Palm oil	4,448.0	0.8	5,817.9	1.0	30.8
Chemicals & chemical products	3,899.9	0.7	4,135.2	0.7	6.0
Crude rubber	1,991.9	0.4	2,949.4	0.5	48.1
Optical & scientific equipment	982.7	0.2	1,441.4	0.2	46.7
Rubber products	290.3	0.1	1,440.1	0.2	*
Machinery, appliance & parts	1,255.4	0.2	1,150.3	0.2	−8.4
Refined petroleum products	928.5	0.2	998.5	0.2	7.5
Saw logs & sawn timber	1,166.5	0.2	991.9	0.2	−15.0
Manufactures of metal	628.0	0.1	876.9	0.1	39.6

Source: http://www.miti.gov.my/cms/content.jsp?id=com.tms.cms.article.Article_e4be6bca-c0a81573-1ca11ca1-6a9d9b92.

Likewise, the bulk of earlier Malaysia's imports from China were goods such as foodstuff, vegetable oil, fruits, livestock, textile yarn and fabrics. However, more recently E and E products, plus machinery appliances represent 65% of total trade. From 2000 the structure of trade goods remained relatively stable: The top four exports of

Table 14.   Malaysia: Imports of top ten products from China, 2005–2006.

Products	2005 RM million	2005 Share (%)	2006 RM million	2006 Share (%)	Change (%)
Manufactured goods	45,965.5	10.6	54,486.5	11.3	18.5
Agricultural goods	1,796.2	0.4	1,966.4	0.4	9.5
Mining goods	1,045.0	0.2	412.0	0.1	−60.6
Total	**49,880.4**	**11.5**	**58,225.7**	**12.1**	**16.7**
Electrical & electronic products	30,723.5	7.1	35,472.0	7.4	15.5
Machinery, appliance & parts	3,505.9	0.8	4,278.3	0.9	22.0
Chemicals & chemical products	2,049.3	0.5	2,830.8	0.6	38.1
Manufactures of metal	1,365.8	0.3	2,100.7	0.4	53.8
Iron & steel products	1,774.0	0.4	1,976.1	0.4	11.4
Textile & clothing	1,504.8	0.3	1,877.3	0.4	24.8
Optical & scientific equipment	999.1	0.2	1,281.7	0.3	28.3
Manufacture of plastics	755.2	0.2	992.2	0.2	31.4
Vegetables, roots, tubers	600.9	0.1	680.5	0.1	13.3
Transport equipment	468.5	0.1	578.6	0.1	23.5

Source: http://www.miti.gov.my/cms/content.jsp?id=com.tms.cms.article.Article_90af0953-c0a81573-4f994f99- 7fda78a3.

China to Malaysia are: E and E products, machinery and mechanical parts, chemical products, and textiles.[8]

This shift in bilateral trade pattern underline the rapid growth of capital-intensive products especially electrical machinery and

---

[8] Loke, W-H (2007). Malaysia's and China's comparative advantages in selected manufacturing goods. In *Emerging Trading Nation in an Integrating World: Global Impacts and Domestic Challenges of China's Economic Reform*, EK-K Yeoh and E Devadason (eds.), pp. 153–170. Kuala Lumpur: Institute of China Studies, University of Malaya.

mechanism appliance which are also the largest export category for China and Malaysia. It also underlines how significant intra-industry trade is between the two countries. Many of the components and products requiring less skill and are cheaper to produce in China are exported to Malaysia to be used for assembly and testing. Malaysia acts as value-added manufacturer and designer in the E and E supply chain. This complementary trade keeps costs down in a thriving regional production platform.[9]

2. Investments

Mutual investments by Malaysia and China have increased though not as spectacular in extent as bilateral trade. China ranked sixth in its investments in Malaysia in 2010, behind major Western and Asian countries (Tables 15–19). In 2002, it was reported that there were 50 China-based companies operating in the manufacturing and non-manufacturing sectors in Malaysia. These companies were involved in the production of mild steel products, ceramics, cut thread, palm-oil based products, gloves, marine gearboxes, power presses and parts, mobile cranes, truck cranes, and rough terrain cranes.

In 2002, Malaysia approved 80 investment applications from China with a capital outlay of US$1billion. But actual amount invested was much lower. This can be compared to 2009 when it was reported that Malaysian Industrial Development Authority approved 17 projects from China which amounted to only US$47.4 million.[10] Likewise, Malaysia's investments of US$385 million in China in 2004 were very small compared to Singapore's US$2 billion over. Still,

---

[9]Devadason, E (2007). Malaysia–China trade patterns in manufactures: How big is production sharing? In *Emerging Trading Nation in an Integrating World: Global Impacts and Domestic Challenges of China's Economic Reform*, EK-K Yeoh and E Devadason (eds.), pp. 138–152. Kuala Lumpur: Institute of China Studies, University of Malaya.

[10]"China's investment in Malaysia insignificant (2010). *IntellAsia News Online*, 20 May.

Table 15. Approved FDI projects in Malaysia: Top 10 sources, 2001–2005 (RM million).

Country	2001	2002	2003	2004	2005	Total
United States	3,412	2,668	2,182	1,059	5,155	14,476
Germany	2,603	5,055	170	4,724	388	12,940
Japan	3,366	587	1,295	1,011	3,672	9,931
Singapore	2,228	1,019	1,225	1,515	2,920	8,907
UK	123	168	3,870	151	99	4,411
UAE	—	0.9	3,952	—	—	3,952.9
Republic of Korea	1,703	369	447	325	674	3,518
China	**2,923**	**55**	**247**	**187**	**40**	**3,452**
Taiwan	1,140	252	622	415	431	2,860
Netherlands	69	607	316	99	1,674	2,765

Sources: IDE-Jetro and MITI.

Malaysia is the second largest among ASEAN countries in investments in China.

As the Malaysian economy recovered from the 1997 Asian Financial Crisis, its companies ventured abroad. The Malaysian government encouraged overseas expansion and former Prime Minister Dr. Mahathir Mohamed led many trade missions to explore investment opportunities. The growing number of Malaysian companies venturing abroad coincided in a period when China was opening up its economy.[11] This created high expectations among Malaysian businessmen who saw the potential of the vast Chinese market.[12]

---

[11] Kwek, K-T and Tham, S-Y. *Op. cit.* pp. 123–137.
[12] Wang, W and Lin, Z (2008). Investment in China: The role of Southeast Asian Chinese businessmen. In *China in the World: Contemporary Issues and Perspectives*, EK-K Yeoh and JH-L Loh (eds.), pp. 147–160. Kuala Lumpur: Institute of China Studies, University of Malaya.

Table 16. Foreign investment in approved projects by country, 2006–2009 (RM million).

Country	2006 RM	No.	2007 RM	No.	2008 RM	No.	2009 RM	No.
USA	2,476.6	38	3,020.0	33	8,669.0	22	2,345.0	19
Australia	2,560.1	20	1,685.1	17	13,105.8	20	323.1	13
Netherlands	3,284.2	13	1,690.4	9	1,795.7	19	479.7	21
Hong Kong	84.5	9	59.8	14	83.6	7	5,315.7	7
China	**134.1**	**19**	**1,883.2**	**13**	**35.7**	**17**	**162.2**	**17**
Japan	4,411.6	81	6,522.7	60	5,594.9	63	7,041.4	54
Germany	232.3	15	3,756.8	26	4,438.3	19	425.0	14
Switzerland	46.1	7	61.3	7	873.2	8	85.9	8
Singapore	1,884.7	130	2,952.2	108	2,004.3	112	1,992.5	92
Taiwan	405.5	70	408.7	41	911.6	32	716.1	32
United Kingdom	642.0	17	385.3	20	850.5	23	325.8	24
Others *	4,066.4	188	11,000.6	167	7,736.4	179	2,932.3	129
Total	**20,227.9**	**607**	**33,425.9**	**515**	**46,098.8**	**521**	**22,144.7**	**430**

Note: *Includes West Asian countries, Austria, Belgium, Brunei, Canada, Denmark, France, India, Indonesia, Italy, New Zealand, Norway, Sweden, Switzerland, Thailand, Philippines, Republic of Korea and other unspecified countries.
Source: Ministry of Finance Malaysia, Economic Report 2010/2011.

The August 2006 issue of *Malaysian Business* listed some 54 companies that had gone abroad or have expanded their overseas business.[13] Most of these were publicly-listed companies in the KLSE. But in fact the number of those that have gone overseas is much larger as the list did not include small companies, and many of the smaller ones are Chinese-owned. Table 22 shows the *Malaysian Business* list of companies venturing overseas. Some 16 Malaysian companies had invested in China. China then was the third largest destination for

---

[13] Kaur, G (2006). Taking on the World (Cover story: Global Malaysians). *Malaysian Business*, 1–15 August, 24–28.

Table 17.   Projects approved by major country, January–July 2011 and 2010 (USD).

Country	January–July 2011		2010	
	No. of projects	Foreign Investment (USD)	No. of projects	Foreign Investment (USD)
Japan	48	824,319,439	61	1,308,235,280
USA	14	788,283,988	47	3,811,229,070
Singapore	54	659,374,419	81	700,237,991
Netherlands	11	399,379,690	13	303,436,321
Taiwan	14	398,740,714	41	407,757,853
Korea, Rep.	6	343,926,427	7	64,689,128
China	**13**	**339,303,351**	**20**	**207,640,938**

Notes: To avoid the disclosure of confidential information, the list excludes countries with less than three (3) approved projects. 2011: US$1 = RM2.95, 2010: US$1 = RM3.08.
Source: Malaysian Industrial Development Authority (MIDA).

Table 18.   Foreign direct investment by Malaysia in China (US$ million).

Year	No. of Projects	Changes %	Actual amount	Changes %
2003	350	9.72%	251	−31.76%
2004	352	0.57%	385	53.38%
2005	371	5.40%	361	−6.14%
2006	336	−9.43%	451	24.93%
2007	285	−15.18%	397	−11.96%
Total	**4,232**	—	**4,681**	—

Source: http://my.mofcom.gov.cn/aarticle/zxhz/zhxm/200802/20080205401564.html.

Malaysian companies, coming after Indonesia and India where both had attracted 17 companies. Malaysian investments in China are concentrated in the coastal cities with three-quarters in the cities of Shanghai, Guangzhou, Jiangsu, Beijing, and Tianjin.[14]

---

[14] Trade, investment and economic cooperation between China and Southeast Asia: The case of Malaysia. Unpublished report of Joint Research between the Institute of Developing Economies (Japan External Trade Organization) and Socio-Economic and Environmental Research Institute, Penang), November 2003–February 2004, p. 12.

Table 19. Actual foreign direct investment by ASEAN countries in China (US$ million).

	1997	1998	2003	2004
Singapore	2,606.4	3,404.0	2,058.4	2,008.1
Malaysia	381.8	340.5	251.0	385.0
Philippines	155.6	179.3	220.0	233.2
Thailand	194.0	205.4	173.5	178.7
Indonesia	80.0	69.0	150.1	104.5
Brunei	0.1	1.8	52.6	96.1
Cambodia	5.5	2.9	12.5	20.7
Burma	2.7	5.1	3.5	8.8
Laos	0.4	1.1	0.4	4.3
Vietnam	1.5	14.1	3.3	1.1
Total	3,428.0	4,223.2	2,925.4	3,040.5

Source: HKTDC, 2006.

There were also push factors for companies going abroad. Rising labor costs at home as well as a small domestic market with limited investment opportunities were major factors. Thus Indonesia is particularly attractive especially for the plantation sector where many Malaysian companies have opened up oil palm estates. Lower labor costs in Vietnam and Cambodia have also drawn Malaysian investments there and in China its gargantuan market. Simply put, returns from investments at home are seen as less attractive. This is aggravated by the government's liberalization policy which led to the entry of foreign companies seeking a larger share of the domestic market. And in anticipation of the entry of foreign banks, local institutions such as Malayan Banking, Public Bank and Hong Leong Bank are establishing overseas branches or buying banks abroad.[15]

Moreover, Malaysian Chinese companies are concerned with what they regarded as the increasingly limited domestic market due to NEP-related policies. They find increasing difficulties competing

---

[15] Malaysia's intrepid companies (2006). *Malaysian Business*, 1–15 August, pp. 30–40.

against *bumiputra*-owned companies or government-linked corporations for government projects.[16] Chinese companies also encounter high costs in doing business including acquisition of land, delays in approval, and the need to surrender 30% of equity to *bumiputra* participation. Investing overseas particularly China is, therefore, an attractive option or hedge.

A few who invested early in China did relatively well especially in retail, hotel, and property sectors. Two of the biggest are William Cheng (the Lion Group) and Robert Kuok (Shangrila Hotels and others). William Cheng's Parkson Stores had very early success. The other big groupings are the Genting Group (oil and gas exploration), Hong Leong Group (property development), Kuala Lumpur–Kepong (edible oil), and Tan Chin Nam's Ipoh Garden (property development).[17] Several Malaysian private colleges such as Inti International College also set up institutions in China.

Robert Kuok has many businesses in China and elsewhere. His most well-known is the hotel chain associated with the Shangri-La Group. By March 2005, Kuok has acquired 21 Shangri-La Hotels in China, (not including two in Hong Kong) which is a sizeable percentage of their worldwide total of 55 Shangri-La Hotels. In the hotel business, a very core business of the Robert Kuok Group, the China involvement is, therefore, very important.

A number of Malaysian companies investing in China, through their investment and expansion of business overseas, would now be considered as transnational companies (TNCs). Robert Kuok's business would be one of them. But Petronas[18] will certainly be the largest

---

[16] The New Economic Policy (NEP) was an affirmative action policy coordinated by the state that was put in place as a result of ethnic riots Kuala Lumpur in 1969. The policy accorded preferential treatment to the indigenous population known as *Bumiputera* (primarily Malay) from education to employment and ownership of stocks in efforts to reduce economic disparity among the various ethnic groups.

[17] Kuala Lumpur Stock Exchange Website. http://www.bursamalaysia.com/website/listing/lcwebsites.htm.

[18] Petronas (Petroleum Nasional Berhad) is a Malaysian company set up in August 1974 and wholly owned by the Malaysian Government entrusted with developing the entire oil and gas resources of the country.

of Malaysia's TNC. It recently was ranked 56th among the world's top 100 non-financial TNCs in terms of foreign assets. Other Malaysian non-financial companies that made it to the list were YTL Berhad and Sime Darby.

II. Projects by Government-linked Companies

Government-linked companies of Malaysia, during this period 2000 to 2010, embarked on large and ambitious joint projects with Mainland Chinese companies in Malaysia and China. These and other ventures abroad require huge funding, skills and technology which only government-linked companies have the capacity to offer. In the context of Malaysia's domestic politics, these largely Malay-dominated government-linked companies also ensured *bumiputra* (indigenous) participation in China's trade and business ventures. Hence during Prime Minister Najib's visit to China in 2009, an MOU was signed between the Malay Chamber of Commerce Malaysia and the China Council for the Promotion of International Trade for the business communities of both countries.

Probably the most important and successful joint venture of the two countries' government-linked companies is that between Petronas, Malaysia's national oil company, and two Chinese oil and gas companies. These companies entered into a 25-year agreement signed in July 2006 which obliges Petronas to provide China with up to 3.03 million metric tones of LNG per year. In October 2009, Petronas made the first delivery to Shanghai LNG Company which is jointly owned by Shenergy Group (55%) and CNOOC Gas and Power (45%). The agreement marked Petronas' first long-term contract with China, and represented a major breakthrough for Petronas in China's energy sector. Petronas and Sinopec, China's oil company are also involved in joint oil exploration in several countries including Sudan and Iran.

Another government-linked Malaysian company involved in China is Sime Darby Berhad. Sime Darby is one of the largest conglomerates in Southeast Asia. In November 2005, it formed the Weifang Sime

Darby Port Company to operate Weifang port.[19] In July 2009, it signed an agreement with Weifang City to develop a 700-square km area to cater for the 13 surrounding universities. Described by Prime Minister Najib as an "iconic milestone project", the proposed Weifang City project is one of the biggest ventures ever undertaken by a foreign company in China and the first in Malaysia–China economic ties.[20]

The participation of a Chinese engineering firm in the construction of the second bridge linking Penang to the mainland highlights the growing participation of China in Malaysia's infrastructure development. Construction work on the bridge started in late November 2008). The 24 km-long bridge is constructed by China Harbor Engineering Company, a subsidiary of China Construction and Communication Group, and United Engineering Bhd, a subsidiary of Khazanah, Malaysia's state investment body. When completed the bridge would be the longest in Southeast Asia. The project, financed by a loan of US$800 million from the Chinese government, reflects the growing role of China in Malaysia's infrastructure development. The first Penang bridge was built by a Korean company.

Indeed, agreements signed between Malaysia and China during President Hu Jintao's visit to Malaysia in November 2009 will see greater involvement of Chinese companies in Malaysia's construction projects. One of the first agreements signed was the awarding to a company from China the contract to build the 250 km rail double-track between Johor Baru in southern Malaysia to Gemas costing US$2.5 billion. This project is part of the Malaysian government's program of eventually double-tracking the entire rail system in the country.

Companies from China have also been invited to invest in the Mengkuang Dam project in Penang while a Malaysia–China Hydro JV Consortium has been formed to complete the Bakun Dam in Sarawak. Companies from China will also be involved in setting up a RM4 billion pulp and paper mill in Sarawak in East Malaysia and an

---

[19] OSK Malaysia Equity (2005). *Investment Research Daily News*, 21 November.
[20] Sime Darby looking at 100 sq km development near Weifang City, China (2009). Bernama, the Malaysian National News Agency, 21 July.

aluminum smelting plant.[21] Some of these joint venture projects are funded by soft loans taken from the US$10 billion fund that China had set up as Beijing seeks greater economic presence in the Southeast Asian region. The performance record of Chinese companies such as China Hydro which completed the Three Gorges Dam in China, has also helped them to gain projects in Malaysia.

III. Trends in Investment

When Malaysians first invested in China, the latter had yet to integrate into the international economy. Furthermore, many Western and Japanese investors avoided China in the aftermath of the 1989 Tienanmen Incident. However, in an about turn, many Western and Japanese investors have since sought to take advantage of cheaper Chinese labor and to penetrate the burgeoning Chinese domestic market. They brought in larger investment funds and expertise in technology and marketing which Malaysian companies could not match, and they proved more attractive as partners to local Chinese corporations.

Malaysian investments in China are likely to fall into the following categories. One will be the continuation of investment by small-scale businesses in food, cosmetics, textiles, and rubber products. A second category takes advantage of being a first mover or having a niche or boutique business. A third category is the manufacturing of component parts for companies operating in China and/or for Malaysian manufactures in Malaysia.

William Cheng's Parkson Stores is an example of the first mover. Despite facing recently-arrived competition from big Western departmental chains such as Carrefour and Tesco, the Parkson chain in China may thrive because it has already established a reputed brand in Beijing, and is making its presence felt in many of the smaller cities in China ahead of other bigger department chains.[22]

---

[21] More Malaysia–China MoUs taking off (2009). *The Edge*, 11 November.

[22] Lee, PP and Lee, KH. China's economic rise and its impact on Malaysian Chinese business. In *Southeast Asia's Chinese Business in an Era of Globalisation*, L Suryadinata (ed.), pp. 162–190. Singapore: Institute of Southeast Asian Studies.

Niche investments range from hotel development of the highest value, such as the Shangri-La chain to the building of a few apartment blocks carried out by the Tan Chin Nam group. The Tan Chin Nam group seized on the idea that there were many Russians doing trading business in Beijing and hence needed suitable facilities and accommodation. Thus, this group constructed a building in Beijing with the lower floors being used by Russians doing business in Beijing and the upper floors as a hotel for them to stay in.[23]

Such investments are likely to survive for two reasons. First, there is an increasing demand for property and retail business from a growing Chinese middle class. Second, property development and the retail business have remained the key strengths of Malaysian Chinese business here in Malaysia. These are areas where they can compete in China. Malaysians are unable to compete with the Taiwanese in manufacturing given the Taiwanese strength in this sector and the impressive success record they have in China in such investments. And for big entrepreneurial and trading deals involving China and the Western world, the Malaysian Chinese cannot match the Hong Kong Chinese. And they are unable to undertake big state sponsored projects like Singapore can with the Singapore–Suzhou project.

Malaysian companies face other major problems. China has become increasingly a competitive place to do business not only because of the entry of Western corporations but also from local companies which are able to produce or offer similar products at lower costs.[24] Malaysians also complain about the lack of transparency of business conducted in China, the frequent amendment of local laws, the difficulties experienced in finding the right Chinese partners, and the need to deal with a powerful and arbitrary bureaucracy. But as China becomes more exposed to international norms of doing business, it is likely that doing business will become more transparent for Malaysians than what they had experienced in the early 1990s. Indeed, Robert Kuok advised Malaysian Chinese investors not to rely

---

[23] Interview with Dato Tan Chin Nam, 15 March 2006.
[24] Kuok, R (2004). Western China[is] full of business opportunities. *Malaysia–China Business Magazine* (publication of Malaysian-China Chamber of Commerce), 12, p. 91.

too much on *guanxi* but to be straight in their dealings with the Mainland Chinese.[25]

It is not easy to evaluate the performance of Malaysian private investments and business in China. According to one interviewee, the successful investors tend not to highlight their success to avoid attracting competition while the less successful ones would frequently voice their complaints about business conditions in China. For Malaysian Chinese investors particularly William Cheng and Robert Kuok, their business operations in China continue to be important. For William Cheng's Lion Group, one indicator is the number of employees the Group has in China. The figures, as of August 2004, show that of the total number of 40,576 employees in their Group, 24,691 are in China.[26] This comes to 60.9%. Another indicator is in the number of retail outlets in China the Lion Group has. There are 15 such outlets (well known as Parkson stores) in China out of 41 in total of their operations, and this is quite a significant percentage.[27]

IV. Financial Services: Banks, Currency and Stock Exchange

Malaysia and China have taken several measures in the financial services sector to enhance bilateral trade and investments. Certainly, the most important move was to allow the Bank of China to reopen in Malaysia. The Bank of China which had a branch in then Malaya in 1939 reopened in December 2000 after it had ceased earlier operations in 1959. Since its reopening in Kuala Lumpur, it set up several branches including in Penang and Muar. On a reciprocal basis, Malayan Banking Bhd set up a branch in Shanghai.[28]

---

[25] *Ibid.*, p. 81.
[26] Corporate Information, Lion Group, 1 March 2005.
[27] Chia, OP (2008). Malaysian investments in China: Market forces or political needs? In *China in the World: Contemporary Issues and Perspectives,* EK-K Yeoh and JH-L Loh (eds.), pp. 61–69. Kuala Lumpur: Institute of China Studies, University of Malaya.
[28] Bank of China resumes operation in Malaysia (2000). *China Daily,* 16 December; Bank of China reopens its branch in Northern Malaysia (2009). *China Daily,* 17 October.

In April 2010, the Industrial and Commercial Bank of China (Malaysia) Berhad (ICBC Malaysia), a subsidiary of ICBC China (the world's largest bank by market capitalization) opened another branch in Malaysia. The opening was witnessed by Prime Minister Najib.[29] The presence of ICBC is significant because many of its customers have economic and trade ties with Malaysian enterprises. Some has direct investments in Malaysia, and thus ICBC Malaysia could service these bilateral economic and trade exchanges. Furthermore, ICBC has a network of branches across the Middle East and Asia, including the ASEAN region. This enables ICBC customers in Malaysia to access the bank's operation network across Asia.[30]

To facilitate bilateral trade, the central banks of both countries signed on 8 February 2009 a three-year 80-billion-yuan ($11.7-billion or RM40 billion) currency swap agreement. This currency swap will boost the amount of yuan that Malaysian banks can draw on while servicing local companies that use the Chinese currency to trade.[31] This currency swap is the third signed by China after similar agreements in January with Hong Kong for a 200-billion-yuan swap agreement and with the central bank of South Korea earlier in December 2008 to expand a currency swap deal to the equivalent of US$26 billion from an existing US$4 billion. The agreement will certainly ease present liquidity problems for banks and traders in the Malaysia–China trade.

Steps have also been taken by Malaysia and China to encourage investments in the two countries' bond and share markets. In September 2010, Malaysia's central bank bought yuan-denominated bonds for its reserve. This move is significant. Even though China has been signing trade currency deals with trading partners like Malaysia it has remained cautious about opening up its capital markets across borders. The Malaysian central bank manages some US$100 billion

---

[29] Industrial and Commercial Bank of China (Malaysia) formally opens (2010). Industrial and Commercial Bank of China, 28 April.

[30] China's ICBC gets nod to open 4 branches in Malaysia (2010). *Business Times*, 29 April.

[31] Malaysia and China establish currency swap (2009). *Star*, 8 February.

of reserves.[32] In August 2010, Beijing announced that the Chinese yuan would be allowed to accumulate abroad as a result of trade settlement or central bank swaps and for it to be funneled back into the mainland's interbank bond market. China's banking regulator has recognized Malaysia as an approved investment destination, paving the way for an inflow of Chinese funds into this country. Malaysia, having promoted itself well as an international Islamic finance hub, might attract Chinese investors looking for exposure into syariah-compliant investment products.

An equally significant development was the listing of several China-based companies in the Kuala Lumpur Stock Exchange. The listing of these China-based companies allows them to tap into funds of Malaysian investors. The first listing was in 2006. Since August 2010, five China-based companies have been trading in the main board of the KLSE. These are: K-Star Sports Ltd, Multi Sports Holdings Ltd, Xidelang Holdings Ltd, Sozo Global Ltd and Xingquan International Sports Holdings.[33] All these companies are manufacturing consumer products such as sports wear. Financial analysts reported that the companies have sound fundamentals and were making good profits.

The initial market response to the listing was favorable. However, share prices of these companies soon afterwards fell below the initial offering price.[34] Analysts suggest that the poor performance of China-based portfolios was due to promoters of the companies selling their shareholdings immediately on listing. The public perception was that promoters and major shareholders were cashing out and this rattled the Malaysian investing public. Furthermore, there had been a sell-down earlier of Singapore-listed China companies following reports of their accounting irregularities. Attempts were made especially by officials of

---

[32] *Star*, 21 September 2010.

[33] Chinese companies seeking to list in Malaysia must lift investors confidence (2010). *Star*, 10 May; Malaysia welcomes more listings by Chinese firms (2010). *Star*, 31 August.

[34] Chinese sportswear firms on expansion trail: Malaysian-listed China sportswear companies (2009). *The Edge*, 28 December.

the KLSE to assure that the KL-listed China companies have proper governance including its annual company reports to its shareholders.[35]

V. Tourism and Education

With the opening of China to Malaysians coupled with the rising wealth of Mainland Chinese, bilateral tourism and education have expanded.

1. *Tourism*

Over the last ten years, the number of tourists from China to Malaysia has doubled from 501,590 in 2000 to more than one million in 2009. Other than travelers from Malaysia's close neighbors especially Singapore, the number of Chinese visitors are vastly larger than those from Japan, Korea, the US, Australia, and UK. Southeast Asia is the most popular destination for Chinese tourists and Malaysia ranks high among ASEAN countries for Chinese tourists

The Chinese tourist, increasingly, is also spending more on purchases, food and hotels. While not the number one spender in per diem terms, Chinese tourists are among the top ten, with those from the Middle East ranking higher. But because the Chinese tourists come in such large numbers, the financial impact of their tourism is very significant. Table 2 shows gross tourist receipts from the Chinese in 2010 totaling RM 3,129 million or US$985 million. It is no wonder that Malaysia is keen to tap into this Chinese tourist market. Tourism from Malaysia to China is also considerable. According to the China National Tourism Association, about 440,000 Malaysians visited China in 2000. Indeed, Malaysian visitors are the fifth largest among countries in China. The Chinese Mainland also attracts Malaysian Muslims who can now visit Islamic sites in China rather than have to go through, since September 2001, immigration hassles in the US and Europe.

---

[35] Don't stereotype China companies here, says Yusli (KLSE CEO) (2009). *The Edge*, 8 October.

Table 20. Tourist arrivals in Malaysia by country 2000–2010.

	2000	2005	2006	2007	2008	2009	2010
Singapore	5,420,200	9,634,506	9,656,251	10,492,692	11,003,492	12,733,082	13,042,004
Thailand	940,215	1,900,839	1,891,921	1,625,698	1,493,789	1,449,262	1,458,678
Indonesia	545,051	962,957	1,217,024	1,804,535	2,428,605	2,405,360	2,506,509
Brunei	195,059	486,344	784,446	1,172,154	1,085,115	1,061,357	1,124,406
Philippines	81,927	178,961	211,123	327,140	397,884	447,470	486,790
Vietnam	7,969	52,543	63,866	119,973	122,933	149,685	159,271
China	501,590	432,570	532,914	789,783	949,864	1,019,756	1,130,261
Japan	455,981	340,027	354,213	367,567	433,462	395,746	415,881
Taiwan	213,016	172,456	181,829	201,311	190,979	197,869	211,143
S. Korea	72,443	158,177	189,464	224,867	267,461	227,312	264,052
India	132,127	225,789	279,046	422,452	550,738	227,312	690,849
West Asia	49,179	153,282	186,821	245,302	264,338	284,890	228,668
USA	184,100	151,354	174,336	204,844	223,249	228,571	232,965
Australia	236,775	265,346	277,125	320,363	427,076	533,382	580,695
UK	237,757	240,030	252,035	276,213	370,591	435,091	429,965

Source: Tourism Malaysia, various years.

2. Education

Between 2000 and 2010, more Chinese students were studying in Malaysia. In 2008, the immigration department recorded 10,355 students from China with valid international student pass. This figure is, however, far less than the 62,582 in the US, 63,543 in Australia and 50,755 in the UK in 2006. But with rising fees and living costs in Western countries, the number of those coming to Malaysia is expected to grow. In turn, 3,000 Malaysian students studied in Chinese universities. This figure may go up when the Malaysian government recognizes a number of Chinese universities (Table 21).

The coming of Chinese students to study in Malaysia followed the liberalization of higher education and establishment of twinning colleges and private universities. With educational liberalization,

Table 21. International students statistics: Number of valid international student passes to Malaysia (as at 31 December 2008).

No.	Country	Private higher education institutions	Public higher education institutions	Total
1.	**China**	**2,385**	**7,970**	**10,355**
2.	Indonesia	3,828	6,192	10,020
3.	Iran	2,998	3,247	6,245
4.	Nigeria	538	5,516	6,054
5.	Bangladesh	418	3,168	3,586
6.	Yemen	1,212	1,846	3,058
7.	Botswana	4	2,358	2,362
8.	Sudan	632	1,407	2,039
9.	Iraq	1,186	467	1,653
10.	Pakistan	175	1,475	1,650
	Total	**20,343**	**49,916**	**70,259**

Source: Immigration Department — 14 January 2009.

Table 22. Malaysian companies abroad, 2006.

Company	Country/region invested
AP Land Bhd	Australia
Astro All Asia Networks PLC	Indonesia, Hong Kong, Brunei
Berjaya Group	Cayman Islands, Singapore, UK, Hong Kong, Guyana, Australia, US, British Virgin Islands, Indonesia, Brunei, China, India, Vietnam, Argentina, Colombia, Mexico, Brazil, Peru, Philippines, Portugal, the Netherlands, Thailand, South Africa
Bina Puri Holdings Bhd	India, Thailand
Bumi Highways Bhd	India
Century Logistics Holdings Bhd	Thailand
Chemical Company of Malaysia Bhd	Indonesia, Singapore, Vietnam
CIMB Bhd	Singapore, Indonesia, Hong Kong
Dato Ishak Ismail	South Africa, Australia, Cambodia, UK, Indonesia, Gabon
Eversendai Corporation Sdn Bhd	Thailand, Indonesia, Hong Kong, Bahrain, Saudi Arabia, UAE
Fraser and Neave Holdings Bhd	China, Thailand
Gamuda Bhd	India, Taiwan, Qatar, Indochina, South Asia, Middle East
Genting Group	Asia, UK, Australia, the Americas, Indonesia, India, China
Goldis Bhd	China, Singapore, Hong Kong
Golden Hope Plantations Bhd	Indonesia
Green Packet Bhd	China
Ho Hup Construction Bhd	India
Hong Leong Group	Hong Kong, Singapore, UK
Hovid Bhd	India
IJM Corporation Bhd	India
IngressCorporation Bhd	Thailand, India, Indonesia
IOI Corporation	Netherlands, US, Egypt, Canada

(Continued)

Table 22. (*Continued*).

Company	Country/region invested
Kerry Group	Hong Kong, Singapore, Thailand, China, Indonesia, Fiji, Australia
Khazanah Nasional Bhd	India, Indonesia, Singapore, Hong Kong
Kuala Lumpur Kepong	Indonesia, China, UK
Kulim (M) Bhd	Indonesia, Papua New Guinea, Singapore
Kumpulan Guthrie Bhd	Indonesia, Thailand
LCL Corp Bhd	Kazakhstan
Lion Group	China, Vietnam
MAA Holdings Bhd	Sri Lanka, India, Indonesia, Philippines
Malayan Banking Bhd	Bahrain, Brunei, Cambodia, China, Hong Kong, Singapore, UK, US, Vietnam
Malaysia National Insurance Bhd	Pakistan
Maxis Communication Bhd	India, Indonesia
MTD Capital Bhd	Indonesia
MUI Group	Asia Pacific, Australia, US
M-Touche Technology Bhd	China
PECD Bhd	UAE
Petronas	In 32 countries (including China)
Petra Perdana Bhd	Singapore, British Virgil, Brunei, Myanmar, Vietnam, Indonesia
PPB Oil Palm	Indonesia
Proton Holdins Bhd	Europe, Indonesia
Public Bank Bhd	Hong Kong, Cambodia, Vietnam, Laos, Sri Lanka
Redtone International Bhd	China, Pakistan, Indonesia
Road Builder (M) Holdings Bhd	India
Salcon Bhd	China
Sime Darby Bhd	China, Hong Kong, Macau, Singapore, Australia, Brunei, Indonesia, Thailand, Vietnam, Philippines, UK, Egypt, New Zealand, Solomon Islands, Papua New Guinea, New Caledonia

(*Continued*)

Table 22. (*Continued*).

Company	Country/region invested
Sunway Group	Australia, Cambodia, China, India, Indonesia, Singapore, Thailand, Trinidad and Tobago, Vietnam
Tanjung PLC	Germany
Telekom Malaysia Bhd	Sri Lanka, Bangladesh, Pakistan, India, Indonesia, Singapore, Cambodia, Thailand, Malawi, Guinea
Tenaga Malaysia	Indonesia, Pakistan, Saudi Arabia
Tun Daim Zainuddin	Indonesia, Eastern Europe, Africa
UEM Group	India, Qatar, UK, China, New Zealand, Australia, Canada
WCT Engineering Bhd	India
YTL Group	Singapore, Indonesia, Australia, UK
Leader Universal Holdings	Cambodia
SapuraCrest	India (oil and gas)

Source: Malaysian Business, 1–15 August 2006, pp. 24–28.

Malaysia aims to be a regional hub of education.[36] Many students from China seeking a Western degree often have difficulties entering universities in the West. Malaysia, on its part, has a fairly liberal visa policy for these students.

Second, the twinning colleges and private universities offer degrees from Western universities, thus enhancing their attractiveness to these Chinese students. Third, the cost in Malaysia is less than in the West. Finally, Chinese students find the Malaysian environment easy to adapt to because of the presence of a large Malaysian Chinese population. Thus from what figures that can be obtained from the Higher Education Ministry, the percentage of students from China of total

---

[36] Based on discussion with Dr. Paul Chan, executive director of Higher Education Learning Program College (HELP), which is one of the top twinning colleges in Malaysia. See also Tan, YS (2004). Partnering China in education. *Malaysia–China Business Magazine*, 13, July.

foreign students in tertiary institutions is significant. For the year 2008 some 14.7% of total foreign students in Malaysia were from China.

In many of the more reputable twinning colleges, students from China constitute a sizeable percentage of not only the foreign student population but also the entire student population. HELP University College in Kuala Lumpur has about 600 students from China out of a total student population of 8,000.[37] This is about 8%. In Nilai College in Negeri Sembilan, the percentage is as high as 35%.[38] It is thus clear that the profitability and indeed survival of many of these colleges depend on students from China. Increasingly there is competition from other countries such as Singapore which are also keen on attracting students from China. Second, many Western universities are setting up branches in China directly. Thus, similar to the challenge of retaining investment from multinationals which are increasingly being diverted to China, Malaysia will have to "upgrade" its private higher education.

VI. Conclusion

China–Malaysia economic relations face several serious challenges in the coming years. These are due in large part to the expected growing strength of the Chinese economy which will shift the balance in bilateral economic relations to China's favor. With China's huge supply of low cost, skilled labor, Malaysian products will face tough Chinese competition for markets. The problem becomes even more serious as China moves up the value chain with advances in technological innovation and thereby threatens that sector in which Malaysia currently enjoys some advantage. With China improving its production technology, there is the risk that Malaysia would lose its comparative advantage within the regional production network.

---

[37] Interview with Dr. Paul Chan, Founder-President of HELP University College, 12 March 2006.
[38] Interview with Dr. Tan Yew Sing, Managing Director of INTI International College, 10 March 2006.

This, in turn, has serious implications for Malaysia in attracting FDIs. There has been a diversion of FDIs to China since the opening up of its economy. And this will continue if Malaysia is unable to match the technological advances of China. Already in 2009, FDI to Malaysia had dropped by some 81% to US$1.4 billion from US$7.3 billion in 2008. There are those who contend that this shift away of FDI from this Southeast Asian country has to do also with its investment and economic environment.

Given the lower labor costs in China, many Malaysian manufacturers especially the SMEs are already unable to compete against Chinese imports which are by far cheaper. Certain industries producing shoes, garments and apparels have been badly hit. The worst affected are Chinese-owned SMEs. William Cheng, President of the Chinese Chamber of Commerce, has lobbied for the implementation of tariff reduction under CAFTA to be delayed. Moreover, multinational manufacturers in Malaysia have relocated their production units to China. The response of SMEs in Malaysia is to upgrade their technology and to move up the value chain. Others have relocated to countries where cost of labor and other production factors such as land is lower. Others have simply closed down production and turned to being traders of products they once manufactured.

This chapter traced the growing Malaysia–China trade between 2000 and 2010, and also how each has become important in the export and import trade of the other. However, the nature and content of this trade have significantly changed. Primary products including timber, oil and gas from Malaysia are still important to feed China's industries. But where once primary products such as rubber and palm oil were major items in Malaysia's exports to China, they are no longer so. Rather, electronic and electrical products represent the bulk of Malaysia's exports to China. Electrical and electronic products also form a major part of Malaysia's imports from China. These changes underline the thriving regional production platform within the East Asian region in which Malaysia and China are integrated into and of the growing bilateral trade of the two countries.

Another observable trend is the increasing participation of state-supported companies particularly in infrastructure projects in both countries. These huge projects are generally beyond the funding resources and technological skills of private companies. It has also to do with the nature of the enterprise. One of the first Malaysian state-linked companies involved in China is Petronas which entered into agreements to supply gas to China and for oil exploration with Chinese oil companies. In turn, Chinese companies and concessionary loans are engaged in Malaysia's infrastructure construction of which the second Penang bridge, the Bakun Dam, and the Gemas-Johor Bahru double tracking program are to date the largest.

Involving state-linked companies can be seen as consistent with Malaysia's efforts toward a limited "bandwagoning" approach in dealing with China. Wariness of a rising China, noted among the dominant Malay political elites, is blunted by a growing involvement in China's trade by the mainly Malay-led state-linked companies. China's companies are also largely state-linked. But more importantly perhaps Beijing sees increased trade as well as joint venture projects with Malaysia's state-linked companies as essential to its quest for an expanding presence in Southeast Asia.

Bibliography

Chia, OP (2008). Malaysian investments in China: Market forces or political needs? In *China in the World: Contemporary Issues and Perspectives*, EK-K Yeoh and JH-L Loh (eds.). Kuala Lumpur: Institute of China Studies, University of Malaya.

Devadason, E (2007). Malaysia–China trade patterns in manufactures: How big is production sharing? In *Emerging Trading Nation in an Integrating World: Global Impacts and Domestic Challenges of China's Economic Reform*, EK-K Yeoh and E Devadason (eds.). Kuala Lumpur: Institute of China Studies, University of Malaya.

Institute of Developing Economies. Trade, investment and economic cooperation between China and Southeast Asia: The case of Malaysia. Unpublished report of Joint Research between the Institute of Developing Economies (Japan External Trade Organization) and Socio-Economic and Environmental Research Institute, Penang), November 2003–February 2004.

Ku, SCY (2006). China's changing political economy with Malaysia: A regional perspective. In *China and Malaysia in a Globalizing World: Bilateral Relations, Regional Imperatives and Domestic Challenges*, EK-K Yeoh and HK Chung (eds.). Kuala Lumpur: Institute of China Studies, University of Malaya.

Kuik, C-C (2008). The essence of hedging: Malaysia and Singapore's response to a rising China. *Contemporary Southeast Asia: A Journal of International and Strategic Affairs*, 30(2), 159–185.

Kwek, K-T and Tham, S-Y (2007). Trade between Malaysia and China: Opportunities and challenges for growth. In *Emerging Trading Nation in an Integrating World: Global Impacts and Domestic Challenges of China's Economic Reform*, EK-K Yeoh and E Devadason (eds.). Kuala Lumpur: Institute of China Studies, University of Malaya.

Lee, PP and Lee, KH (2006). China's economic rise and its impact on Malaysian Chinese business. In *Southeast Asia's Chinese Business in an Era of Globalisation*, L Suryadinata (ed.). Singapore: Institute of Southeast Asian Studies.

Li, Y (2006). An analysis of recent Sino–Malaysian trade relations. In *China and Malaysia in a Globalizing World: Bilateral Relations, Regional Imperatives and Domestic Challenges*, EK-K Yeoh and HK Chung (eds.). Kuala Lumpur: Institute of China Studies, University of Malaya.

Lim, TS (2009). Renewing 35 years of Malaysia–China relations: Najib's visit to China. *EAI Background Brief*, No. 460, East Asia Institute, National University of Singapore, 23 June.

Liow, JCY (2000). Malaysia–China relations in the 1990s: The maturing of a partnership. *Asian Survey*, XL(4), 672–691.

Loke, W-H (2007). Malaysia's and China's comparative advantages in selected manufacturing goods. In *Emerging Trading Nation in an Integrating World: Global Impacts and Domestic Challenges of China's Economic Reform*, EK-K Yeoh and E Devadason (eds.). Kuala Lumpur: Institute of China Studies, University of Malaya.

Wang, W and Lin, Z (2008). Investment in China: The role of Southeast Asian Chinese businessmen. In *China in the World: Contemporary Issues and Perspectives*, EK-K Yeoh and JH-L Loh (eds.). Kuala Lumpur: Institute of China Studies, University of Malaya.

Chapter 14

THE PHILIPPINES AND CHINA: TOWARDS A STRATEGIC PARTNERSHIP?

Andrea Chloe WONG

In recent years, relations between the Philippines and China have been active in various areas of cooperation. This development is underpinned by the Philippines with regard to China as an important partner with a stronger economic, military and diplomatic clout in East Asia and the world. However, this bilateral relationship has also experienced dramatic setbacks that caused mutual tension, mistrust and unease. Aside from territorial and maritime disputes with Beijing in the West Philippine Sea (South China Sea),[1] Manila also faces challenges in its various economic dealings with its giant partner. While prudently promoting long-term cooperation and engagement with a rising China, the Philippines is an ally of the US superpower. Moreover, the Philippines seeks to gain economic benefits from China, given that the US and EU are mired in economic crisis since 2008.

---

[1] The current administration of Philippine President Benigno Aquino III has officially used "West Philippine Sea" to refer to the sea present in the Western side of the country where the Philippines has overlapping territorial claims with other nations, instead of the all-embracing tag of "South China Sea". For the purpose of this paper on Philippines–China relations, particularly from a Philippine perspective, the author will use both "West Philippine Sea" and "South China Sea".

This chapter focuses on the important developments in Philippines–China relations from a Philippine perspective. It argues that the Philippines strives to compartmentalize economic and security issues in its bilateral relations and seeks to reflect a stronger posture towards China that will ultimately advance its national interests. The Philippines is maximizing economic benefits and minimizing security concerns that lead to continued diplomatic goodwill and enhanced strategic partnership with a rising global power. At the same time, despite the asymmetry in power relations, the Philippines is developing a tougher stance on important issues in relation to its assertive neighbor in the region.

The first part examines how China views the Philippines and how the Philippines perceives China, which serves as an important guide in understanding the dynamics of the bilateral relations. Next, it analyzes the various economic issues and the long-standing security challenges that contribute to the complexities in the relationship between the two countries. Lastly, it concludes with prospects in the bilateral partnership as the Philippines strives to proactively manage its relations with China.

I. China's Perception of the Philippines

Essentially, China regards the Philippines as having more political than economic value. More specifically, Beijing views Manila as:

1. *A close ally of Washington*

The Chinese government is aware of US perceptions of China as a rising power that will eventually threaten US interests.[2] Thus, the possibility of China being targeted in a US containment strategy through its alliances looms large. For China, these alliances thwart the

---

[2] For China's leaders, the retreat to the backburner of the "China threat theory", due to US preoccupation on the war on terrorism, is temporary rather than long-term. They believe that the US will continue to see China as a dissatisfied and aspiring great power that will challenge US global preponderance. See San Pablo-Baviera, A (2003). The China factor in US alliances in East Asia and the Asia Pacific. *Australian Journal of International Affairs*, 57(2), 339–352.

advancement of its political-security interests in the Asia Pacific. It is in this context that China is wary of US alliances in the region. Because of its long-standing security US alliance, the Philippines is thus strategically important to China. Along with other US allies (Japan, South Korea, and Thailand), the Philippines is generally deemed as a "proxy" for US efforts in its policies to curtail China's influence and "peaceful development". Therefore, China has been very watchful and cautious of the Philippines because of its US links.

2. A principal member of ASEAN

China prefers a multi-polar world order through an active and inclusive regional organization, given the increasing economic interdependence and similar security challenges faced by various East Asian countries in recent years. This perception is evident in China's eminent regard for ASEAN — its significance and its role in Asia. Aside from its economic value as China's important market for its export products, ASEAN also represents a valuable avenue for China to advance its diplomatic influence, as well as political and security interests in the region.

An integral part of ASEAN, the Philippines is a key Southeast Asian player that China needs to deal and "get along" with in the region. The country is deemed as an important player in the grand scheme of China's strategy to pursue its various interests in Southeast Asia. Thus, China seeks to develop stable bilateral ties with the Philippines that would most likely translate to an overall cordial relationship with ASEAN.

Currently, ASEAN is largely receptive of China's increasing influence, particularly the promotion of its "soft power" in the region. In particular, the Philippines is considered as an active recipient of this "soft power", by accepting various economic investments, development aid and financial assistance from China. This bilateral approach suits well for China in advancing cooperation with individual ASEAN countries such as the Philippines towards a stable region that is friendly to China. Simply put, good and amiable relations between the Philippines and China would strengthen Chinese foreign policy pronouncements of its "peaceful rise".

3. *A major stakeholder in the West Philippine Sea (South China Sea)*

As one of the claimant countries in the territorial disputes in the West Philippine Sea (South China Sea), the Philippines is regarded as an important stakeholder that China needs to cooperate with. Thus, China constantly reassures the Philippines that it is "committed to settling international disputes through peaceful means and to preserving international and regional security".[3] As part of its charm offensive, China and ASEAN signed the Declaration on the Conduct of Parties (DoC) on 4 November 2002 that seeks to preserve the status quo and encourages the claimants to pursue confidence-building measures to ease tensions.

Eventually, the DoC paved the way for the signing of the Joint Marine Seismic Undertaking (JMSU) to conduct joint seismic studies for three years (2005–2008) on the extent of oil and gas deposits in the disputed waters of the West Philippine Sea (South China Sea). The Philippine National Oil Company (PNOC) and the China National Offshore Oil Company (CNOOC) signed this landmark agreement in September 2004. Meanwhile, after initially condemning the agreement, Vietnam's PetroVietnam joined the JMSU in March 2005. For China, this three-year commercial agreement among the three oil companies is an important undertaking to shelve the sovereignty dispute in favor of joint exploration and the extraction of resources. Evidently, this reinforces China's regard for the Philippines as a major player it needs to deal with in its policies in the disputed area.

II. The "Duality" of China to the Philippines

Meanwhile, for the Philippines, China has a dichotomous image: A source of economic opportunities and potentially a strategic threat to its national security. Specifically, Manila regards Beijing as:

---

[3] China reaffirms commitment to resolve South China Sea claim peacefully (2010). *The Philippine Daily Inquirer*, 29 September.

1. *A vital strategic power*

According to the "Eight Realities of Philippine Foreign Policy" put forward by the past administration of Gloria Macapagal-Arroyo, the Philippines considers China as one of its most important partners, along with the US and Japan.[4] It recognizes China as an economic partner with the largest growing economy in the world and a major political and diplomatic player in regional and global affairs. Moreover, the Philippine government increasingly views China as a considerable factor in its alliance with the US, particularly on important security matters.

2. *A major trade partner*

Since 2000, trade between the Philippines and China has increased rapidly with an average growth rate of more than 35% annually.[5] In 2010, trade between the Philippines and China reached US$27.7 billion, a remarkable increase from the US$20.5 billion trade in 2009.[6] Because of this significant trade volume, the Philippines currently ranks China as its third largest trade partner after the US and Japan. It also regards China as a big market for its export products such as electronic products and semi-conductors that resulted in a trade surplus in favor of the Philippines. Moreover, the Philippines is expected to export more products to China such as minerals and metals (iron ore, copper, and nickel) that are considered essential commodities to fuel China's growing economy. This trend is predicted to overtake Japan and make China the Philippine's number one destination for its exports in 2011, following a 94% growth in 2010.[7]

---

[4] Chapter 24 responsive foreign policy. *Medium-Term Philippine Development Plan (2004–2010)*, National Economic and Development Authority (NEDA), pp. 269–273.

[5] 2007 trade surge being repeated in 2008 despite global slowdown (2008). *The Sunday Times*, 29 June.

[6] Philippines-China trade continues to increase (2010). Republic of the Philippines Department of Foreign Affairs, Public Service Information Unit, 1 September.

[7] China emerges as major export for Philippine products (2011). *China Daily*, 15 February. http://www.chinadaily.com.cn/bizchina/2011-02/15/content_12019922. htm [accessed 23 September 2011].

3. *A significant investor and loan provider*

China is a vital source of loans and investments, and a financer of the country's various development projects. Chinese investments to the Philippines peaked at US$86 million, with a 112% increase compared to previous investments in 2009.[8] Apart from ventures in the mining and agriculture sectors, the biggest Chinese investment in the Philippines is in infrastructure development. China has provided the Philippines with loans and investment provisions with low interest rates and flexible payment schemes for railroad rehabilitation, as well as other multimillion-dollar infrastructure development projects, such as airports, seaports, railway systems, and waterworks and sewerage systems.

4. *An intermittent security threat*

Despite their active economic ties, Manila and Beijing's overlapping territorial claims in the West Philippine Sea (South China Sea) occasionally undermine their bilateral relations. These territorial disputes have become a critical source of tension between the two countries, as well as with other parties in the region.

This long-standing territorial dispute was recently evident in the various provocations of China, much to the consternation of the Philippines. These irritants include China's temporary occupation of small islands, building of structures, erection of posts, laying down of markers, and intimidation of Philippine fishing vessels in the disputed areas in the South China Sea. These incidents greatly reinforced Philippine perceptions of China as a national security threat.

Moreover, the Philippines also consider this security dilemma as a "litmus test" of China's great power ambition.[9] This is in the context

---

[8] Wee, D (2011). Philippines, China upgrade bilateral trading agreement. *Minda News*, 16 August.

[9] Storey, I (2007). China and the Philippines: Moving beyond the South China Sea dispute. *China Brief*, 6(7), 9 May.

of rapid advances in Chinese capability and a clear intent to project naval power in the East China Sea and South China Sea. China utilizes its growing military to assert its sovereignty in various areas that were enclosed in its nine-dashed line map, even in areas close to the coastlines of other claimant states. The Chinese government eventually registered this map with the United Nations indicating its official claims in the disputed areas.

III. Addressing Vital Issues and Recurring Challenges

In recent years, there were several setbacks in Philippines–China relations. These problems include a sluggish expansion in bilateral trade; a major scandal involving Chinese investments in development projects in the Philippines; territorial disputes in the West Philippine Sea (South China Sea); and concerns over US influence in Philippines–China relations.

1. *Slow growth in bilateral trade*

Despite their active trade, the Philippines and China have experienced an apparent slowdown in trade volume. In 2008, bilateral trade was at US$28.6 billion, further decreasing in 2009 to US$20.5 billion following the global economic crisis.[10] Despite bilateral trade significantly increasing to an estimated US$27.7 billion in 2010, it has yet to considerably surpass its pre-economic crisis level, specifically its trade volume in 2007 valued at US$30.6 billion.[11]

Aside from the global economic crisis, the similar nature of items and products traded between the Philippines and China has resulted in a decline in trade volume. The Philippines imports from China include electronic products, textiles and clothing, steel, and light industrial products, among others. Meanwhile, the Philippines exports to China

---

[10] Lee-Brago, P (2010). RP–China trade seen to expand. *The Philippine Star*, 5 September.

[11] *Ibid.*

are highly concentrated, with semi-conductors and electronic products comprising the bulk of its imports.[12] The high share of electronics in the traded aggravated trading volatility during the economic downturn as evidenced in its bilateral trade in 2008 and 2009.

It is apparent that trade complementary between the two sides needs to be enhanced. Both countries should cooperate to expand bilateral trade, and diversify it away from competing mechanical and electrical products. Despite bilateral trade which is mostly in favor of the Philippines, Manila is expected to diversify its exports by selling more agricultural products, processed food, and minerals to Beijing, since these items merely comprise less than 5% of China's imports from the Philippines.[13]

2. Controversies in China's ODA to the Philippines

In recent years, the Philippines has become an eager recipient of Chinese overseas development assistance (ODA). Aside from its low interest rates and flexible terms, China's ODA reflects its development paradigm of trade and investment in infrastructure and social institutions with an adherence to the principle of non-interference in a recipient country's internal affairs and sovereign integrity.

This is in sharp contrast to US imposition of preconditions in its aid programs such as political, social and economic reforms. For example, the Philippine's access to more grant assistance from the US hinges on its ability to implement government reform, especially in the area of mitigating corruption. Thus, China's "no-strings attached" approach to its ODA is more attractive to the Philippines.

However, the general notion of China's ODA without conditionalities, particularly those concerning multi-million dollar projects, is a

---

[12] China's top 10 exports to the Philippines and China's top 10 imports from the Philippines. General Administration of Customs of China (GACC), April, taken from the Philippine Embassy in the People's Republic of China, http://www.philembassychina. org/downloads/Bilateral/bilateral_economic_relations_tabels.pdf [accessed 25 January 2011].

[13] Philippines–China trade continues to increase (2010). Republic of the Philippines Department of Foreign Affairs, Public Service Information Unit, 1 September.

misconception. Similar to other countries' development assistance, Beijing provides tied-in loans with stipulations in business transactions that seek to benefit Chinese industries. This actually reinforces criticisms against Chinese ODA as basically self-serving since a significant portion of its ODA funds and loans to other countries eventually goes back to China through its own corporations. In most bilateral agreements, Chinese state banks provide recipient countries with concessional loans to finance infrastructure and other development ventures while Chinese state-owned corporations implement and build these projects.

An example of this is the North Rail project. Considered as China's largest ODA commitment to the Philippines, the North Rail project seeks to rehabilitate and upgrade the North Luzon Railway in order to provide mass transport services connecting Metro Manila to provinces in the North. It is a concessional loan agreement worth US$503 million that will be financed by the Export–Import Bank of China, with China National Machinery and Equipment Corporation and China National Technical Import and Export Corporation automatically designated as the project's contractors.[14]

Despite these realities, the Philippines prefers to accommodate China's offers because it also stands to benefit from its loans and assistance. This is in addition to the Chinese government offering "cheaper rates, faster approval, and fewer questions".[15]

However, what seemed to be a mutually beneficial endeavor became a major source of controversies that rocked relations between the Philippines and China. During the previous Arroyo administration, there were various corruption scandals that involved multi-billion dollar government ventures financed by China.

One such scandal is the National Broadband Network (NBN) project. The Philippine government and the Chinese telecommunications firm Zhongxing Telecommunication Equipment Co. (ZTE) signed

---

[14] Tadem, E (2007). The crisis of official development assistance to the Philippines: New global trends and old local issues. Asian Center, University of the Philippines. http://www.mode.org/oda/pdf/Crisis%20of%20ODA%20to%20the%20Philippines.pdf [accessed 27 April 2010].

[15] Naim, M (2007). Help not wanted. *The New York Times*, 15 February. http://www.nytimes.com/2007/02/15/opinion/15naim.html [accessed 30 April 2010].

the NBN contract on 21 April 2007 in Hainan, China. However, before it was implemented, the NBN project was mired with allegations of corruption after awarding the contract to ZTE for US$329.5 million. It was perceived as hugely overpriced by US$197 million to "fund" commissions for Filipino government officials. Following the uproar against the irregularities, former President Arroyo then cancelled the NBN deal on 2 October 2007 in Shanghai, where she informed Chinese President Hu Jintao about her "difficult decision".[16] This scandal evidently produced national embarrassment for the Philippines and painted a negative image for China.

3. *Tensions in the South China Sea*

Another issue that has perpetually haunted Philippines–China relations is the overlapping territorial claims in the West Philippine Sea (South China Sea). As mentioned earlier, there were bilateral efforts to cooperate on the disputed territories with the signing of the Declaration on the Conduct of Parties (DoC) and the JMSU. However, while Beijing is keen on promoting cooperation, it does not tolerate actions implying sovereignty claims by other countries. Because of China's aggressive claims, there have been sporadic hostilities in the disputed area.

- In February 1995, Chinese forces occupied and built structures on the Mischief Reef, a tiny land situated within 135 miles West of Palawan. It is part of the disputed Spratly Islands but well within the Philippine Exclusive Economic Zone (EEZ). It created further tensions after it increased the presence of Chinese naval vessels and replaced the original structures on Mischief Reef with a three-story fortress in 1998.
- In March 2009, China raised security alarms in the Philippines after Beijing sent one of its modern vessels to the Spratly Islands, "prompting complaints of provocative display of military might to

---

[16]See The NBN-ZTE: A Primer. March 2008. http://www.ateneansact.net/dl/ GMA%20Primer%20on%20ZTE-NBN%20Deal.pdf [accessed 5 May 2009].

thwart attempts by any state to lay claim to the disputed territories in the South China Sea".[17]

This incident was interpreted as China's objection against the Philippines' signing of Republic Act 9522, or the Philippine Archipelagic Baselines Law on 10 March 2009. The law reaffirms the country's claims over the 7,100 islands in its archipelago, including outlying territories in the disputed Spratly Islands. It also states that the Kalayaan Group of Islands and Scarborough Shoal in the Spratlys are considered as "regime of islands" under the Republic of the Philippines.[18]

The Chinese government expressed strong opposition and solemn protest against the law. Beijing categorically stated that Manila's territorial claims were "invalid and illegal".[19]

- In February 2011, a Chinese frigate reportedly fired shots at three Philippine fishing vessels that were operating in the waters off Jackson (Quirino) atoll, 140 nautical miles West off Palawan.[20]
- In March 2011, two Chinese patrol boasts ordered the Philippine's *MV Veritas Voyager* (a survey vessel operating in the Reed Bank off Palawan Island), to leave and twice maneuvered close in what appeared a threat to ram the vessel.[21]
- In May 2011, Chinese ships reportedly unloaded building materials, erected an undetermined number of posts, and placed a buoy near the Iroquois Bank.[22] Eventually, the Philippine Navy and

---

[17] China reaffirms commitment to peaceful settlement of Spratlys dispute (2009). *GMA News*, 24 March.

[18] *Ibid.*

[19] China opposes Philippine claim on islands (2009). *China Daily*, 11 March. http://www.chinadaily.com.cn/china/2009-03/11/content_7569668.htm. [accessed 5 May 2009].

[20] Calica, A (2011). PHL to take Chinese incursions to the United Nations. *The Philippine Star*, 4 June.

[21] Philippines halts tests after China patrol challenge (2011). *BBC News Asia Pacific*, 8 March. http://www.bbc.co.uk/news/world-asia-pacific-12672889. [accessed 23 September 2011].

[22] Lee-Brago, P (2011). China building in PHL waters, DFA summoned envoy. *The Philippine Star*, 2 June.

Coast Guard reportedly removed "foreign markers" and plastic buoys installed on Amy Douglas Bank, Reed Bank, Boxall Reef that were all located in the waters claimed by the Philippines.[23]

- In April 2012, the Philippines dispatched its largest warship to inspect a group of Chinese fishing vessels in the Scarborough Shoal after a Philippine Navy surveillance plane detected them poaching. Two Chinese maritime surveillance ships eventually sailed towards the mouth of the shoal, placing themselves between the Philippine warship and the Chinese fishing vessels, effectively preventing the Philippine Navy from arresting the Chinese fishermen. This resulted in a long naval and diplomatic standoff between the two countries over the Scarborough Shoal.

Indeed, these altercations in the West Philippine Sea (South China Sea) have dampened bilateral ties. For the Philippines, the recent incidents with China in the area proved unsettling. Philippine National Defense Secretary Voltaire Gazmin observed, "It is alarming in the sense that the intrusions are increasing. They are staking claim on the areas where we do not have a presence. They want to hoist their flag so they can claim the area".[24]

Because of these, the Philippines made several actions in response to the recent tensions and skirmishes (particularly in the first half of 2011) in the West Philippine Sea (South China Sea). These included the following:

3.1. *Filing diplomatic protests*

The Philippine Department of Foreign Affairs lodged a diplomatic protest with the Chinese Embassy in the Philippines over the "increasing presence and activities of Chinese vessels including naval assets in the West Philippine Sea... undermining the peace and stability in the

---

[23] Navy removes Chinese markers in reed bank (2011). *Manila Standard Today*, 16 June.
[24] Pazzibugan, D (2011). Chinese intrusions in PH-claimed parts of Spratlys alarming. *Philippine Daily Inquirer*, 2 June.

region".[25] China responded with a statement from its Ministry of Foreign Affairs: "Chinese vessels were cruising and carrying out scientific studies in waters under China's jurisdiction and their activities were in line with the law... China asks the Philippine side to stop harming China's sovereignty and maritime rights and interests, which leads to unilateral actions that expand and complicate South China Sea disputes".[26]

The Philippines also filed a formal complaint to the United Nations in May 2011 over China's definition of its territorial claims in the West Philippine Sea (South China Sea). It would also complete some data on about six to seven Chinese incursions in its territory since February 2011 that would be formally lodged to the United Nations.[27]

Meanwhile, at the height of the dispute in the Scarborough Shoal in April 2012, the Philippines' Department of Foreign Affairs proposed to bring both the Philippines and China's territorial claims to the International Tribunal on the Law of the Sea (ITLOS). However, the Chinese government rejected the proposal, arguing that Scarborough Shoal is China's inherent territory. Despite China's rejection, the Philippines decided to unilaterally bring its case to the international court. According to Secretary del Rosario: "The whole world knows that China has myriad more ships and aircraft than the Philippines. At day's end, however, we hope to demonstrate that international law would be the great equalizer."[28]

---

[25] Statement of the department of foreign affairs on the presence of chinese vessels in the West Philippine Sea (South China Sea) (2011). Republic of the Philippines Department of Foreign Affairs, 4 June.

[26] China rejects Philippines' Accusation on South China Sea issue (2011). *People's Daily Online*, 7 June. http://english.peopledaily.com.cn/90001/90776/90883/7403021. html. [accessed 25 September 2011].

[27] Landingin, R and K Hille (2011). China and Philippines tensions mount. *The Financial Times*, 1 June.

[28] Mateo, J (2012). Scarborough dispute to be brought to international court even without China's approval. *Philippine Online Chronicles*, 3 May. http://thepoc.net/ breaking-news/world/15830-scarborough-dispute-to-be-brought-to-intl-court-even-without-chinas-approval.html, [accessed 13 June 2012].

Aside from filing a formal complaint to the United Nations, the current administration of President Benigno Aquino III is supporting two legislative measures in response to China's assertiveness. The Philippine House of Representatives is drawing up the Philippine Maritime Zones bill to delineate the country's maritime zones, while the Philippine Senate is drafting the Archipelagic Sea Lanes Bill, that prescribes the rights and obligation of foreign ships and aircraft exercises as well as the right of archipelagic passage through an established archipelagic sea lanes.[29]

3.2. *Improving military and naval defense*

The Armed Forces of the Philippines (AFP) had increased air and naval patrols in the West Philippine Sea (South China Sea). It also allocated US$183 million in funds from its Capability Upgrade Program to purchase two offshore fast patrol boats, long-range maritime aircraft, surveillance and communication equipment, including air defense radar to better protect its territory.[30]

In addition, the AFP planned to set up a coast watch system on the Western seaboard in the next two to three years to monitor and secure maritime borders and natural resources. It also announced a new US training program for its naval forces to enable them to better carry out its mission of providing security for oil exploration activities in the West Philippine Sea (South China Sea).[31]

3.3. *Lobbying ASEAN*

President Aquino lobbied his ASEAN colleagues to unify as a regional bloc and has proposed for an integrated position in the West

---

[29] DFA: Stronger Sea Code to prevent repeat of mischief reef (2011). *GMA News*, 2 June.

[30] Villanueva, M (2011). Keeping Philippine navy afloat. *The Philippine Star*, 16 May and Philippines set to deploy new patrol ship to Kalayaan islands (2011). *Manila Bulletin*, 14 April.

[31] Escalante, S (2011). Philippines increase security for oil exploration. *Australia Network News*, 28 April. http://www.radioaustralianews.net.au/stories/201104/3201767.htm [accessed 25 September 2011].

Philippine Sea (South China Sea) dispute among ASEAN claimant states. According to him: "Instead of one country having a bilateral agreement with China and the other having another one, let us come together as a body. Why do we have to fight or increase all of these tensions when it profits nobody?"[32]

President Aquino also called for the adoption of the implementing guidelines on the DoC, which was signed at the ASEAN–China meeting in 21 July 2011. Eventually, the Philippine Department of Foreign Affairs expressed hope for a "more binding Code of Conduct for Parties in the South China Sea".

These actions indeed reflect a stronger Philippine stance against recent Chinese aggressions in the West Philippine Sea (South China Sea). Though it has soured bilateral relations, the Philippines is expected to protect its security interests and strengthen its territorial claims in the area.

4. Dilemmas in balancing the Philippines ties with China and the US

The relationship of Philippines with China is occasionally affected by strong influence of the US over the Philippines. The seemingly competitive nature of the US–China relations, however implicitly portrayed in their bilateral ties, impacts the Philippines' partnership with both countries.

For the US, the Philippines' increasingly active relationship with China might result in the Philippines' shift from depending on the US to relying more on China. Likewise, the US views this "growing closeness" as a worry trend, which may slowly reduce American influence on the Philippines.

Indeed, the US is strengthening its commitments, particularly its military and security agreements with the Philippines. During tensions between the Philippines and China over the Spratlys in 2009, US President Barrack Obama talked to former President Arroyo and

---

[32] Poblete, J (2011). Philippines preparing issues for UN about China intrusions. *Business World*, 2 June.

reaffirmed the Philippines–US alliance and his country's commitment to the Visiting Forces Agreement (VFA). The actual intent of this affirmation is open to interpretation, but the timing suggests it was a gesture of support for the Philippines in its possible altercation with China.[33] As a result, some Filipino officials called for American support by playing up the importance of the US as the Philippine's treaty ally. These officials also campaigned for the extension of the VFA as a deterrent against perceived Chinese expansion in the West Philippine Sea (South China Sea).

Recent Chinese provocations in the West Philippine Sea (South China Sea) have also reaffirmed the US commitment to support the Philippines. At the height of tensions, Philippine Secretary of Foreign Affairs Albert del Rosario met with his US counterpart to confirm American support and ask for assistance in upgrading its naval capabilities. In response, US Secretary of State Hillary Clinton affirmed her country's commitment to its ally: "We urge all sides to exercise self-restraint, and we will continue to consult closely with all countries involved, including our treaty ally the Philippines. We are determined and committed to supporting the defense of the Philippines".[34]

Moreover, at the state visit of President Aquino to the US in June 2012, President Obama pledged US support for Aquino's efforts to upgrade the antiquated Philippine military and build a "minimum credible defense posture." Against the backdrop of a tense standoff in the Scarborough Shoal, the two leaders "underscored the importance of the principles of ensuring freedom of navigation, respect for international law and unimpeded lawful commerce."[35]

To China, however, the Philippine's long-standing alliance with the US is a hindrance to its political-security interests in the region. Apparently, China perceives the Philippines as a "proxy" for the US efforts to curb Chinese influence in the Asia Pacific. During the US-led war on terrorism, the Philippines benefited from American

---

[33] Storey, I (2009). Impeccable affair and renewed rivalry in the South China Sea. *China Brief*, IX(9), 30 April, 7–10.

[34] US backs Philippines on the South China Sea. *The Financial Times*, 24 June.

[35] Obama backs Philippines on sea freedom (2012). *Philippine Daily Inquirer*, 9 June.

economic and military aid after it supported the US, and China found this rejuvenated alliance as unsettling. However, when the Philippines withdrew its military personnel in Iraq, Philippines–US relations suffered.[36] China took advantage of this to increase its economic concessions and security interaction with the Philippines. The Philippines in turn reciprocated to Chinese goodwill — possibly signaling to the US that it should not be taken for granted.

Evidently, the Philippines is temporarily benefiting from its position, exploiting benefits from competing parties to serve its national interests. However, it is conceivable that walking the tightrope between the two great powers may negatively affect the Philippines' vital relationship with China as well as its long-standing partnership with the US.

IV. Philippine Approach to China: Compartmentalizing Areas of Concern

Just as it has a dichotomous image of China both as a source of opportunities and threats, the Philippines has thus put forward its strategy of compartmentalizing issues that segregate economic and security matters. This is perceived to be ultimately advancing the Philippines' overall national interests. Essentially, the Philippines is seeking to maximize economic opportunities and minimize security problems with China.

This approach is reflected in the state visit of President Aquino to China from 30 August to 3 September 2011. During the visit, President Aquino opted to highlight the long-standing friendship of the Philippines and China rather than talk about "some

---

[36] To support the US war on terror, the Philippines sent a humanitarian assistance mission to Iraq in June 2003. However, an Iraqi insurgent group captured Angelo dela Cruz, a Filipino truck driver, in July 2004. The Iraqi insurgents demanded the immediate withdrawal of the Philippine mission in exchange for the life of dela Cruz. Fearing a major political backlash against her administration, President Arroyo gave in to the demand of the insurgents. The US government criticized the Philippine government's position as sending a wrong message to encourage more kidnappings in Iraq.

disagreements".[37] While his state visit came at a time of looming tensions in the West Philippine Sea (South China Sea), President Aquino chose to be more optimistic and agreed to "peacefully settle" the issue. "About the West Philippine Sea, I am excited to tell you that our exchange of ideas with them on how to move forward and agree on differences of the two sides on this issue went well and was meaningful".[38] he said. Details on the "peaceful settlement" however were not provided.

Instead, President Aquino emphasized more on the trade and investment benefits his delegation acquired from the Chinese government and the business community. His state visit reportedly generated an estimated US$13 billion worth of Chinese investments: US$1.3 billion in actual investments, US$3.8 billion in planned projects, and US$7.9 billion in pledged ventures[39] These Chinese investments are expected to flow into various sectors in the Philippines particularly in mining, agriculture, energy, tourism, and infrastructure, among others.

Similarly, China did not let the territorial dispute stand in the way of deeper cooperation with the Philippines, fully aware that economics usually trump politics in diplomacy. Its antagonistic behavior in the security realm is tempered with an ever-increasing trade with neighboring countries. China has deliberately used its soft power to its advantage by building relationships based on financial inducements and gestures of goodwill, which have proven to be effective during President Aquino's visit. This resulted in temporarily neutralizing China's aggressive image in the Philippines by likewise highlighting opportunities and downplaying hostilities.

Overall, President Aquino's approach of compartmentalizing bilateral matters is evident in his productive state visit to China that ultimately set the tone for a more cordial bilateral relation despite looming tensions. His visit is perceived by some analysts to be more like a family

---

[37] Kabiling, G (2011). China awaits Aquino state visit. *Manila Bulletin*, 14 June.
[38] Maningat, J (2011). Why Spratlys is a non-issue in Aquino's China trip. *Philippine Online Chronicles*, 5 September. http://www.thepoc.net/commentaries/13428-why-spratlys-is-a-non-issue-in-aquinos-china-trip.html [23 September 2011].
[39] *Ibid.*

member visiting third degree relatives. They are like relatives "distant enough to be forgotten until problems arise, but close enough to demand respect and courtesy for the sake of family harmony".[40]

V. Promoting Philippine Efforts in the Bilateral Partnership

Given these developments in the bilateral relations, there are positive forecasts in strengthening ties between Manila and Beijing. The Philippines is poised to continue compartmentalizing trade and security issues with China, trumping economics over politics towards a stronger strategic partnership. With the current Aquino administration, the Philippine government seeks to develop a broader and deeper relationship with China.

In the next five years, Manila is expected to implement the *Joint Action Plan for Strategic Cooperation* (2012–2016) that was signed on 29 October 2009 as a guide to its relations with Beijing. The agreement is intended to strengthen the Philippines–China relations through various initiatives for collaboration including Trade, Investment, and Financial Cooperation; Agriculture and Fisheries Cooperation; Infrastructure Cooperation; Transportation Cooperation; Mining and Energy Cooperation; Tourism Cooperation; Defense and Security Cooperation; Cultural, Education, and Media Cooperation; and Cooperation on Sustainable Development, among others.

Aside from advancing its relations with China, the Philippines is also looking to promote its national interests and development agenda through the following areas:

1. *Bilateral trade and investments*

Both countries expect a more diversified product mix for trade as the China–ASEAN free trade agreement (FTA) takes effect. Under the

---

[40] Cruz-del Rosario, T (2011). Win–win For President Aquino's China visit? *People's Daily Online*, 29 August. http://english.peopledaily.com.cn/90780/91343/7582304.html [accessed 23 September 2011].

agreement, duties of more than 7,000 trading items will be reduced to zero starting on 1 January 2010.[41] Given its regard for China as a valuable trade partner, the Philippines is already preparing for expansion of its export items to China, particularly to satisfy its growing demand for Philippine agricultural, mining, and aquatic products.

In addition, the Philippines is expected to benefit from the Philippines–China Five Year Development Program for Trade and Economic Cooperation (2012–2016). It serves as the blueprint for future bilateral efforts in the following sectors: Agriculture and fishery, infrastructure and public works, processing and manufacturing, among others. The Philippines also agreed to further expand its trade volume with China and accordingly set a target of US$60 billion in total two-way trade by 2016.[42]

Meanwhile, despite controversies over China's ODA and investments to the Philippines, there is still a significant amount of Chinese funds pouring into various infrastructure and development projects in the country. The current Aquino administration, which won an electoral mandate for its principles of integrity and honesty, will strive to implement transparency in the negotiation, management and implementation of the loans, investments, and development assistance that the Philippine government regularly receives. At the same time, it is expected to address the Philippine's immediate needs by placing a priority on demand-driven projects (such as road and railway projects based on the country's development plans) rather than supply-driven projects (such as the national broadband network project that was contracted to accommodate a Chinese company's business interests and some Filipino officials' personal motives and political agenda). In addition, the Philippines is also committed to implement its Public Private Partnership program to govern the planning and implementation of development projects

---

[41] Xu, L (2009). China to become 2nd largest trade partner of Philippines as recovery takes hold. *China View*, 30 December. http://news.xinhuanet.com/english/2009-12/30/content_12728233.htm [accessed 28 January 2010].

[42] Joint statement of the Republic of the Philippines and the People's Republic of China (2011). Republic of the Philippines Department of Foreign Affairs, 1 September.

by encouraging qualified companies to participate in the competitive bidding processes.

2. Security in the West Philippine Sea (South China Sea)

Despite recent tensions, the Philippines is committed to a peaceful resolution with China in their overlapping claims in the West Philippine Sea (South China Sea), particularly in the Spratly Islands. It welcomed the adoption of the implementing guidelines of the DoC that is considered "a step forward towards the development of a more binding Code of Conduct".[43]

More importantly, the Philippines has also proposed the concept of a *Zone of Peace, Freedom, Friendship, and Cooperation* (ZoPFFC) as an initiative to transform the West Philippine Sea (South China Sea) from a region of conflict to an area of cooperation. President Aquino first announced this initiative at the 18th ASEAN Summit and Related Meetings in May 2011 in Jakarta, Indonesia and explained that "what is ours is ours, and with what is disputed, we can work towards joint cooperation".[44]

According to the Philippine Department of Foreign Affairs, the ZoPFFC provides a framework for segregating the disputed territorial features that may be considered for collaborative activities, on the one hand, and the non-disputed waters in the West Philippine Sea (South China Sea), on the other. This will be in accordance with international law in general and the UNCLOS in particular. According to the ZoPFFC, a disputed area could be turned into a "Joint Cooperation Area" for the development and the establishment of marine protected area for biodiversity conservation. Areas not in dispute, such as the Reed Bank that lies within the Philippines' continental shelf can be developed exclusively by the Philippines or

---

[43] Romero, P (2011). ASEAN–China adopt guidelines on Spratlys. *Newsbreak*, 22 July.
[44] Quoted in a speech by Albert del Rosario, Secretary of the Department Foreign Affairs, Republic of the Philippines (2011). A rules-based regime in the South China sea. Republic of the Philippines Department of Foreign Affairs, Public Information Services Unit, 7 June.

with the assistance of foreign investors invited to participate in the area's development.[45]

The Philippines' proposal of a ZoPFFC aims to achieve this vision by providing a framework from which multilateral cooperative endeavors could be undertaken, while isolating the complexities and tensions that overlapping territorial claims create. Currently, the Philippines is proactively conducting dialogue among claimant states and other stakeholders on the feasibility of the ZoPFFC to prevent further tensions in the West Philippines Sea (South China Sea).

3. *Philippine relations with US and China*

During the previous Arroyo administration, the Philippines enjoyed the best of both worlds as it bolstered its security relations with the US, while obtaining economic and politico-diplomatic concessions from China. However, the Philippines under the present Aquino administration, is expected to advance a stronger and more "independent" foreign policy that seeks to promote an "equidistance" in its relations with the US and China. How the Aquino administration will operationalize it remains to be seen as the Philippines grapples with a more fluid and complex global environment. Nonetheless, the Philippines trusts that implementing such foreign policy will enhance cooperation abroad while obviating aggressiveness by these major powers.[46]

VI. Strengthening Philippines–China Relations

For the Philippines, enhancing strategic partnership with China is critical in its foreign policy. It is precisely because of this that the country strives to compartmentalize economic and security issues in the bilateral relations by acquiring economic goodwill in an attempt to diffuse recent security tensions with China. This is evident during the

---

[45] *Ibid.*

[46] Valero, VAJ (2010). US in focus: Changing the dynamics of a longstanding partnership. *Vital Partners and Influential Players: A Review of Philippine Bilateral Relations*, Republic of the Philippines Foreign Service Institute, June.

previous Arroyo administration and the current Aquino government in how both related with China. Meanwhile, despite its show of amity, the Philippines is at the same time seeking to develop a stronger Philippine posture given the asymmetry in power relations in the bilateral relations. This is particularly reflected in the Philippine efforts to defend its territorial claims in the West Philippine Sea (South China Sea). Through these endeavors, the Philippines hopes to strike a balance and achieve its goals of promoting its national interests while developing a mutually-beneficial partnership with China.

Alongside its ASEAN counterparts, the Philippines aims to anchor its relations with China within an incipient East Asian Community (EAC). Despite their differences in size and power, the Philippines and China are developing countries yearning for peace, stability and prosperity. In the midst of regional tensions, the East Asian community remains accommodating and cordial. There are already efforts to pacify hostilities and establish guidelines in promoting security cooperation. In spite of global economic downturn, a rising tide of economic prosperity in East Asia (underpinned by China's phenomenal economic growth poised to overtake US GDP by 2020) is expected to raise the economies of big and small countries. In the coming years, this will undoubtedly create a sunny scenario for the economies in East Asia, in stark contrast to the dark clouds looming over the US and EU economies.

Bibliography

2007 trade surge being repeated in 2008 despite global slowdown (2008). *The Sunday Times*, 29 June. http://www.manilatimes.net/national/2008/june/29/yehey/top_stories/20080629top4.html [accessed 4 May 2009].

Calica, A (2011). PHL to take Chinese incursions to the United Nations. *The Philippine Star*, 4 June.

Chapter 24 responsive foreign policy. *Medium-Term Philippine Development Plan (2004–2010)*. National Economic and Development Authority (NEDA), pp. 269–273.

China emerges as major export for Philippine products (2011). *China Daily*, 15 February. http://www.chinadaily.com.cn/bizchina/2011–02/15/content_12019922.htm [accessed 23 September 2011].

China opposes Philippine claim on islands (2009). *China Daily*, 11 March. http://www.chinadaily.com.cn/china/ 2009–03/11/content_7569668. htm [accessed 5 May 2009].

China reaffirms commitment to peaceful settlement of Spratlys dispute (2009). *GMA News*, 24 March.

China reaffirms commitment to resolve South China Sea claim peacefully (2010). *The Philippine Daily Inquirer*, 29 September. http://globalnation. inquirer.net/news/breakingnews/view/20100929-295018/ RP-reaffirms-commitment-to-resolve-South-China-Sea-claim-peacefully [accessed 25 September 2010].

China rejects Philippines' accusation on South China Sea issue (2011). *People's Daily Online*, 7 June. http://english.peopledaily.com.cn/90001/90776/ 90883/7403021.html [accessed 25 September 2011].

China's top 10 exports to the Philippines and China's top 10 imports from the Philippines (2010). General Administration of Customs of China (GACC), April, taken from the Philippine Embassy in the People. http://www.philembassychina.org/downloads/Bilateral/bilateral_ economic_relations_tabels.pdf [accessed 25 January 2011].

Cruz-del Rosario, T (2011). Win–win for President Aquino's China visit? *People's Daily Online*, 29 August. http://english.peopledaily.com. cn/90780/91343/7582304.html [accessed 23 September 2011].

del Rosario, A (2011). A rules-based regime in the South China sea. Republic of the Philippines Department of Foreign Affairs, Public Information Services Unit, 7 June.

DFA: Stronger sea code to prevent repeat of mischief Reef. *GMA News*, 2 June.

Escalante, S (2011). Philippines increase security for oil exploration. *Australia Network News*, 28 April. http://www.radioaustralianews.net. au/stories/201104/3201767.htm [accessed 25 September 2011].

Joint Statement of the Republic of the Philippines and the People's Republic of China (2011). Republic of the Philippines Department of Foreign Affairs, 1 September.

Kabiling, G (2011). China awaits Aquino state visit. *Manila Bulletin*, 14 June.

Landingin, R and K Hille (2011). China and Philippines tensions mount. *The Financial Times*, 1 June.

Lee-Brago, P (2010). RP–China trade seen to expand. *The Philippine Star*, 5 September.

Lee-Brago, P (2011). China building in PHL waters, DFA summoned envoy. *The Philippine Star*, 2 June.

Maningat, J (2011). Why Spratlys is a non-issue in Aquino's China trip. *Philippine Online Chronicles*, 5 September. http://www.thepoc.net/commentaries/13428-why-spratlys-is-a-non-issue-in-aquinos-china-trip.html [23 September 2011].

Naim, M (2007). Help not wanted. *The New York Times*, 15 February.

Navy removes Chinese markers in Reed bank (2011). *Manila Standard Today*, 16 June.

Pazzibugan, D (2011). Chinese intrusions in PH-claimed parts of Spratlys alarming. *Philippine Daily Inquirer*, 2 June.

Philippines halts tests after China patrol challenge (2011). *BBC News Asia Pacific*, 8 March. http://www.bbc.co.uk/news/world-asia-pacific-12672889 [accessed 23 September 2011].

Philippines–China trade continues to increase (2010). Republic of the Philippines Department of Foreign Affairs, Public Service Information Unit, 1 September.

Philippines–China trade seen ending year at $30 billion (2010). *Business World*, 22 December.

Poblete, J (2011). Philippines preparing issues for UN about China intrusions. *Business World*, 2 June.

Romero, P (2011). ASEAN–China adopt guidelines on Spratlys. *Newsbreak*, 22 July.

San Pablo-Baviera, A (2003). The China factor in US alliances in East Asia and the Asia Pacific. *Australian Journal of International Affairs*, 57(2), 339–352.

Statement of the Department of Foreign Affairs on the Presence of Chinese Vessels in the West Philippine Sea (South China Sea) (2011). *Republic of the Philippines Department of Foreign Affairs*, 4 June.

Storey, I (2007). China and the Philippines: Moving beyond the South China Sea dispute. *China Brief*, 6(7), 9 May.

Storey, I (2009). Impeccable affair and renewed rivalry in the South China Sea. *China Brief*, IX(9), 30 April, 7–10.

Tadem, E (2007). The crisis of official development assistance to the Philippines: New global trends and old local issues. Asian Center,

University of the Philippines, March. http://www.mode.org/oda/pdf/ Crisis%20of%20ODA%20to%20the%20Philippines.pdf [accessed 27 April 2010].

The NBN-ZTE: A Primer. March 2008. http://www.ateneansact.net/dl/ GMA%20Primer%20on%20ZTE-NBN%20Deal.pdf [accessed 5 May 2009].

US backs Philippines on the South China Sea (2011). *The Financial Times*, 24 June.

Valero, VAJ (2010). US in focus: Changing the dynamics of a longstanding partnership. *Vital Partners and Influential Players: A Review of Philippine Bilateral Relations*, Republic of the Philippines Foreign Service Institute, June.

Villanueva, M (2011). Philippines set to deploy new patrol ship to Kalayam islands. Manila Bullekin, 14 April.

Villanueva, M (2011). Keeping Philippine navy afloat. *The Philippine Star*, 16 May.

Wee, D (2011). Philippines, China upgrade bilateral trading agreement. *Minda News*, 16 August.

Xu, L (2009). China to become 2nd largest trade partner of Philippines as recovery takes hold. *China View*, 30 December. http://news.xinhuanet. com/english/2009–12/30/content_12728233.htm [accessed 28 January 2010].

INDEX